This is a beautiful book which convincingly weaves the lives and religious development of the Wesley brothers and their mother with relevant psychoanalytic concepts. This examined life illuminates their human struggles and seeks to offer a narrative in which religious experience and the use of psychoanalytic thinking and theory can be used both to avoid internal experience but also to transcend it. The tracking of their human struggles and the travails of their souls are put in the context of psychoanalytic theory and religious understanding. It offers hope of resolution and salvation.
—**Jan McGregor Hepburn, Psychoanalytic Psychotherapist,
Registrar of the British Psychoanalytic Council**

Genuinely inter-disciplinary books are much to be appreciated especially when they throw fresh light on people of major significance. Dr Pauline Watson's very considerable achievement is to have drawn on her professional experience of understanding how human beings become what they are to illuminate the different characters of John and Charles Wesley. In her sympathetic portraits, both come alive anew for all those of us who in different ways are heirs of their many gifts and graces.
—**Professor Ann Loades, CBE, Professor Emerita of Divinity,
University of Durham, and Honorary Professor,
University of St Andrews**

'Two Scrubby Travellers':
A Psychoanalytic View of Flourishing and Constraint in Religion through the Lives of John and Charles Wesley

The ways in which people change and grow, and learn to become good, are not only about conscious decisions to behave well, but about internal change which allows a loving and compassionate response to others. Such change can take place in psychotherapy; this book explores whether similar processes can occur in a religious context.

Using the work of Julia Kristeva and other post-Kleinian psychoanalysts, change and resistance to change are examined in the lives of John Wesley, the founder of Methodism, and his brother Charles, the greatest English hymn-writer. Their mother's description of them as young men as 'two scrubby travellers' was a prescient expression indicating their future pilgrimage, which they negotiated through many struggles and compromises; it points towards the 'wounded healer', a description which could be applied to John in later years. The use of psychoanalytic thought in this study allows the exploration of unconscious as well as conscious processes at work and interesting differences emerge, which shed light on the elements in religion that promote or inhibit change, and the influence of personality factors.

'Two Scrubby Travellers': A Psychoanalytic View of Flourishing and Constraint in Religion through the Lives of John and Charles Wesley enriches our understanding of these two important historical figures. It questions the categorising of forms of religion as conducive to change and so 'mature', and other forms as 'immature', at a time when many, particularly young people, are attracted by fundamentalist, evangelical forms of belief. This book will be essential reading for researchers working at the intersection of psychoanalysis and religious studies; it will also be of interest to psychotherapists and psychoanalysts more generally and to researchers in the philosophy of religion.

Pauline Watson graduated in medicine from Glasgow University, UK, and holds a PhD in theology from Durham University, UK. She worked as a General Practitioner before training in psychiatry. As a consultant psychiatrist and psychotherapist, she set up a local psychiatric service in Consett, Co. Durham. She has also worked as a psychotherapist with asylum seekers.

'Two Scrubby Travellers':
A Psychoanalytic View of Flourishing and Constraint in Religion through the Lives of John and Charles Wesley

Pauline Watson

LONDON AND NEW YORK

First published 2018
by Routledge
2 Park Square, Milton Park, Abingdon, Oxon OX14 4RN

and by Routledge
711 Third Avenue, New York, NY 10017

Routledge is an imprint of the Taylor & Francis Group, an informa business

© 2018 Pauline Watson

The right of Pauline Watson to be identified as author of this work has been asserted by her in accordance with sections 77 and 78 of the Copyright, Designs and Patents Act 1988.

All rights reserved. No part of this book may be reprinted or reproduced or utilised in any form or by any electronic, mechanical, or other means, now known or hereafter invented, including photocopying and recording, or in any information storage or retrieval system, without permission in writing from the publishers.

Trademark notice: Product or corporate names may be trademarks or registered trademarks, and are used only for identification and explanation without intent to infringe.

British Library Cataloguing-in-Publication Data
A catalogue record for this book is available from the British Library

Library of Congress Cataloging-in-Publication Data
Names: Watson, Pauline, author.
Title: 'Two scrubby travellers' : a psychoanalytic view of flourishing and constraint in religion through the lives of John and Charles Wesley / Pauline Watson.
Description: New York : Routledge, 2018.
Identifiers: LCCN 2017056922 (print) | LCCN 2018005567 (ebook) | ISBN 9781315281490 (Master e-book) | ISBN 9781138241046 (hardback)
Subjects: LCSH: Christianity—Psychology. | Change (Psychology)—Religious aspects—Christianity. | Psychoanalysis and religion. | Wesley, John, 1703–1791. | Wesley, Charles, 1707–1788.
Classification: LCC BR110 (ebook) | LCC BR110 .W37 2018 (print) | DDC 287.092/2—dc23
LC record available at https://lccn.loc.gov/2017056922

ISBN: 978-1-138-24104-6 (hbk)
ISBN: 978-1-315-28149-0 (ebk)

Typeset in Times New Roman
by Apex CoVantage, LLC

Printed and bound in Great Britain by
TJ International Ltd, Padstow, Cornwall

To Dick with love and gratitude.

Contents

Acknowledgements x
Abbreviations, permissions xi

Introduction 1

PART I
'Growth to goodness' 9

1 Why Kristeva? 11
2 The search for the good 24
3 Interaction with an 'emotionally available' object 32
4 The search for deep truth through symbolisation 41
5 Resonances: psychic space in a religious context 56

PART II
John and Charles Wesley 75

6 Evangelical nurture 77
7 John Wesley (1703–91) 93
8 Charles Wesley (1707–88) 133
9 Theological differences 165

Conclusion 183

Index 191

Acknowledgements

This book brings together two aspects of my experience over many years: Christianity in the Methodist tradition has been a valued part of my life from childhood onwards, and psychoanalysis has been an important element in my professional life as a psychiatrist and psychotherapist. They have often been difficult for me to reconcile, and it is this which has given rise to the present book.

I owe a debt of gratitude to people from both traditions who have ensured my ongoing critical appreciation of their value. In Methodism, I think of my mother and my grandmother, Alan Davies, John Farley and Ralph Waller. With regard to psychoanalysis, the patients I was privileged to help in both psychiatry and psychotherapy repeatedly responded in ways which reinforced my sense of its value and importance. I often felt they gave more to me than I could give them. I was greatly helped and inspired by the wisdom and generosity of my consultant colleagues; of Jan McGregor Hepburn, my psychotherapy supervisor for many years; and of the psychiatric staff with whom I worked.

I am also grateful for my time in the Department of Theology at Durham University. For me, the years from 2002 to 2009 were very exciting intellectually, and I would particularly like to thank Professor David Brown, Professor Paul Murray and Dr Marcus Pound: their experience, clarity of thought and challenging but kind analyses of my writing were essential. In the early stages David and Alison Jasper, and Gareth Lloyd of the John Rylands University Library, Manchester, provided useful discussion and encouragement, as did Henrietta and John Batchelor and Charles Lund who kindly read early versions; at a later stage Adrian Bullock has been a valuable guide and inspiration.

I would like to thank several people who have read the final version: Ann Loades, Jan McGregor Hepburn, Ralph Waller, Anne Stevenson and Peter Lucas. Their interest, generosity and advice have been invaluable.

David, Elizabeth and Rachel Watson have given advice and showed unflagging tolerance and loving encouragement of their parent's preoccupations. It is difficult to express how grateful I am to my husband, Dick Watson, to whom the book is dedicated. He has lived with it for a long time and has never lost patience; without his advice, his expertise on hymns and his consistent love and encouragement, I doubt it would have appeared. I hope that this attempt to bridge the two worlds will be useful to others on their pilgrimage.

Abbreviations, permissions

BEJ: Ward, W. and Heitzenrater, R., eds., 1988–90. *The Bicentennial Edition of The Works of John Wesley*, vols. 18 and 19, *Journals and Diaries I, 1735–1743*, Nashville: Abingdon Press. Copyright © 1988–90. Used by permission. All rights reserved.

BEL: Baker, F., ed., 1980–2. *The Bicentennial Edition of the Works of John Wesley*, vols. 25 and 26, *Letters I and II, 1721–1755*. Oxford: Oxford University Press. Copyright © 1980–2. Used by permission.
Campbell, T. and Maddox, R., eds. 2015. *The Bicentennial Edition of the Works of John Wesley*, vol. 27, *Letters III, 1756–65*. Nashville: Abingdon Press.

BES: Outler, A.C., ed., 1984–7. *The Bicentennial Edition* of *The Works of John Wesley*, vols. 1–4, *Sermons I*. Nashville: Abingdon Press.

CWL: Newport, C. and Lloyd, G., eds., 2013, *The Letters of Charles Wesley: A Critical Edition, with Introduction and Notes*, vol. I, 1728–56. Oxford: Oxford University Press. Used by permission of Oxford University Press.

MJCW: Kimbrough, S., and Newport, K, eds., 2007–8. *The Manuscript Journal of the Reverend Charles Wesley, M.A.* Nashville: Kingswood Books. Copyright © 2008 Abingdon Press. Used by permission. All rights reserved.

SW: Wallace, C., ed., *Susanna Wesley: The Complete Writings*. New York/Oxford: Oxford University Press. Copyright © 1997. Used by permission.

Telford: Telford, J., ed., 1931. *The Letters of John Wesley A.M*, vols. I–VIII. Standard Edition, London: Epworth Press, 1931.

Kristeva: Quotations from the works of Julia Kristeva by kind permission of Columbia University Press.

Images: Used courtesy of the General Commission on Archives and History, The United Methodist Church, Madison, New Jersey.

Use of pronouns

In this book, masculine and feminine third-person pronouns and possessive pronouns are used on a random basis. They are mainly necessary to refer to a developing child in relation to an adult, a patient in relation to a therapist, or a human being in relation to God. The individual nature of these relationships makes the use of the individualised pronoun inescapable, but the random use of pronouns is considered the least biased method in terms of gender and the power differentials of the relationships.

Introduction

> O wad some Pow'r the giftie gie us To see oursels as ithers see us!
> —Robert Burns, 'To a louse'

Nathan, the Old Testament prophet, knew that self-deception was easy and ubiquitous and that seeing ourselves as we are was more challenging. King David had lusted after and bedded Bathsheba, and then engineered the death of her husband Uriah by putting him in the forefront of a battle. Nathan told him a parable (2 Samuel 12:1–13). A rich man who owned a flock of sheep would not kill one of his own sheep to feed a traveller but took the only possession of a poor man, his beloved 'little ewe lamb'. When he heard the parable, David was outraged. He said that the rich man deserved to die and should be made to restore the lamb fourfold. Nathan replied simply, 'Thou art the man'.

This book is about the struggle to see ourselves as we are, as it might take place in both a psychotherapy and a religious context. It arose from my experience working as a psychiatrist and psychoanalytic psychotherapist in an acute hospital setting. I worked with patients who often made contact with the service at times of crisis. This meant that the old-fashioned luxury of being able to select people as 'suitable' for psychoanalytic psychotherapy was not usually available. Many of them had severe personality disorders, addictions or psychosomatic disorders; there were many who had 'borderline' or 'narcissistic' pathology, and some who might be termed 'difficult to reach' (Joseph, 1989, p. 75).

My experience confirmed what Joseph had found: that such patients, if they were engaged psychotherapeutically, were often able to begin to know themselves better only after a prolonged struggle with intense and negative feelings towards the therapist. It was not uncommon for both patient and therapist to have a sense of being pushed to the brink of catastrophe and to have a sense of a life-and-death battle (Joseph, 1989, pp. 127–38). I also met a different group of people: they saw themselves as deeply committed Christians, who subscribed to the Christian ideals of love and forgiveness, but, in spite of these beliefs and their regular religious practices, were unable to give up destructive behaviour towards themselves and/

or others. They would either turn a blind eye to the effects of their behaviour or attempt to legitimise it by invoking God's will. They felt that their actions were good, morally right and justifiable; as a result, they saw no necessity for change.

Members of the first group may or may not have been willing to engage with psychotherapy, should they be offered it. The second group would usually see no need for it, expecting that any necessary change would be identified and brought about in the context of their religious experience. On first acquaintance, the people in these groups would appear to have little in common, but in fact, like King David, they share considerable resistance to accessing unconscious conflicts, wishes and motives.

The book explores possible elements in religion which might lead to change by facilitating access to the unconscious. Are there processes within an individual's relationship with religion that can be compared to the facilitating elements in psychotherapy, which allow increased awareness of deep truths about the self, and lead to freedom to act in more loving ways? Are there *forms* of religion which are more likely to facilitate change than others, and are there some which tend to hinder change and growth?

My concern is not only with those whose lives are constrained by mental disorders of some kind or by their own extreme destructive behaviour but also with all those, including ourselves, who turn a blind eye to some of our hurtful behaviour and who feel a need to grow and to live life 'more abundantly'.

I explore these questions using post-Freudian psychoanalytic theory and particularly the psychoanalytic concepts of Julia Kristeva, the French psychoanalyst and professor of linguistics. Although Kristeva privileges art, poetry and psychoanalysis over religion as enablers of growth and change (offering what she calls 'alternatives to narcissism'), she is interested in the personal use of Christian symbolism by believers, and her insights are enlivening and enlightening but also disruptive. I use her theory in relation to two specific examples: the lives and personalities of John Wesley, the founder of Methodism, and his brother Charles, thought by many to be the greatest English hymn writer. The book is titled *'Two Scrubby Travellers'* because their mother described them as such in an affectionate and intimate way, but it also represents two aspects of their lives. 'Travellers' is a recognition that they were, like most people, on a pilgrimage through life; and 'scrubby' indicates their humanity, their ways of dealing with the inevitable struggles and compromises on the way. It points towards the 'wounded healer', a description which could be applied to John in particular in later years.

This exploration of the Wesley brothers has been undertaken to try to learn more about how the personalities of different people affect the way they interact with the religious cultures surrounding them. Are there forms of religion which are more likely to encourage more 'mature' or 'immature' kinds of religious experience, as has been previously suggested by psychologists? And to what extent do people use or exploit aspects of their religious culture, of whatever sort, in helpful or unhelpful ways, according to their own particular needs? Both of these questions are of great significance at a time when large numbers of people, particularly young people, continue to embrace 'fundamentalist' forms of religion, traditionally thought by many psychologists to promote 'immature' relating. The purpose of the study is to shed light on these difficult questions. Theological and psychoanalytic ideas about the human struggle to maturity and goodness are used to elucidate differences in the brothers' lives. By using Kleinian, post-Kleinian and Kristevan theory, elements have been highlighted which would have been less evident in a study using the developmental methods that are more often used in the study of religion, in which there is less emphasis on the unconscious.

I have chosen the Wesley brothers because Methodism is the form of Christianity with which I am most familiar and because early Methodism as preached by John and Charles Wesley would be categorised by some psychologists and psychoanalysts as an 'immature' form of religion (Symington, 1994, pp. 22–7). An extreme form of this view is found in the work of someone who is not a psychologist or a psychoanalyst but a Marxist social historian, E.P. Thompson. Thompson (who came from a Methodist missionary family) saw Methodism in the late eighteenth and early nineteenth century as damaging and oppressive, as enforcing obedience and submission through fear and as sapping revolutionary fervour from the gullible masses. He suggested that emotion was seen by Methodists as dangerous to the social order and that it was safe to release it, only harmlessly, in a religious meeting, usually after a rousing sermon, as 'a ritualised form of psychic masturbation' (Thompson, 1963, p. 368). If Thompson is right, this form of religion would be expected to lead to an 'immature', infantilising and stultifying response, rather than to an opportunity for growth among its believers.

John and Charles Wesley were both Anglican priests. They devoted their lives to the reform of the church into which they had been ordained, and which was, in many places, lacking in dedication and inspiration. They travelled through the whole country, preaching and writing, and clearly had a powerful effect on many people, especially those who felt themselves ignored by the church. John Wesley was anxious at the outset not to separate from the Church of England, insisting that his followers should attend their parish church, but his field preaching, and his conduct of worship in the fledgling Methodist societies, provided many with their first hope and purpose in a society in which they seemed to be ignored and forgotten. This may have been interpreted by Thompson as frustrating a natural aspiration towards a necessary revolution, but this study shows the real situation to be more complicated.

Much has previously been written about the Wesley brothers, and a great deal of it is hagiographical. Adam Clarke, in his *Memoirs of the Wesley Family* (Clarke, 1823, p. 543), ended by saying that never 'since the days of Abraham and Sarah, and Joseph and Mary of Nazareth, has there ever been a family to which the human race has been more indebted'. In the present book, I hope to avoid such unqualified praise and to question some of the myths and legends. The use of psychoanalytic theory addresses not only conscious but possible unconscious factors which may have affected their lives. In order to achieve this, I have relied as far as possible on their own writings and those of their mother, Susanna. I have also made use of letters and other information from their contemporaries.

It may seem foolhardy to attempt to understand the inner worlds of two people whose lives extended throughout most of the eighteenth century; there are obvious hazards in having to rely on material, some of which is inevitably second-hand. But the present study has the advantage, unusual at this distance in time, of access to the extensive writings about the Wesleys' early lives by their mother, as well as their own personal journals and letters. Although the ideas and speculations drawn from these sources cannot be checked out repeatedly with each brother, as would happen if they were in therapy, and although there can be no information gained from non-verbal or counter-transference sources, there are records of a wide range of interactions with family members, with other people, with their work and with religious and cultural elements. These can be used to add to weight to the suppositions made from their subjective writings. In many ways, the Wesleys' situation is a ready-made experimental setting for a comparison between the two brothers. While they had very similar cultural, educational, religious and family influences, their *individual* experiences within the family would have been different. In addition to their genetic make-up, these individual experiences, particularly with their parents, would have contributed significantly to their personality differences. There is sufficient documentation and detail about their early lives for this to be usefully explored, and it is these personality factors which are of interest in comparing their responses to their faith.

The book is separated into two parts: Part I (Chapters 1, 2, 3, 4 and 5) outlines psychoanalytic understandings of an individual's growth to emotional, mental and moral maturity. It is concerned mainly with mechanisms of change in the early life of an individual and in psychotherapy. In addition, it looks at parallel opportunities for change in a religious context, attempting to understand them psychoanalytically. It includes a discussion of some forms of religion which in conventional terms might be expected to encourage defensiveness rather than growth.

Chapter 1 describes the context in which ideas about growth and change in psychoanalysis and in theology have developed. It focuses on Melanie Klein, the child psychoanalyst who wrote between the 1920s and the 1960s, and Julia Kristeva (the main theorist used in this book), who was greatly influenced by Klein. It looks at some parallel changes in psychoanalytic and theological thinking in the post-modern era, and also at the changes in psychoanalytic attitudes to religion over the second half of the twentieth century and in the twenty-first century.

Chapter 2 is concerned with the search for 'goodness' and 'maturity' in religion and in psychoanalysis. It examines what is meant by 'growth' and 'goodness' in theology (through the work of Rowan Williams (2000) and Ellen Charry (1997)) and in psychoanalysis (through the work of Margot Waddell, 1999). It concentrates on the relationship between ideas about 'growth' or 'development' and ideas of the 'good'. Two elements necessary to promote growth and change emerge from Waddell's study, and these two facilitators of change are used in subsequent chapters as a framework to re-examine important psychoanalytical ideas about development.

Chapter 3 is concerned with first of these facilitators: the interaction with an emotionally available object.[1] It outlines ideas about the development of the moral sense in the context of a relationship with a good object, as they have evolved through Kleinian thought and subsequently. Although I have taken a mainly Kleinian focus, relevant, illuminating insights are included from Fairbairn's object-relations theory, Kohut's self-psychology and from analysts in the Independent tradition such as Winnicott and Bollas. The chapter also considers some of the consequences for a subject's relationships with other people, philosophies or religion, when these processes go awry.

In Chapter 4 the second of the facilitators of change is explored more fully. This relates to the search for increased awareness of the 'deep truth' about the self, achieved in repeated confrontation with the truth in everyday interactions with other people in life, or in the particularities and detail of therapy. Truth is described as food for mental growth (Bion, 1965, p. 38), but accessing the 'deep truth' about the self is no easy matter. It depends on the capacity to 'symbolise', which in psychoanalytic theory includes not only the use of material symbols and rituals but also the capacity to conceptualise and verbalise unconscious content.

This chapter is concerned with the development of this capacity and also with the ways in which the use of symbols can facilitate the search for 'deep meaning'. It introduces Kristeva's understanding of very early infantile development, and her view that culture (religious or secular) must provide opportunities to 'symbolise' disturbing unconscious contents arising from pre-verbal experiences, if an individual is to grow and develop. Her thoughts on the entry into what she terms the 'symbolic' realm (a realm of language and rules), through identification with a loving, supportive object, which facilitates the separation from the mother/child dyad, add another layer of understanding to the more conventional ideas about the relationship with a good object. Her emphasis on the need for a dialogue between the 'symbolic' and the 'semiotic' (a term she uses idiosyncratically to indicate the realm of the body, of sensation and fragmented affect) is important for the study of how religion might promote growth.

In Chapter 5, following the analysis of processes of change in Chapters 2, 3 and 4, four elements emerge which are important in facilitating the process of growth. They are all important in the work of Kristeva and can be understood in her terms. In this chapter, they are considered in relation to religion.

They include interactions with transforming objects; opportunities to experience 'intersections' (between the universal and the particular, the known and the unknown, the human and the divine, or the 'symbolic' and the 'semiotic'); the use of religious symbols, narratives, sacraments and rituals to symbolise the 'semiotic' (this section is mainly concerned with Kristeva's thought on symbolism and ritual, and introduces her concept of the 'abject'); and the availability of triadic spaces.

In Part II (Chapters 6, 7, 8, 9 and 10), the lives of John and Charles Wesley are explored in the light of the theories about growth and transformation discussed in Part I.

Chapter 6 outlines their shared cultural and religious heritage and their family background. An examination of the sermons and the character of their maternal grandfather, Dr Samuel Annesley, an eminent dissenting preacher, provides evidence of the beliefs, values and expectations which they inherited, many of which appear in their writings and those of their mother. Her writings are the source of a great deal of information about their immediate family, early experience and education.

Chapters 7 and 8 explore the individual lives, relationships and spiritual journeys of the Wesley brothers. Using psychoanalytic theory, and particularly Kristevan theory, an attempt is made to understand their mental structures and psychological defence mechanisms from their own writings and from the writings of others close to them. Ways in which these personality features affected their responses to the religious faith they shared are considered.

Chapter 9 explores the theological differences between the Wesley brothers. It is concerned with their conversion experiences, their attitudes to mysticism, their ideas on Christian Perfection and their positions on the meaning of suffering and on the Trinity. As far as is possible, these are related to their psychological needs.

Chapter 10 draws together the findings from these chapters, outlining the differences between the two brothers and the implications of these differences in understanding the ways in which individual personality factors and psychological defences influence the practice of religion. The merits of employing Kristeva as the main theorist in the book are considered, and her privileging of art and psychoanalysis over religion is readdressed in the light of the findings. This final chapter also returns to the classification of forms of belief by psychologists as 'mature' and 'immature', which is inevitably dismissive and denigrating of 'immature' forms. The differences between two people within the same religious context demonstrate that each person's response is complicated and idiosyncratic and that classification of forms of religion in terms of their being conducive to mature or immature relating is too simplistic to be useful.

Note

1 *Object* is used here in the psychoanalytic sense to mean a person, a part of a person, or a symbol of either, to which a subject relates; it can be internal or external (Rycroft, 1972).

References

Bion, W., 1965. *Transformations: Change From Learning to Growth*. London: Heinemann, quoted in Waddell, M. (1999).

Charry, E., 1997. *By the Renewing of Your Minds: The Pastoral Function of Christian Doctrine*. New York/Oxford: Oxford University Press.

Clarke, A., 1823. *Memoirs of the Wesley Family*. London: Printed by J. and T. Clarke.

Joseph, B., 1989. The Patient Who Is Difficult to Reach. In eds. M. Feldman and E. Bott Spillius, *Psychic Equilibrium and Psychic Change*, 1st ed. London/New York: Tavistock/Routledge.

Rycroft, C., 1972. *A Critical Dictionary of Psychoanalysis*. Harmondsworth: Penguin Books.
Symington, N., 1994. *Emotion and Spirit: Questioning the Claims of Psychoanalysis and Religion*. London: Cassell.
Thompson, E., 1963. *The Making of the English Working Class*. London: Victor Gollancz Ltd.
Waddell, M., 1999. On Ideas of 'The Good' and 'The Ideal' in George Eliot's Novels and Post-Kleinian Psychoanalytic Thought. *American Journal of Psychoanalysis*, 59(3), pp. 271–86.
Williams, R., 2000. *On Christian Theology*. Oxford: Blackwell.

Part I

'Growth to goodness'

Chapter 1

Why Kristeva?

Julia Kristeva

This chapter considers the psychoanalytic and theological contexts within which the ideas concerning growth and change used in the book have developed. In exploring ideas at the interface of psychoanalysis and Christianity, the first impulse would usually be to turn to C. G. Jung. While Freud and many other early analysts and psychiatrists saw religious beliefs as illusional or even delusional and as based on infantile wishes for care and protection from a loving father, for Jung religious myth was central to his thought. He emphasised the integrating function of symbols, and much of his work was related to processes of spiritual growth and transformation. He decided to embark on a career in psychiatry because he believed it to be a discipline which involved both the biological and the spiritual, a combination he had sought but failed to find elsewhere (Jung, 1963, p. 130).

It is in this biological/spiritual territory that the present explorations take place, so why employ Kristevan ideas rather than Jung's? Kristeva's early writings were in the field of linguistics, where her interests were in the nature of subjectivity, the ambiguity of signs, intertextuality, and poetic language. In the 1970s, she became interested in psychoanalysis and trained as an analyst. In her subsequent work, she combined her linguistic interests with psychoanalytic understandings of early child development and applied her ideas to the symbolism of religion. The first reason for a Kristevan analysis is that for her, while many other factors are involved in the motivation of behaviour, the biological/bodily drives stressed by Freud are very important. While Jung also acknowledged their importance, he could not accept the prominence Freud had given them. He believed that by wanting to turn his ideas about sexuality into dogma, Freud had rejected religion and replaced it with sexuality (Jung, 1963, pp. 173–4). In the psychoanalytic theories of Kristeva used here, these biological aspects are preserved; they give detailed attention to very early experience, including the development of the moral sense and the capacity to symbolise.

Second, while Jung had attempted to adhere to empirical methods in arriving at his theories, his powerful experiences of dreams, visions and sudden inspirations, and his witnessing of 'psychic' phenomena, sometimes undermined this attempt. He had a sense that some 'forms of being which are commonly called spiritual' arose from an external source, from 'behind a veil' (Jung, 1963, p. 385). On the other hand, Freud, as a neurologist, arrived at his theories, as far as possible from clinical observation. The theories I have drawn on similarly originate from experiences with patients in therapy rather than from 'behind the veil'.

A third reason for deciding on a Kristevan reading is related to the need to understand patients such as those mentioned previously, whom Kristeva describes as suffering from 'new maladies of the soul' ('borderlines, psychosomatics, substance abusers, vandals and so forth'; Kristeva, 2001, p. 202), whom Freud would have seen as not susceptible to analytic treatment. Kristeva is particularly interested in such patients and acknowledges that she owes a great debt to Melanie Klein in her thinking about them; it is therefore important to see Kristeva's work in the context of Kleinian thought. Melanie Klein (1882–1960) did not depart from Freud's biological drive theory; she believed that the 'death drive' was of central importance, but she also asserted that from the beginning of life there were no mental processes which did not involve external or internal objects: 'love and hatred, phantasies, anxieties, and defences are also operative from the beginning and are *ab initio* indivisibly linked with object-relations' (Klein, 1952, p. 53). She had a capacity to interact deeply with children, opening up her own unconscious to that of the child. However, empathy was not merely a supportive, compassionate therapist stance: it involved a recognition and interpretation of the negative aspects of the transference (Klein, 1926, pp. 128–38; Klein, 1957, pp. 230–5). Klein has been criticised for her focus on interpreting the negative and on destructiveness, sadism and envy, and many prefer a more holding, maternal stance in the therapist, which facilitates self-discovery (Wright, 2009, p. 30). However, envy and gratitude were both aspects of her work, and she had an exceptional ability to confront but be 'merciful' rather than judgemental with negative aspects of the child's experience.

Kristeva vividly describes Klein's capacity to work in a 'deep and intense' way with a child, in which the focus on the body and its acts led to a feeling of a 'digging into our guts'. She quotes Lacan as describing this work as like that of 'an inspired gut-butcher' (Kristeva, 2001, p. 148). Klein's understanding of early Oedipal dynamics and her emphasis on drives, affect, actions, and bodies, is echoed in Kristeva's work. Kristeva's concept of the 'abject', which is discussed later, describes the mother from whom the child is beginning to separate as a locus of the 'abject' (not yet an object). She is felt as a 'magnet of gratification and repulsion' and as belonging to a realm of orality, torn bodies, bodily fluids, desire, hatred and death (Kristeva, 2001, p. 151). Although Kristeva regrets Klein's relative neglect of the father in a child's development (2001, p. 177), Klein remains influential in the development of Kristeva's ideas about the separation of the child from the mother, the entry of the child into the world of language and rules, and the importance of aggression in the child's development and in therapy. Like Klein, Kristeva has been criticised for concentrating on the negative, and as with Klein, this has been attributed to her own depression. Indeed, Kristeva begins her study of melancholia, *The Black Sun*, by suggesting that for those who are 'wracked by melancholia, writing about it would have meaning only if writing sprang out of that very melancholia' (Kristeva, 1987, p. 3).

The final reason for using Kristevan theory is that Kristeva applies her thought in an instructive way to religious symbolism and its place in stabilising or transforming the individual. She is often described as a 'French Feminist', but she was born and brought up in Bulgaria under communism. She was accustomed to examining religion critically from an early age. On interview, she has talked about her father, an Orthodox Christian, and her mother, a Darwinian, and of how as a child she used her mother's ideas to attack her father's religious beliefs. She learned French at an early age in a school run by Dominican nuns and subsequently moved to France, where she felt welcomed by the intellectual community but nevertheless experienced life as an 'exile' (Kristeva, 2013). These early experiences were influential on her work on religion, and she has said that they also led her to reflect on the ways in which 'foreignness' is dealt with in the world, 'culturally and psychologically' as well as 'poetically and pathologically' (Kristeva, 1988, p. 4). Like Freud, she is an atheist and often refers to the inadequacies, errors and hazards of religion, turning to psychoanalysis and art instead as sources of healing and growth (Kristeva, 1983, pp. 379–83). Nevertheless, a great deal of her work explores in depth the capacity of Christian symbols to represent unconscious material and thus to perform a psychologically valuable function. Many scholars have found her writings, which involve not only psychoanalysis but also art, literature and linguistics, a rich amalgam of ideas through which to read theological concepts.

It is her capacity to explore the human interaction with religious dogma, narrative and symbols that I have found fascinating in Kristeva's work. Her emphasis on biological drives and affect and the parallels she draws between the Christian narrative and very early infant experience demonstrate great rigour in her examination of religious experience, but she is by no means reductive. She writes that Freud saw religion as an illusion, 'albeit a glorious one', in that like early scientific ideas, which were misunderstandings, such 'illusions' might lead to future benefits. The idea of religion as illusion persists in her work, but less as a distortion, than as something creative and as a source of sustenance. She does not advocate religious faith, but neither does she promote atheism, as Freud did. She sees religious belief as able to offer support and a kind of coherence, allowing an individual to carry on with life (Kristeva, 1985a, pp. 11–13). While she is very challenging towards it, she speaks, as if with an inside knowledge, of the richness and depth of religious belief. This is particularly the case in her understanding of both the Christian narrative and psychoanalysis as based on love: God as a God of love, and the Agape of the cross; and the transference love of psychoanalysis. It is her rigour, combined with her knowledge of the deep meaning of religion, which is never denigrating or dismissive, that adds to this examination.

Her attitude to religion has resulted in a multitude of appreciative as well as critical responses. Some, whose views I would endorse, regard her theories as offering possibilities for changes which would be beneficial in religious practice

(Reineke, 2003, p. 114). Her writings on the lives of 'exemplary' women (Arendt, Klein and Colette) are seen as potentially instrumental in the development of a changed notion of ethics (Beardsworth, 2004, pp. 274–5). In her book *Strangers to Ourselves*, psychoanalysis is offered as a model for a 'reconceived ethics', based on her belief in the 'divided self', where a capacity to embrace the 'stranger within' leads to a willingness to embrace the marginalised (Oliver, 1993, p. 8). There is widespread appreciation of her thought on poetic language, which is also relevant to religious belief: for instance, Beattie encourages its use in new explorations of liturgy and sacramentality, which might include space for both male and female (sexual as well as maternal) bodies (Beattie, 2006, p. 291).

Although she is usually described as a 'feminist' and embraces many feminist ideals, she does not consider herself as part of any particular group and is regarded with suspicion by many feminists. Her ideas on the 'abject' are seen by some as complicit with the denigration and fear of the sexual woman in patriarchal systems; however, she sees herself as describing rather than condoning patriarchal institutions. While she is concerned about the plight of women in patriarchal societies, she nevertheless re-examines Freud and retrieves those concepts she sees as valuable from his theories and from other 'patriarchal' systems. She regards all human beings, male and female, as having to negotiate a painful struggle to separate from the mother. Her concern is with the individual, and she is aware that the tendency of some feminists to think in terms of *groups* of women risks the overriding of subtle individual differences among them. She is suspicious of 'feminism in a herd' (Kristeva, 1980, p. 117).

After Klein, there has developed what Kristeva calls a psychoanalytic 'ecumenism', where ways of working with particular sorts of patients and particular symptoms may involve theories from a variety of sources, though many of these theories are developments of Klein's ideas. In addition, psychoanalysis has become more open to social and cultural influences (Kristeva, 2001, p. 245). I want to uphold this spirit of psychoanalytic ecumenism in this exploration of the processes of change in therapy and religion. It cannot be a solely Kristevan narrative, as contributions from Klein, Bion and Winnicott and contemporary analysts such as Wright, Bollas and Britton have to be included if a comprehensive picture is to emerge. Kristeva is however the most prominent theorist. Her engagement with the question of whether Christian symbols can adequately symbolise unconscious contents is central to an understanding of the processes of change. As a clinician who sees theory as a framework or an internalised set of tools which help in the thinking about an individual patient, I find her ecumenical, pragmatic approach a familiar one.

Change in psychoanalysis

Since Klein, there have been developments in psychoanalysis which have resonances with developments in theological thinking over the same period. In both there is an increased understanding of accessing truths through means that are not merely cognitive. As such, they are important for this book and are briefly highlighted here. They do, however, threaten the status of psychoanalysis as a science, which Freud was so keen to preserve.

The first development was a shift in psychoanalytic theory, starting with Klein, from its empirical/deterministic origins to a more subjective, imaginative approach. As such, this shift could be seen as a return to Jung's subjective ways of arriving at his theories, but in fact, it does not rely on the individual subjective experiences of one person but derives from and relates to experiences in therapy with patients. Nevertheless, the 'subjective' has become more prominent.

As described by Black, there has also been an increasing emphasis on the capacity to appreciate 'higher values' in psychoanalysis, which are necessary for psychological growth, rather than for survival and reproduction. The development of this capacity in a child depends on a process which is affective as well as intellectual, facilitated by a loving relationship with the other (Black, 1996, p. 315). Its development is important in the work of Klein and Kristeva.

Since Klein there has been more emphasis on the gaining of knowledge through interpersonal processes in therapy, what Kristeva would describe as 'between the imaginaries' of the patient and those of the therapist (Kristeva, 2001, p. 148). This development can be clearly shown in the change which has been undergone in the notion of 'countertransference'. This term was first used to describe the feelings arising in the therapist during therapy, owing to the therapist's neurosis. They were regarded as an obstacle to treatment, and the therapist's own analysis was aimed at enabling her to abolish or deal with them. However, a paper by the Kleinian analyst Paula Heimann (1950) brought about a change. She argued that countertransference might be used as a tool rather than an obstacle. There was a shift from seeing the patient as a sealed unit to seeing two individuals with feelings and responses, open to each other. The therapist's feelings, stirred up in the therapy, became a useful source of information about the patient's feelings and internal world.

Wilfred Bion explored these interpersonal exchanges between analyst and patient in detail. He fought in the First World War, and worked with traumatised soldiers in the Second World War, before having a training analysis with Klein and becoming an analyst. In the early phase of his work, he struggled to express therapeutic processes in mathematical terms but found that the concepts which were most difficult to elucidate were best expressed using terms and ideas from philosophy, mysticism and aesthetics. He began his book *Attention and Interpretation* by intimating his suspicion of relying only on reason and by pointing out the limitations of words to describe some kinds of experience. He regretted the inadequacies of everyday language, believing that poetic and religious expressions were more able to portray what was otherwise difficult to access (Bion, 1970, pp. 1–2).

Although he was not religious, he used the language of religious mystics to describe the processes of therapy through which the unknown psychic truth of an individual could be arrived at by the therapist, and through the therapist by the patient: for instance, in his choice of 'O', which he used to denote 'that which is the ultimate reality, absolute truth, the godhead, the infinite, the thing-in-itself'. He used religious language to describe the therapist's apprehension of the patient's inner truth. The therapist can observe and hear what the patient does and says, but it is only through 'attention' and 'intuition' that the truth of the patient's inner world can be approached. He described this process in such terms as the 'evolving' of 'O', 'becoming' 'O', incarnating 'O' or 'at-one-ment' with 'O' (Bion, 1970, pp. 26–30). The truth is approached through the 'reverie' of patient and therapist. Fragmented and incomprehensible material brought by the patient is thought about and symbolised, or 'metabolised', before being put into words and offered back to the patient. It is a process likened to the 'container/contained' relationship which occurs between a mother and her baby, in which the mother holds and contains what feel like unbearable distressing feelings for the baby. They are made sense of and offered back in a more bearable and comprehensible form and then can be 'borne' or 'suffered' rather than expelled. Similarly, in analysis, the analyst shares what has become *knowable truth* with the patient who 'allows it to be transformed into wisdom, personal "O"' (Grotstein, 2004, pp. 1087–92).

In order for 'O' to evolve, Bion advocated that the therapist's 'memory' and 'desire' be abolished. He described a necessary state of attention, which he compared to Keats's 'negative capability': 'that is when man is capable of being in uncertainties, Mysteries, doubts, without any irritable reaching after fact and reason' (Keats, 1817, p. 370). This seemingly impossible state of mind had to be achieved by 'a positive discipline of eschewing memory and desire'. In addition, Bion asserted that 'faith' was required: 'a faith that there *is* an ultimate reality and truth – the unknown, "formless infinite"'. There had to be a willingness and openness to know, but without an insistence on knowing. Memory and desire in the analyst, he claimed, interfered with the capacity to be receptive to present experiences, to the shifts and new meanings in the here and now of the relationship, in the process of which 'O' was evolving. There had to be a giving up of certainties, past beliefs, predictions and expectations (Bion, 1970, pp. 31–2).

Subsequently, psychoanalysts have sought to open up and examine the processes occurring in therapy more deeply and critically. This has involved a focus on the position, attitude and attunement of the therapist; on intersubjectivity rather than the study of the patient as object; and on the nature of empathy. All these areas of focus involve attempts to understand how the patient's truth can be arrived at by means other than the purely rational or cognitive.

Change in theology

The period of change in psychoanalysis described above has coincided with the development of 'post-modern' thinking in art, literature, philosophy and theology. The term *post-modern* is used here in the theologian Graham Ward's sense; it describes a philosophical position which is critical of modernism and suspicious of metanarrative. He acknowledges the ways in which post-modern thought can 're-imagine' the world and lead to an opening up of ideas, for instance, the role of the unsayable, 'rupturing' what is presented; the self as divided, or 'abysmal', and so open and *en proces*; the role of desire, 'initiated and fostered by the other'; all interlacing in the body. There is a questioning of old dichotomies, such as 'body/soul, body/mind, form/content, sign/signified' and the recognition that the meanings of words are determined by their situation in the text, the cultural setting and the response of the reader. There is an awareness of layers of and shifts in meanings: in this sense, Ward suggests, post-modern thought can be seen as restoring a sense of mystery which had been lost because of the emphasis on the 'logic' and rationality of modernity. He points out that the thinking of many 'post-modern' theologians draws heavily on the thinking of the early fathers (Ward, 1997, pp. 588, 594). One example of this connection is evident in the work of Rowan Williams. In discussing the praise of God, he insists that not only 'euphoric fluency' is required but also toleration of the work and pain of the 'negative'. He describes this as a dispossession, a 'suspension of the ordinary categories of "rational" speech'. The use of the word *dispossession*, he suggests, evokes the 'most radical level of prayer, that of simple waiting on God, contemplation'. In contemplation, there is a recognition that no verbal or visual form can depict God and this recognition is expressed in 'silence and attention' (Williams, 2000, pp. 10–11). Such descriptions which include non-cognitive ways of apprehending the 'sacred beyond', are reminiscent of the descriptions of the 'apophatic' search for God given by the mediaeval mystics, which will be discussed later. In their emphasis on the subjective and on the attitude of the 'openness' and 'attentiveness' required and the use of faculties other than reason to apprehend that which is beyond what can be known through the senses, they also resonate with the descriptions given earlier of the attitude and receptivity of the therapist to the patient's unconscious. Both require a responsiveness to the other and a giving up of preconceptions and expectations. The language used is often similar, and the concern of both is to apprehend a truth which cannot become known by cognitive effort alone. In both, the centrality of such a relationship with the O(o)ther, which allows and facilitates development and change, hints at an underlying commonality.

These aspects are also familiar from Kristeva's work. In this 'post-modern' context where psychoanalysts have sought to open up the processes occurring in therapy and examine them more deeply and critically, the emphases on the imaginative and intuitive are the aspects that are particularly attuned to the unconscious, and to what Kristeva called the 'semiotic' realm of affect and drives, what she describes as 'energies', 'extremely fragile psychic traces' (Kristeva, 1985b, p. 22). These 'fragile psychic traces' respond to what Freud called 'primary process thinking' which is fragmented and lacks rationality and logic. The conscious mind, on the other hand, is involved in 'secondary process thinking' (concerned with rationality, logic, language and cause and effect), the realm of what Kristeva calls the 'symbolic'. Both primary and secondary processes make up the human psyche, and both imagination and reason are necessary to understand it and to interact with it therapeutically. Kristeva's description of her interaction with a text is reminiscent of such an interaction. She describes a 'psychoanalytic position' which is a 'back and forth movement' between a state of close identification with the object, a 'mimetic' relationship, a 'position of osmosis' and a stepping back to 'a position of understanding and of knowledge' (Kristeva, 1985b, pp. 30–1).

Harris Williams describes psychoanalysis as both a science and an art (Williams, 1999, pp. 127–3); Kristeva's different ways of relating to her object lead her to describe psychoanalysis as both a 'science' and a 'fiction' (Kristeva, 1985a, p. 20). For both, a deep understanding of the human psyche requires the bringing together of art and science, reason and imagination, the symbolic and the semiotic.

Religion and psychoanalysis

In addition to the preceding changes in theory and technique in psychoanalysis, a further change has occurred in the attitude of many analysts to religion. Freud's view of religion as illusory wish fulfilment, which encouraged infantilism, was taken up by many in early psychoanalytic circles. More recently, however, theorists have emphasised the positive aspects of religion, seeing religious belief as a possible way of achieving growth and change

Many of the scholars who have examined these processes in religion from a psychological point of view have used 'developmental approaches'. For instance, Erikson's 'ego-psychology' comprises a concept of human development in a form analogous to 'epigenesis', a term used in embryology to describe the physical development of the embryo (Erikson, 1950). He famously described stages of development, in each of which specific necessary tasks were negotiated (Wulff, 1991, p. 371). These ideas, together with elements from Piaget's theories of cognitive and moral development and Kohlberg's stages of moral development, were incorporated into Fowler's 'faith development' theory. This describes stages of faith of increasing maturity, each of which offers not only an enduring 'emergent strength' but also potential hazards (Fowler, 1981).

In W. W. Meissner's 'dialogue' between psychoanalysis and religion, he also incorporated ideas from 'ego-psychology' and from the 'self-psychology' of the American psychoanalyst Heinz Kohut in describing growth and change in a religious context. Using these ideas, he described the believer as having an 'immature' or 'mature' image of God and as relating to religious objects in an 'immature' or 'mature' fashion. He suggested that the whole range of these ways of relating was found well distributed in all forms of religious groups and traditions, and he did not label particular traditions 'mature' or 'immature'. However, he raised the question as to whether there were preferred modalities, in each tradition, which were adhered to and idealised. He issued a challenge, demanding research aimed at understanding the level of interaction between a particular modality and the cultural influences and developmental needs of the individual. It is hoped that the exploration in this book will shed some light on this question. To what extent do the developmental needs of an individual influence an adherence to particular aspects of religious symbolism and/or particular forms of praxis? (Meissner, 1984, pp. 150–9)

Since the 1980s, there has been a great deal of work which explores religious belief psychoanalytically, with more tolerance for the forms of faith which appear at the more 'mature' ends of the developmental spectra just described. However, in 2006, Rachel Blass questioned whether this superficially friendly attitude to religion is actually preferable to Freud's open antagonism. She asserts that the apparent increased tolerance of religion among analysts coincides with a shift in the nature of both psychoanalytical theory and in the kind of religion analysts tolerate. The psychoanalytical shift, already mentioned, is from 'drive' to 'relationality' and 'self-experience' and to an emphasis on the 'transitional' (phenomena seen as neither entirely subjective nor entirely objective). The forms of religion of which psychoanalytic writers are tolerant are those stressing similar aspects: 'interpersonal or cultural relatedness', 'experiencing', and the 'transitional' nature of religious phenomena. Blass suggests that when phenomena are viewed as 'transitional', then Freud's question about whether religious claims are actually true becomes irrelevant. She refers to Stein's book *Beyond Belief* (Stein, 1999), in which essays by twelve psychiatrists, psychoanalysts and psychotherapists are critical of organised traditional religion but value a 'personal, self-determined mysticism, devoid of history, ritual, authority, obligation and mediation, a kind of westernised Buddhism'. Many Christians, she suggests, while reassured that their beliefs are not 'infantile', would not be reassured that the truths of their claims were irrelevant. The vast majority of Christians practise a traditional form of faith and would prefer an honest argument with Freud (Blass, 2006, pp. 27–9).

James W. Jones, who has written a great deal about religion and psychoanalysis, draws on object-relations theory and on self-psychology. He attributes the capacity of religion to inspire great selflessness, on the one hand, or violence and terror, on the other, to the idealisation within it. He explores the possibility of a religion without idealisation and offers the '*via negativa*' as such an alternative, thus supporting Blass's point (Jones, 2002, pp. 106–17). The American scholar of the psychoanalysis and religion Diane Jonte-Pace (1999, pp. 177–8) is concerned that among the many existing theologies and forms of religion, the 'liberal, humanistic, non-authoritarian, ecumenical' form Jones advocates applies only to a limited number. While she sees his use of object-relations theory as helpful in the study of religion, she regrets his relative stress on the conscious and intellectual, and calls for his examination to be pushed further into the unconscious, including an analysis of the *praxis* of religion, the 'material reality in rituals, texts, icons, liturgies and communities'.

The repudiation of institutionalised, traditional religions occurs repeatedly in those authors who see themselves as sympathetic to religion. For example, the psychoanalyst Neville Symington advocated the abandonment of the 'primitive mythology' of Judaism, Christianity and Islam and the replacement of it with a mature structure which would maintain their core values (Symington, 1994, pp. 24–5). Wright shares Symington's approval of what he calls 'natural' religions, which, unlike 'revealed' religions, are less preoccupied with sin and badness but which evoke a pre-Oedipal world offering containment and acceptance (Wright, 2009, pp. 160, 170). While traditional, 'primitive' religion is denigrated, ideas of achieving autonomy, trust, a sense of identity, integrity and a capacity for wisdom are almost ubiquitous. They are seen as goals of healthy development, psychological treatment or a religious journey.

Apart from a relative neglect of unconscious elements, there are other risks in the use of developmental methods to judge the 'maturity' of a person's response to religion. First, as Wallace writes, there is a risk of 'collapsing' 'rich and complicated present-day adult behaviours, motives and meanings, into their infantile precursors'. For instance, a numinous experience may involve the experience of trust originating in infancy, but this is not necessarily evidence of infantile dependency (Wallace, 1991, pp. 274–5). Second, it is tempting to assume, having examined the representations which individuals hold of God in terms of maturity, that 'immature forms' imply defensive forms of relating: for instance, it might be assumed that an idealised, anthropomorphic God, seen as punishing disobedience, would be related to in a defensive way which precluded change. The present exploration should shed light on whether this is a valid assumption.

The tendency of psychoanalysts to sanction private, individualised, non-anthropomorphic forms of religion is illuminated by the work of Jeremy Carrette (2007, pp. 104–6, 130–1), a student of religion and culture. He asserts that much of the psychoanalytic study of religion insulates itself from wider cultural and economic influences and suggests that this is linked to the psychoanalysts' choice of forms of religion that they sanction. He delineates two forms, two 'political orders', of the study of religion. The first is 'the order of the *same*' which he associates with 'dominant American readings of psychoanalysis'. This he sees as ego-driven and individualistic, as separating self and society and as colluding with post-war affluence and ideas of freedom which conceal and ignore the oppressed. It is regarded as allowing itself to be linked with, and therefore as justifying, profitable 'spirituality' movements, which emphasise individual development and the 'American dream'. He laments the separation of American psychoanalysis from Freud's reading of the unconscious. On the other hand, 'the order of the *other*' (which he associates with European psychoanalysis and the voice of the oppressed in America) unites self and society and is focused on unconscious drives and social identity.

Klein remained closely associated with Freud's reading of the unconscious; she stressed the importance of bodily phantasies, biological drives and destructive impulses in her work. Kristeva maintains these emphases in her examination of the unconscious resonances of religious symbolism and *praxis*. She stresses the 'divided self', the persistent 'abject', the intersection of the 'symbolic' and the 'semiotic', and the need in society for opportunities to symbolise 'semiotic' elements of the psyche. Both theorists can be seen in Carette's terms as associated with the second political order of the study of religion – the 'order of the other' – and these are further important factors in the choice of Kristeva (and Klein) as the main theorists in this book.

Early Methodism at the time of the Wesley brothers could be described as dogmatic and authoritarian and as involving a belief in an idealised, anthropomorphic (either punishing or forgiving) God. Good and evil were polarised, and fanaticism or 'enthusiasm' could occur. In Meissner's or Fowler's terms, such a God representation would be expected to result in 'immature', dependent relating, with associated primitive psychological defence mechanisms. The question addressed here is whether a Kristevan reading of transformative factors in child development and in religion, when applied to John and Charles Wesley's experience, would tend to confirm this expectation of immature relating or whether it would elicit additional, unanticipated, processes of change.

Does this exploration of processes of change through a Kristevan reading of the experiences of the Wesleys belong to Carette's 'order of the other'? By studying religion through Kleinian, post-Kleinian and Kristevan eyes, it is hoped that this is the case, that some of the hazards associated with developmental theories will be avoided and that the process of exploration itself will be less 'ego-driven' and more receptive to unconscious factors.

It is also hoped that, as a result, some light will be shed on the degree to which growth and change in a religious context relate to personality factors. This will be linked to whether or not a person can select out 'transformative' elements from a so-called 'immature' religion and, if so, how this happens. This, in turn, relates to the presence or absence of 'psychic spaces' for reflection and growth in early Methodism, and the evidence for these will be sought. As a result of the findings, Kristeva's privileging of psychoanalysis and art over religion as facilitators of growth is revisited. Finally, the usefulness of classifying forms of religions according to their 'maturity' is reconsidered.

Overall, I hope to provide a fresh interpretation of the religious journeys of the Wesley brothers, to revisit Kristeva's thought on symbolisation in religion through the application of her ideas to the two historical figures, and to offer additional perspectives on the psychoanalytical perceptions of the potential for change in different forms of religion.

References

Beardsworth, S., 2004. *Julia Kristeva: Psychoanalysis and Modernity*. Albany: State University of New York Press.

Beattie, T., 2006. *New Catholic Feminism: Theology and Theory*. London/New York: Routledge.

Bion, W., 1970. *Attention and Interpretation: A Scientific Approach to Insight in Psycho-Analysis in Group*. London: Tavistock Publications.

Black, D., 1996. Abiding Values and the Creative Present: Psychoanalysis in the Spectrum of the Sciences. *British Journal of Psychotherapy*, 12(3), pp. 314–22.

Blass, R., 2006. Beyond Illusion. In ed. D. Black, *Psychoanalysis and Religion in the 21st Century*. London: Tavistock Publications.

Carrette, J., 2007. *Religion and Critical Psychology: Religious Experience in the Knowledge Economy*. London/New York: Routledge.

Erikson, E., 1950. *Childhood and Society*, 2nd ed. New York: W.W. Norton, 1963.

Fowler, J., 1981. *Stages of Faith: The Psychology of Human Development and the Quest for Meaning*. San Francisco: Harper and Row.
Grotstein, J., 2004. The Seventh Servant. *International Journal of Psychoanalysis*, 85(5), pp. 1087–92.
Heimann, P., 1950. On Countertransference. *International Journal of Psychoanalysis*, 31, pp. 81–4.
Jones, J., 2002. *Terror and Transformation: The Ambiguity of Religion in Psychoanalytic Perspective*. Hove/New York: Brunner-Routledge.
Jonte-Pace, D., 1999. In Defence of an Unfriendly Freud. *Pastoral Theology*, 47(3), pp. 175–81.
Jung, C., 1963. *Memories, Dreams, and Reflections*. Glasgow: William Collins Sons & Co. Ltd.
Keats, J., 1817. Letter to George and John Keats. In ed. E. Cook, *John Keats*. Oxford: Oxford University Press, 1990.
Klein, M., 1926. Psychological Principles of Early Analysis. In *Love, Guilt and Reparation*. London: Virago Press, 1988.
Klein, M., 1952. The Origins of Transference. In *Envy and Gratitude, and Other Works*. London: Virago Press, 1988.
Klein, M., 1957. Envy and Gratitude. In *Envy and Gratitude, and Other Works*. London: Virago Press, 1988.
Kristeva, J., 1980. Interview With Elaine Hoffman Baruch 'Feminism and Psychoanalysis'. In ed. R. Guberman, *Julia Kristeva Interviews*, 1st ed. New York: Columbia University Press, 1996.
Kristeva, J., 1983. *Tales of Love*. Translated by L. Roudiez. New York: Columbia University Press, 1987.
Kristeva, J., 1985a. *In the Beginning Was Love: Psychoanalysis and Faith*. Translated by A. Goldhammer. New York: Columbia University Press, 1997.
Kristeva, J., 1985b. Interview With I. Lipkowitz and A. Losellee, a Conversation With Julia Kristeva. In ed. R. Guberman, *Julia Kristeva Interviews*, 1st ed. New York: Columbia University Press, 1996.
Kristeva, J., 1987. *Black Sun*. Translated by L. Roudiez. New York: Columbia University Press, 1989.
Kristeva, J., 1988. Julia Kristeva in Person (France-Culture Broadcast). In ed. R. Guberman, *Kristeva Interviews*, 1st ed. New York: Columbia University Press, 1996.
Kristeva, J., 2001. *Melanie Klein*. New York: Columbia University Press.
Kristeva, J., 2013. Interview With Jules Law, *On Julia Kristeva's Couch*. Chicago Humanities Festival. www.youtube.com/watch?v-b-kzikJn-uc.
Meissner, W., 1984. *Psychoanalysis and Religious Experience*. New Haven/London: Yale University Press.
Oliver, K., 1993. *Reading Kristeva: Unravelling the Double Bind*. Bloomington: Indiana University.
Reineke, M., 2003. Our Vital Necessity: Julia Kristeva's Theory of Sacrifice. In eds. M. Joy, K. O'Grady, and J. Poxon, *Religion in French Feminist Thought*. London/New York: Routledge.
Stein, S., ed., 1999. *Beyond Belief: Psychotherapy and Religion*. London: Karnac.
Symington, N., 1994. *Emotion and Spirit*. London/New York: Karnac.
Wallace, E., 1991. Psychoanalytic Perspectives on Religion. *International Review of Psychoanalysis*, 18, pp. 265–78.

Ward, G., 1997. Postmodern Theology. In ed. D. Ford, *The Modern Theologians*, 2nd ed. Oxford: Blackwell.
Williams, M., 1999. Psychoanalysis: An Art or a Science? A Review of the Implications of the Theory of Bion and Meltzer. *British Journal of Psychotherapy*, 16(2), pp. 127–35.
Williams, R., 2000. *On Christian Theology*. Oxford: Blackwell Publishing.
Wright, K., 2009. *Mirroring and Attunement*. Hove: Routledge.
Wulff, D., ed., 1991. *Psychology of Religion: Classic and Contemporary Views*. New York/ Chichester: John Wiley.

Chapter 2

The search for the good

Both John and Charles Wesley aspired to be 'saved from sin', to be 'perfected in love' and to achieve 'perfect holiness'. It was a hope of wholeness and freedom:

> When shall I see the welcome Hour,
> That plants my God in me!
> Spirit of Health, and Life, and Power,
> And perfect Liberty!
>
> (*Hymns and Sacred Poems*, 1740, 'Against Hope, believing in Hope', p. 156)

How do these Wesleyan views of growth and goodness compare with what is understood as spiritual and psychological 'maturity' in psychoanalysis and in Christianity more widely? The present chapter is concerned with the relationship between the idea of development and growth, and the idea of the 'good'. It involves exploring parallels between psychoanalytic ideas of a 'mature' individual, and biblical aspirations to a Christian identity. Philosophers, theologians and psychoanalysts, among others, have long been preoccupied with the necessary or desirable elements required in becoming a 'good' person and in leading a 'good' life. In this context, and as will be obvious below, many authors use the terms 'morality' and 'ethics' interchangeably. Paul Ricoeur, however, differentiates them: for him, ethics refers to the '*aim* for an accomplished life', while morality is 'the articulation of this aim in *norms* characterised at once by the claim to universality and by an effect of constraint'. He defines "ethical intention" as 'aiming at the "good life" with and for others, in just institutions'. For him ethics is a striving for the good in the self, for Aristotle's 'living well'; it involves 'solicitude' for others and a requirement of justice and equality, not only for 'friends' but also for others who are not encountered 'face-to-face'. Morality is a 'limited' but 'indispensable' part of ethics but is encompassed by it (Ricoeur, 1992, pp. 170–2, 194).

It is with a striving for good in Ricoeur's 'ethical' sense that this chapter is concerned: it relates not only to *behaviour* towards others and to adherence to rules but also to responsibility to the self and to others, and to an individual's aspiration towards the 'good life'; this striving requires ongoing personal change.

As Antonaccio has pointed out, much current thinking sees morality in terms of human choice, convention, or the will to power; any ideas related to its deep or 'transcendent' source risk being labelled 'nostalgic' (Antonaccio, 2004, pp. 273–5). She describes the way in which the moral philosopher Iris Murdoch struggled against what she saw as the superficialities, illusions and 'lightness' of much modern philosophy and post-modern thought, by seeking to rescue the 'self' as a 'moral centre of substance' (Murdoch, 1993, p. 153, in Antonaccio, 2004, p. 278). Murdoch saw the moral life as based on the ordinary struggles of everyday life rather than in abstractions. For her, the 'subject' was an opaque and complex individual whose personality manifested not only the conscious and rational but also the darker unconscious and irrational aspects; for such a subject, the striving towards goodness and away from 'sin' could be almost impossible. This view of the personality led to her assertion that 'the idea of the good' was a 'transcendent moral ideal', with an absolute claim on human existence. She saw the 'transformation of the egoistic consciousness [as] the central task of ethics', an emphasis on inner change rather than on acceptable behaviour (Antonaccio, 2004, pp. 278–80). However, she had difficulty in rescuing the 'depth' of value and goodness without resorting to a religious foundation. Although she was an atheist, Murdoch's thought about religion demonstrated a great deal of ambivalence. While she saw the moral life as a struggle from illusion to realism, she also saw the human need for the images and myths, which religion offered:

> high morality without religion is too abstract. High morality craves for religion. Religion symbolises high moral ideas which then travel with us and are more intimately and accessibly effective than the unadorned promptings of reason. Religion suits the image-making human animal.
> (Murdoch, 1993, p. 484, in Antonaccio, 2004, pp. 281–3)

Murdoch saw human consciousness as in a constant relationship with 'the good as its ideal', but she located the Good *within* human consciousness rather than in a transcendent God (Antonaccio, 2004, p. 284).

In both Ricoeur and Murdoch, the emphasis was on inner, rather than behavioural, change. This emphasis persists in the following accounts of Christian and psychoanalytical understandings of the growth to goodness, as does Murdoch's concentration on the 'moral life' as based on everyday interactions.

Christian goodness

A full appreciation of Christian 'excellence' would, require a survey of ethical thought from Aristotle to contemporary Christian ethics. However, it is possible to draw out some features held in common in the search for goodness in Christianity and psychoanalytic thought with reference to Rowan Williams's work on New Testament ethics (Williams, 2000) and Ellen Charry's writing on Christian doctrine (Charry, 1997).

In both theology and analytic thought, a loving relationship is central to the development of a capacity for 'goodness' and for loving others, and it is the working out of love which leads to 'moral' action. 'Good' actions and attitudes, such as concern for others, a capacity for tolerance, forgiveness, a realistic assessment of the self, and a lack of arrogance, are common to both as manifestations of maturity. In neither discipline, however, is 'goodness' judged merely by behaviour: freedom *from* sin is central to Christianity, just as freedom *from* entrenched destructive patterns of behaviour is central to psychoanalytic change, but both also emphasise the need for freedom *for* a richer engagement with life: 'I am come that they might have life, and that they might have it more abundantly' (John 10:10). The letting go of sin or of repetitive destructive actions and relationships allows for a fuller and more loving engagement with new relationships.

Williams (2000, pp. 239–50) dismisses the commonly held belief that an individual's 'good' or destiny is to be found in a unique, hidden, authentic self of integrity, which is free from self-deception. For him, true self-perception and 'what is good' for the self have to be worked out in conversation and negotiation with others; in this way, the self 'grows ethically'. However, he suggests that the 'other', the 'interlocutor', in such conversations cannot be, in the estimation of the subject, an 'ideal' other, that is, one to whom the subject imagines he himself makes perfect sense. If this were the case there would be no challenge to his self-perception. There must be a relationship which involves a 'contentious' exchange, with frustration and resistance, with the discovery that some goals are unattainable, a form of 'self-dispossession'. However, neither can 'ethical growth' occur unless the subject is free from engaging in competition, rivalry, and jockeying for position. There must be a 'non-competitive other'. This other, Williams believes, is a God as shown through Christ, accessible to all, irrespective of privilege or position, whose actions 'do not occupy the same moral and practical spaces, and are never in rivalry' with the believer, a God who is not reactive but whose actions are prior to human activity and who is 'gracious'. Because the believer is 'authentically other' there is no need for a defensive strategy. Interactions and experiences of daily life take place in the sight of this 'non-competitive other'. The description of this relationship is reminiscent of psychoanalytical descriptions of the nourishing relationship with a loving and sometimes frustrating early object.

For Williams, it is not only the teaching of Jesus but also the narrative of his Incarnation, Crucifixion and Resurrection, which mediates the 'non-negotiable and therefore non-competitive presence before which ethical discourse is conducted'. In this context, there is an ongoing process of formation, with the assurance that failure and disaster are not final and where there is always the opportunity for forgiveness and restoration: 'What God's regard, as pronounced by Jesus, establishes is my presence as an agent, experiencing and "processing" experience. I continue to be a self in [the] process of being made, being formed in relation and transaction' (Williams, 2000, p. 249).

Williams goes on to explore the ways in which the Christian narrative can provide a framework for 'an ethic and an anthropology' not based on human argument and rivalry. Drawing on Charry, he examines primary Pauline literature, the letter to the Ephesians, and the Gospel of St Matthew, in terms of their approach to ethics and spirituality. He draws out the paradox in these texts: that while Christian behaviour is that which can be seen as manifesting the nature of God, as seen in Christ (the 'imitation' of Christ), it is not merely the successful performance of behaviour that manifests God. 'Failure' which is recognised and accepted can also be seen as mirroring God, in his kenotic gift in the incarnation and subsequent crucifixion (Williams, 2000, pp. 253–4).

Williams sees this 'ironic strategy' as central to the role of these texts as they might influence the development of a Christian ethic. Generosity, mercy and welcome manifest God as he was seen in Jesus, and this manifestation results in joy and delight in the beauty of God; however, failure, inadequacy and vulnerability also mirror God's giving up control, his 'dispossession'. Consequently, Williams advocates a scepticism towards successful performance. Both the Pauline and Matthean texts are seen as avoiding the idea that success in good behaviour is the means of forming the Christian identity; rather, it is based on a relationship with God as portrayed in the Beatitudes. The Beatitudes do, indeed, urge virtue, which mirrors the nature of God and gives delight, but they also describe situations of vulnerability which require a Christian response. This, for Williams, is neither one of passive acceptance, nor of militant resistance, but a working with the situation in order 'to show the character of God'. Rather than offering a code of morals, this reading of the Sermon on the Mount offers pointers and requires careful thought for every situation (Williams, 2000, pp. 255–9).

Williams describes ethical growth as based on a relationship with the loves and resistances of the world, and held by the love and forgiveness of an ideal object; within this context a wish to emulate the object develops. As such, unlike an adherence to a moral code imposed by a punitive father figure, it is a characterological change based on love.

This idea of the relationship with God, of the individual's 'knowing and loving God' as the basis of the development of Christian excellence, is also the theme of Charry's work. She demonstrates its development in New Testament texts and in pre-modern theology. She also shows how Christian doctrine might be seen as what she calls 'aretegenic' ('conducive to virtue') and as performing a salutary (health-promoting) function; how 'the imitation or assimilation to [God] brings proper dignity and human flourishing' (Charry, 1997, pp. 18–19). As with Williams, the antitheses of the Sermon on the Mount are seen as models for emulation rather than as rules, so that an 'alternative interior purity' is offered, consisting of 'aggressive self-scrutiny, compassion, integrity, selflessness and, finally, love of enemies, traits which are essentially limitless in application' (Charry, 1997, p. 76). It is the knowledge and love of God, as well as the practice of virtue, through the imitation of God as seen in Christ, which form the path to excellence. Coming to 'know' God, as understood by the patristic bishops, was not merely a cognitive process, though the intellect was important, but it required 'sapientia' (wisdom/love). As Charry points out *sapientia* derives from *sapere*, the Latin word which meant 'to taste or smell' and only later 'to discern or be wise'. She describes how St. Augustine encouraged believers to 'taste and enjoy God' and so participate in His justice, wisdom and goodness. It was this 'sapiential' knowledge of God, through a relationship which involved desire, love and enjoyment, which was seen as transformative (Charry, 1997, pp. 132–3, 229).

Examining Paul's letters, Charry emphasises the dramatic transformation of the self which involves both intellect and emotion, and which Paul repeatedly describes: 'be ye transformed by the renewing of your mind, that ye may prove what is good, and acceptable, and perfect will of God' (Romans 12:2). She enumerates the many images and vivid metaphors in Pauline and deutero-Pauline texts to describe this 'participation in Christ'. Changed behaviour (compassion, kindness, humility, meekness, patience, forgiveness and peace (Colossians 3:12) follows as the new self is moulded into the image of God, empowered by the Holy Spirit. The believers are to become newly dressed, to 'clothe [themselves] with love'. Christian 'goodness' here is seen as the striving towards the image of God, in the living out of these virtues through the grace of God, the indwelling of Christ and the guidance of the Holy Spirit (Charry, 1997, pp. 3, 46–50). While the 'imitation of Christ', the adherence to ways of behaving which manifest the nature of God, forms a crucial part of Christian moral codes and a guide to Christian spirituality, the process of transformation as understood by Charry and Williams emphasises inner change based on a relationship. It draws out the formative power of a relationship of trust, truth, acceptance and forgiveness; there is a struggle with a God of justice and mercy, towards a continuously changing but 'better' self.

Psychoanalytic understandings of a search for the good

The psychoanalyst Margot Waddell has written of the search to know 'how a person may be enabled to grow up in the inside as well as the outside'. She points out how, for psychoanalysis, this 'growing up' becomes identified with goodness: 'implicitly, development *is* good'. She bases her study on the characters in George Eliot's novels. This may seem an odd place to begin such a discussion, but as Waddell explains, Eliot's characters 'incarnate' her ideas, so that philosophical ideas about the striving for a good life can be explored through the details of their relationships. Waddell, like Eliot, finds this detailed attention to relationships more enlightening than abstract theorising (Waddell, 1999, pp. 271–2). Eliot's works provide what Ricoeur has described as a 'laboratory of selfhood', providing imaginative variations on individual development (Ricoeur, 1991, p. 350). It is a similar 'incarnation' to that which occurs in individual lives, including those described in the case histories of analytic patients. Like Murdoch, George Eliot's struggle, portrayed in her novels, was to find, in the absence of orthodox religion, a way of understanding and expressing the human wish for self-transcendence, goodness or purpose that fitted with her awareness of the complexity of human experience, particularly in relationships (Waddell, 1999, pp. 272–3).

Waddell uses Kleinian theory to elucidate the ways in which elements essential to the process of growth to mental, emotional and moral maturity emerge from the study of Eliot's characters. As a first essential, she describes the transformational capacity of a relationship with a 'good', emotionally available object in infancy (usually the mother). The child's experience of love and gratitude in response to the mother's love and care is the source of the development of trust and the belief in goodness (Klein, 1957, p. 180). Waddell explores how the infant's early pleasant or unpleasant 'feeling-state', within this relationship (for instance, feeling gratified and full of love, or frustrated and full of hate), come to acquire 'moral status'. She also demonstrates through Eliot's characters that when there has been a lack in this early loving experience, there remains a possibility of 'rescue' and of change and development occurring later in life, in the context of relationships with similar emotionally available objects (Waddell, 1999, pp. 278, 283).

A second essential in the 'growth to goodness' is a capacity to bear the truth about the self. In her discussion of the importance of truth, Waddell explores the difference between the 'ideal', as a source of hope and trust, and the 'idealised' as a distortion of the truth. She compares the way both psychoanalysis and literature engage with the role of truthfulness as an individual develops, and quotes Bion (1965, p. 38) who saw truth as a 'food' for the mind, while falsehood caused it to 'wither' (she does, however, regret that Bion's later work became concerned with theory and abstractions, rather than with details of people's lives). Coming to understand the deep truth about the self is an essential component or 'food', which provides the means by which an individual grows towards maturity. If growth is to occur, the often unpalatable truth about the self must not be denied but painfully addressed; it has to be 'genuinely suffered', rather than avoided. Waddell emphasises that this coming to the truth occurs within the minutiae of human relationships, as shown in Eliot's novels, and may be compared with the engagement of the therapist with the complex details of the patient's material in therapy (Waddell, 1999, pp. 272–3, 285). In both situations, the concentration on the particular in a detailed way, often over a long period of time and involving many interactions, allows the subject's truth to evolve and to become real for the subject.

Waddell uses *Daniel Deronda* as her principal example. I suggest that a similar 'growth to goodness' is apparent in the narrative of *Romola*, another of Eliot's novels. As Romola's awareness of the deep and often painful truths about herself increases, there develops a widened vision, with reduced egocentricity, an increased capacity to appreciate what other people feel, a willingness to take responsibility for her actions, and an ability to see herself as part of a wider universe. This is accompanied by an increased awareness and enjoyment of beauty, which as Waddell suggests reflects a 'changing unconscious relationship to a sense of goodness in the internal world' (Waddell, 1999, p. 276). As Romola describes it, the 'highest happiness' can only be gained by having

> wide thoughts and much feeling for the rest of the world, as well as ourselves; and this sort of happiness often brings so much pain with it, that we can only

tell it from pain by its being what we would choose before everything else, because our souls see it is good.

(Eliot, 1994, p. 547)

At the beginning of the novel, Romola is closely identified with her father, a man who relies almost entirely on intellect and on the strict adherence to rules. Through experience and through her relationships to others, there evolves a capacity to value feeling and to allow herself to become immersed in the physicality of caring for children. She has not ceased to use her mind, but there has been a move to involve the whole of her being in her judgements: affect and intellect, body and mind, unconscious and conscious, material and spiritual. She develops the capacity to be less bound by external codes of behaviour: moral judgements can become based on love rather than fear of punishment. In his introduction to the novel, Brown (1994, p. xviii) describes how Eliot portrays a moral system which constrains purely selfish impulses but without relying on authoritarian abstractions, and for her, this path depends on love, particularly close family relationships: 'She [Romola] felt the sanctity attached to all close relations, and therefore, pre-eminently to the closest, was but the expression in outward law of that result towards which all human goodness and nobleness must spontaneously tend' (Eliot, 1994, p. 442).

This is the kind of morality towards which Romola moves when she becomes involved in the lives and needs of others at the end of the novel. As she becomes aware of the previously unconscious, unpalatable truths about herself, she begins to be able to recognise others as whole people, to have concern for them and to be reconciled with them. There is an involvement in ordinary everyday concerns and actions, and responses to the needs and feelings of others, rather than grand gestures aimed at self-gratification.

Many of the themes in this psychoanalytic understanding of growth to maturity echo those in the work of Williams and Charry and involve change based on love: a loving, nourishing, trusting relationship is central, though not without inevitable frustrations; change occurs in 'ordinary' interactions and negotiations; there is an emulation of a valued good object; and there is a necessity for self-scrutiny through means which are not entirely intellectual. In both there is emphasis on inner and not merely behavioural change.

In the hymn quoted at the beginning of this chapter, we saw that the Wesleys aspired to wholeness and freedom. Two important elements in the striving towards this position have been discussed: the interaction with a transformational object and the development of an increasing awareness of deep truths about the self. In the next two chapters, these processes are discussed psychoanalytically so that this psychoanalytic understanding can be then be used in the subsequent exploration of how the 'growth to goodness' was played out in the Wesleys' lives.

References

Antonaccio, M., 2004. Iris Murdoch's Secular Theology of Culture. *Literature and Theology*, 18(3), pp. 271–91.

Bion, W., 1965. *Transformations: Change From Learning to Growth*. London: Heinemann.
Brown, A., 1994. Introduction. In G. Eliot, *Romola*. Oxford: Oxford University Press.
Charry, E., 1997. *By the Renewing of Your Minds: The Pastoral Function of Christian Doctrine*. New York/Oxford: Oxford University Press.
Eliot, G., 1862–3. *Romola*. Oxford: Oxford University Press, 1994.
Klein, M., 1957. Envy and Gratitude. In *Envy and Gratitude, and Other Works 1946–63*. London: Virago Press, 1988.
Murdoch, I., 1993. *Metaphysics as a Guide to Morals*. New York: Allen Lane/Penguin.
Ricoeur, P., 1991. Narrated Time. In ed. M. Vadez, *A Ricoeur Reader: Reflection and Imagination*. Toronto: Toronto University Press.
Ricoeur, P., 1992. *Oneself as Another*. Chicago: Chicago University Press.
Waddell, M., 1999. On Ideas of "The Good" and "The Ideal". *American Journal of Psychoanalysis*, 59(3), pp. 271–86.
Williams, R., 2000. *On Christian Theology*. Oxford: Blackwell.

Chapter 3

Interaction with an 'emotionally available' object

Psychoanalytic theory has elucidated the processes through which the chaotic infant, who is struggling with overwhelming, passionate, confused and conflicting feelings, can be transformed into someone who can think about and show concern for others. This chapter explores the first requirement for such change as discussed in the last chapter: a child's relationship with its first 'emotionally available', or 'transformational', object (usually the mother). An understanding of these ideas provides pointers in the search for transforming factors in the context of religious experience and in the examination of the Wesley family.

In 'The Ego and the Id', Freud outlined his view of the development of the mental structures (the 'superego' and the 'ego') which had the capacity to manage instinctual drives and so to control behaviour. The functioning of the superego, which he saw as an internal representation of parental figures, included all its prohibiting, censoring and controlling aspects, as well as the standard-setting and the ideal-inspiring aspects. He described the 'superego' or 'ego ideal' as the 'heir to the Oedipus complex' in which the superego 'retained the character of the father' (Freud, 1923, pp. 373–6). Here Freud was using *superego* and *ego-ideal* synonymously, but *ego-ideal* came to embody also those aspects towards which an individual would aspire. Freud was aware that the superego could be harsher and more severe than the parental figures; he attributed this to its harshness being reinforced by the subject's own 'inclination to aggression and destruction', and he compared the disciplining of such a dominating superego to Kant's Categorical Imperative (Freud, 1924, p. 422). Although for Freud, the wish to emulate the loved parents influenced behaviour, the stress was on the tyranny of the superego. He invoked his theory of castration anxiety as integral to the controlling of instincts so that it became a process based largely on fear (Freud, 1923, pp. 399–400).

Melanie Klein

Klein held a different view of the development of the moral sense, based on her understanding of the child's very early experience in the time before Freud's 'Oedipal' period (3–5 years). She explored the early mother/child interaction and the passionate and disturbing feelings which were part of it. She saw the impetus for development as inextricably bound up with the vicissitudes of this relationship and described a process of internalisation of aspects of this very early experience and the affects and defences involved. These she called 'positions'. Her ideas involved an assumption that human beings were 'moral in their *very nature*' and that the evolution of the moral sense was part of normal growth to maturity (Waddell, 1999, p. 283). Klein's concepts of her 'paranoid/schizoid' and 'depressive' positions are outlined below to show her understanding of this development of the moral sense, as the positions alter with maturation (Klein, 1946, pp. 2–16).

From her work in child analysis, she concluded that the child's primary fear was of annihilation, experienced as a fear of persecution; she attributed it to the inborn aggression and destructiveness of the 'death instinct'. The aggression was felt to threaten the early ego, which lacked cohesiveness, with fragmentation and annihilation. Klein believed that there was an immediate 'projection'[1] of these aggressive feelings into an external object (the breast/mother) which was then felt as persecutory because it was full of the infant's frightening feelings. She described a process of 'splitting' in the infant's view of the world: 'in states of gratification love-feelings turn towards the gratifying breast, while in states of frustration, hatred and persecutory anxiety attach themselves to the frustrating breast' (Klein, 1946, p. 7). The child's world is polarised into good and bad according to whether the child is frustrated or gratified. The good is exaggerated as a safeguard against the persecuting breast which is experienced not only as frustrating but also as containing the child's projected hate and aggression. The child's wish is for unlimited gratification and an *ideal* breast is phantasised as the answer to this wish. There is a strong sense of omnipotence, of being able to deny the persecutory breast and to create the ideal one. In addition to the projection of bad feelings, good and bad objects are taken into the ego (or introjected).[2] This results in a splitting of the ego into benevolent and persecutory internal objects. The splitting into good and bad is an essential part of the infant's early attempt to make sense of a bewildering world and a normal part of early mental functioning. Klein called this early position the 'paranoid-schizoid position' (Klein, 1946, p. 2, n1). In the paranoid-schizoid position the child's main anxiety is because of fear of persecution: persecutory or paranoid anxiety.

In the second three months, according to Klein, a process of integration begins. The good and bad aspects of the breast/mother come closer together and there is a gradual increase in awareness that the feeding and frustrating object is one and the same. This awareness leads to the development of feelings of guilt linked to the knowledge that the good mother has been attacked in phantasy, and there is an increased fear of losing this loved object. This stage, which Klein called the 'depressive position', is associated with feelings of depression and mourning. There is decreased splitting in the ego, with a less polarised view of the world, a clearer understanding of reality, decreased omnipotence, and a desire to make reparation out of concern for the previously hated object. The child's concern and reparation improve relationships, which in turn promote further integration of the ego. There is a reduction in the idealisation and denigration of objects, and a consequent reduction in persecutory anxiety. 'Depressive anxiety' predominates at this stage: a fear that the infant's internal hate and aggression will destroy its objects.

As Klein explains, while the child's internal drives, particularly the degree of innate aggression, are central to his success or failure in negotiating these positions, they are also affected by external conditions, particularly the availability of consistent, empathic mothering without traumatic loss, or disappointments too great for him to manage. Success leads to the development of the ability to tolerate ambivalence, to have concern for others and to relate to others as 'whole people' rather than as sources of gratification. There is less need for polarised thinking and an increased capacity to tolerate unpleasant feelings without having to project them immediately into others or to act impulsively to discharge them. There develops an ability to own less acceptable feelings, thoughts and wishes, in other words, a capacity to accept the truth about the self. This move to the depressive position can be considered as central to the development of more mature behaviour and attitudes; through this shift a 'natural' morality based on concern for the welfare of others is achieved. Some of the characteristics of this change, resonate with those associated with religious conversion (to be addressed later).

As we have seen, Klein stresses the difference between the 'ideal' and the 'idealised' object. The 'ideal' breast is seen as the focus for all the infant's desires and forms the 'core' around which its development occurs. If the child is faced with early experiences of deprivation, or disappointments too great to cope with at a particular stage, the 'ideal' object can be *idealised* and clung to for too long. Because there are unrealistic expectations that such an object will fulfil all the subject's desires, it will inevitably disappoint, and there will be repeated disappointments leading to disillusionment (Waddell, 1999, pp. 282–3).

Both 'persecutory' and 'depressive' anxiety have to be overcome. When this happens, the characteristics of the idealised and of the harsh, critical, persecutory internal figures are modified:

> Good objects – as distinct from idealized ones – can be established in the mind only if the split between persecutory and ideal figures has diminished, if aggressive and libidinal impulses have come close together and hatred has become mitigated by love.
>
> (Klein, 1950, p. 47)

This is achieved partly by the child's reparative urges, driven by guilt, towards the object she has damaged in phantasy, and also through continued consistent, loving, maternal care. There remains, however, an underlying fear of inflicting damage, which stimulates the impetus for continuing reparative impulses and actions. There is also a continuing fluctuation between the 'paranoid-schizoid' and the 'depressive' positions (Klein, 1948, pp. 34–8).

Klein made the important observation that if persecutory anxiety was not sufficiently overcome, the boundary between the conscious and unconscious would become 'rigid' rather than 'porous', with excessive repression of unconscious material. As a result, impulses, phantasies and thoughts, which might otherwise repeatedly become conscious, and so able to be judged and accepted or rejected by the ego, remain repressed (Klein, 1952, p. 87). This will affect development and further maintain the split between 'good' and 'bad' internal objects. As we will see, this was important to John Wesley's experience.

Unlike a morality based on the fear of a primitive father-figure as described by Freud, for Klein, 'depressive anxiety', the fear of *internal* aggression, which is felt as capable of damage, and guilt about damaging a loved object, is the impetus for reparative action. It is the basis of a more mature morality based on self-knowledge and self-awareness, which tends to negate the need to identify with an external figure or system of rules as a source of control. George Eliot described this change to a state in which the thinking self makes moral decisions, as 'the soul daring to act on its own warrant' (Eliot, 1994, p. 442). Britton has called it the 'emancipation' of the ego (Britton, 2003, pp. 104–16).

It is clear, then, that the success or failure in negotiating this stage of development will have a profound effect on an individual throughout life. In general, people function for much of the time in the depressive position, but at times, particularly when under pressure or threat, or when traumatised, they retreat to the paranoid-schizoid position. Some, however, will function mainly in a paranoid-schizoid mode.

Divergence from Klein

Since Klein other analysts have differed from her theories and there has been emphasis on other aspects which are important in the understanding of the Wesleys. Many, for instance, Fairbairn (1952, p. 166) and Winnicott (1965, p. 47), saw negative feelings (hate and aggression) as resulting from insult, frustration or deprivation, rather than as innate. There has also been criticism, among Independent analysts, of theories about early development, such as Klein's, in which the baby is said to be seen as a 'bundle of impulses seeking discharge' and in which the mother/child interaction involves the child's 'projecting' or 'evacuating' chaotic material into the mother (Wright, 2009, p. 77). Bion's theory of the mother as container could be viewed in this light. He described the way the child projects confused and fragmented images, impulses and feelings into the mother; these are contained by the mother, and through her 'reverie', are somehow altered and taken back in by the baby in more manageable form (Bion, 1962). Wright points out that exactly how this transformation is achieved is not described by Bion. For illumination, he turns to analysts for whom the child's primary aim is to relate and communicate, rather than to deal with destructive urges (Wright, 2009, pp. 76–81). He cites the work of Winnicott and Stern, who attribute a more 'active' role for the mother. Winnicott suggests that *form* is given to the child's emotional state by the mother's receptive holding, by her feeding the child and by her facial expression which 'mirrors' the child's experience (Winnicott, 1971, pp. 130–8). Stern describes as 'attunement' the mother's continuous tracking of the child's inner state, a non-verbal process of which the mother is largely unaware, in which the infant's inner state is enacted in her reactions so that the child feels in constant contact with her (Stern, 1985, pp. 138–61). For Wright, through these subtle forms of relating, the mother's capacity to be in touch with the child becomes the basis of the child's capacity to 'be in touch with himself'. He suggests that 'the external relationship might be internalised, thus providing the basis of inner containment' (Wright, 2009, pp. 22–6).

Winnicott introduced the term 'good-enough mother', a term that has entered everyday language, to describe a holding and mirroring mother who facilitates the development of the child's 'true self', rather than a falsely compliant self. She does this not by being perfect but by being able to respond repeatedly to the child's needs and gestures; she is a mother who can to judge the degree of frustration the child can manage at each stage (Winnicott, 1965, p. 145). The consistent care of this 'good-enough' mother is essential for the development of the child's moral sense. Like Klein, Winnicott links it to the child's struggle to integrate loving and destructive feelings towards the mother. He stresses her role as one of repeatedly surviving and remaining loving in the face of the child's destructiveness. She is also receptive to his reparative and loving behaviour, which is driven by guilt, the beginnings of his moral sense (Winnicott, 1965, pp. 102–3). The child internalises the 'good-enough' maternal image, and this enables the child to develop a psychological structure so that he is able to care for (or mother) himself; he develops the capacity to be alone and has trust in a 'benign environment' (Winnicott, 1965, p. 32).

Fairbairn's understanding of 'frozen' parts of the ego is helpful here. He also believed that the core of normal development was the child's relationship with a good mother and that the child's search for social relationships was its *primary* need. He suggested that the child's relationships with 'over-exciting' and 'over-frustrating' aspects of objects were repressed and came into being in the unconscious as 'bad' internal objects. The parts of the child's ego, which related to these internal objects, were split off from the central ego and were engaged with them in the unconscious (Fairbairn, 1952, p. 135). These split-off parts of the ego were in effect 'frozen', and so the ego was deprived of some of its power to relate to new events or objects in the external world in a realistic way. The greater the amount of ego, which was split off and engaged with the bad objects, the more the individual was prone to struggle with and re-enact early conflict in a new situation (Clarke, 2006, pp. 153–6). Clarke points out similarities with the ideas of the philosopher, John Macmurray, who saw morality in terms of the need to react to objects 'as they really are, and not in terms of our subjective inclinations and private sympathies' (Macmurray, 1935, p. 23). For Fairbairn, only an individual whose ego has become more integrated by letting go of its bad objects is able to interact in this way (Fairbairn, 1952, p. 145).

As discussed in Chapter 2, Eliot's novel *Daniel Deronda* 'incarnates' a process in which interactions with a 'good object' after infancy, can 'rescue' a subject and allow further transformation. Christopher Bollas writes about the mother as the first 'transformational object', but in addition discusses such transforming interactions at a later stage of life. He describes how the memory of the early relationship with the mother is important in the person's search for a future object '(a person, place, event or ideology) that promises to transform the self'. He suggests that, for the infant, 'the mother is less significant and identifiable as an object than as a process that is identified with cumulative internal and external transformations'. Subsequent relating to 'transformational objects' occurs when the adult seeks out a repetition of the early experience with an object recognised as potentially transforming. The search continues through life, and in Bollas's view a psychosomatic sense of recognition and 'fit', sometimes a sense of the 'uncanny' or the numinous, is evoked by the resonance with the previous experience. He suggests that the promise of change inspires a sense of reverence, and the subject then 'tends to nominate such objects as sacred' (Bollas, 1987, pp. 14–17).

As we have seen, Klein saw idealisation as a defensive response to a failure of progression from the paranoid-schizoid to the depressive position. The self-psychologist, Heinz Kohut, had a more optimistic view. Jones charts Kohut's understanding of the *evolution* of idealisation from the child's early or 'archaic' experience of the mother as a state of 'narcissistic bliss' in which both the self and the parents are idealised. It becomes modified to the 'mature narcissism' of adulthood, in which idealisation persists but is tempered with reality, and where relationships are characterised by 'freedom, spontaneity, and realism' (Jones, 2002, pp. 18–23). Kohut describes a further alteration of narcissism, into what he calls 'cosmic narcissism'. There is a shift from a preoccupation with the self to a feeling that one is part of a wider, timeless context, enabling one to see life 'sub specie aeternitatis': an 'abiding attitude', not a transient experience (Kohut, 1978, pp. 455–6 in Jones, 2002, pp. 27–8). (This state corresponds to 'wide thoughts 'of Eliot's heroine in *Romola*.)

Jones elucidates Kohut's term 'object hunger', which is important in understanding how individuals relate to their faith: if in the early stage of the mother/child relationship, there is a loss of the mother, or there are too sudden or too large disappointments in her, then the process of disillusionment is unmanageable. The process of internalisation of the good mother is hampered, and a longing for the original 'archaic' experience with the ideal mother persists. The self then feels empty, depleted and depressed and becomes dependent on external sources to boost self-esteem. There is an intense striving for a substitute for the missing segments of the psychic structure (Jones, 2002, p. 20). This state of affairs, this aptly named 'object hunger', can persist into adulthood: there is a searching for people, philosophies or religions to idealise and with which to identify. They become a source of increased self-esteem and a confirmation of the subject's goodness. Drugs or alcohol are tempting as self-soothers. These 'replacement' objects are not valued for their own qualities but because they fulfil a need to re-create the archaic relationship.

When a person fails to develop adequate psychological structures in this way, he may embrace a form of religion or a philosophy with intense 'hunger' so that it acts as a substitute for an early relationship (an 'archaic object'). It is then unlikely that he would be able to explore any hazards, weaknesses or disadvantages of his religion of choice or to consider any possible good aspects of alternative philosophies or religions. Any differences from the chosen beliefs would be denigrated. In order to fulfil its function as an archaic object, the discovered substitute must be idealised and unquestioned. Such is the power of the fixation on the replacement archaic 'self-object', and the need for it, and the heady increase in self-esteem when such a substitute object is engaged that a thoughtful, realistic consideration of associated moral issues becomes impossible.

The theorists in this chapter vary in their understanding of the vicissitudes of the child's relationship with the early 'emotionally available' object. Freud and Klein emphasised innate destructive, aggressive impulses (the death instinct), while Winnicott, Fairbairn and Kohut attributed the infant's rage and aggression to its response to failures in the environment, particularly in the mother/child relationship. For Freud, moral behaviour was subject to a rigid paternal law, internalised as the superego, and it resulted from fear; in Klein and Kohut, the development of a more mature conscience depended on the internalisation of a reliable parental object, which was not idealised, but was more like Winnicott's 'good-enough' mother. Klein and Winnicott saw the capacity for moral behaviour as arising from guilt and concern for good objects, and the integration of good and bad internal and external objects as enabling an increased freedom to relate to objects in an undistorted and empathic way, as integration proceeds, As described by Fairbairn, freedom and flexibility in new situations are possible only when previously split-off or 'frozen' parts of the ego have been released from 'bad objects' and integrated into the central ego.

Many elements in George Eliot's characters that are intrinsic to the capacity to lead a 'good life' have appeared in the work of the previously mentioned authors. A later examination explores how John and Charles Wesley fared in relating to potentially transformational objects in their early lives and subsequently. For instance, how successful were they in establishing a 'good-enough' internal, maternal object, and to what extent were they dominated by 'bad' internal objects? When there is a failure successfully to negotiate these transformational processes, when defensive mechanisms such as splitting and projection predominate, and when there is no integration of split-off parts of the ego, there is an avoidance of awareness of inner feelings. The boundary between the conscious and unconscious is less porous, and the perception of inner and outer reality is distorted. As a result, moral judgements depend on placating an external lawgiver, and the emphasis is on self-justification or achieving the moral high ground, rather than on any attempt to accept and manage feelings which are felt as bad. The defensive processes and the internalised relationships with 'bad' objects are unconscious:

in Jung's terms the 'shadow' is outside consciousness but has to be confronted: 'One does not become enlightened by imagining figures of light, but by making the darkness conscious' (Jung, 1967, p. 265). After Freud, the emphasis has been increasingly on internal change rather than obedience to moral codes: on love and concern rather than fear and on freedom to relate to others pleasurably and flexibly, in other words, to flourish. All these features mirror Charry's 'aretegenic' features of Christ's narrative and teaching referred to earlier.

Notes

1 *Projection* is used here to describe a process by which feelings, impulses or parts of the self are imagined to be located in an object outside the self (Rycroft, 1972, pp. 125–6).
2 Ego is understood as that part of the personality which relates to objects and is experienced as oneself (Rycroft, 1972, p. 39).

References

Bion, W., 1962. A Theory of Thinking. *International Journal of Psychoanalysis*, 43, pp. 306–10.
Bollas, C., 1987. *The Shadow of the Object: Psychoanalysis of the Unthought Known*. London: Free Association Press.
Britton, R., 2003. *Sex, Death and the Superego: Experiences in Psychoanalysis*. London/New York: Karnac.
Clarke, G., 2006. *Personal Relations Theory: Fairbairn, Macmurray and Suttie*. London/New York: Routledge.
Eliot, G., 1862–3. *Romola*. Oxford: Oxford University Press, 1994.
Fairbairn, W., 1952. *Psychoanalytic Studies of the Personality*. London/Boston: Routledge and Kegan Paul.
Freud, S., 1923. The Ego and the Id. In *On Metapsychology: The Theory of Psychoanalysis*. Harmondsworth: Penguin, vol. 11, 1984.
Freud, S., 1924. The Economic Problem of Masochism. In *On Metapsychology: The Theory of Psychoanalysis*. Harmondsworth: Penguin, vol. 11, 1984.
Jones, J., 2002. *Terror and Transformation: The Ambiguity of Religion in Psychoanalytic Perspective*. Hove: Brunner-Routledge.
Jung, C., 1967. *Alchemical Studies*. Princeton: Princeton University Press.
Klein, M., 1946. Notes on Some Schizoid Mechanisms. In *Envy and Gratitude, and Other Works, 1946–1963*. London: Virago Press, 1988.
Klein, M., 1948. On the Theory of Anxiety and Guilt. In *Envy and Gratitude, and Other Works, 1946–63*. London: Virago Press, 1988.
Klein, M., 1950. On the Criteria for the Termination of Analysis. In *Envy and Gratitude, and Other Works, 1946–63*. London: Virago Press, 1988.
Klein, M., 1952. Some Theoretical Conclusions Regarding the Emotional Life of the Infant. In *Envy and Gratitude, and Other Works, 1946–63*. London: Virago Press, 1988.
Kohut, H., 1978. Forms and Transformations of Narcissism. In ed. P. Ornstein, *The Search for the Self*, vol. 1. New York: International Universities Press.
Macmurray, J., 1935. *Reason and Emotion*. London: Faber and Faber.
Rycroft, C., 1972. *A Critical Dictionary of Psychoanalysis*. London: Penguin Books.

Stern, D., 1985. *The Interpersonal World of the Infant*. New York: Basic Books.
Waddell, M., 1999. On Ideas of "The Good" and "The Ideal". *American Journal of Psychoanalysis*, 59(3), pp. 271–86.
Winnicott, D., 1965. *The Maturational Processes and the Facilitating Environment*. London: Karnac, 1990.
Winnicott, D., 1971. Mirror Role of Mother and Family in Child Development. In *Playing and Reality*. Harmondsworth: Penguin Books, 1986.
Wright, K., 2009. *Mirroring and Attunement*. Hove: Routledge.

Chapter 4

The search for deep truth through symbolisation

The search for the 'deep truth' about the self, of the facing up to and 'suffering' often unpalatable truths, is an essential part of a growth to goodness (see Chapter 2). The child with its mother, the patient in therapy or the Christian believer has to learn to think about and make meaning out of largely unconscious fragmented thoughts, images, chaotic feelings and impulses.

Psychoanalysts see this creation of meaning out of chaos as depending on the individual's capacity to 'symbolise'. The term is used in a particular way to describe not only the use of objects as symbols, and in rituals, but also for the conceptualising and verbalising of unconscious content. This chapter considers psychoanalytic theory about 'symbolisation' and the processes involved in the development of the capacity to form and use symbols. It will also become apparent what problems and difficulties arise if the capacity to symbolise is inhibited.

Kristeva's discussion of a subject's interaction with Christian narrative, ritual and symbol is introduced in this chapter. It offers insight into the ways a believer can be affected by Christian symbol at a deep level. In spite of Kristeva's reservations about religion, and the ambiguity which emerges from her writing about its effects, I find her interpretations helpful in understanding the responses of John and Charles Wesley to their faith.

The capacity to use symbols

The development of the capacity to symbolise is closely related to the way an infant familiarises herself with the world and endows it with meaning, and also with the ways in which she makes sense of her own inner world. Provided the child has been lucky enough to have a 'good-enough' mother, she becomes secure enough to turn her attention to the world. A secure and confident infant begins to encounter other objects and people and to endow them with personal meaning. Bollas has written of the processes through which the outer world gradually becomes populated with meaningful objects and the inner world with equally meaningful representations of them (Bollas, 1993, pp. 33–46, 55–6). *Early* experiences of objects make them particularly powerful and evocative, but the internal world continues to be enriched as layers of meaning are added.

The endowing of objects with particular significance is intrinsic to their use in negotiating the inevitable losses involved in a child's achieving independence. Such 'transitional' objects symbolise the mother during the gradual separation from her and until an internal image of a reliable mother is formed (Winnicott, 1971, pp. 1–6). This is the basis of the development of 'the capacity to be alone' (Winnicott, 1990, pp. 29–36). Although transitional objects symbolise the mother, they retain their own qualities. The child does not mistake the teddy bear for the mother but is comforted by what it represents. Winnicott also described the development of an *area* in which 'transitional phenomena' occur, a 'transitional space': a potential space between the mother and the child where the boundary between subjectivity and objectivity is blurred so that it functions as a place of 'illusion'. In this area of illusion, between subjectivity and objectivity, there is no pressure to differentiate between what is a product of phantasy and what is objectively real. As weaning occurs, a gradual process of *dis*illusionment proceeds, which has to be at a rate which is bearable for the child so that the task of accepting reality can be negotiated (Winnicott, 1971, pp. 10–14). For Winnicott, transitional space persists into adulthood, as an area where there is a relative freedom from the struggle to differentiate between the subjective and the objective. He described children's play and adult art, culture and religious practices, as occurring in transitional space: a space where reflection and experimentation and play with ideas, images, symbols and material objects can occur. 'Illusion' was not used by Winnicott in the sense of something distorted or false but as a product of creativity, with elements of both the subjective and the objective, and as offering an opportunity for growth (Winnicott, 1971, pp. 11–14).

Symbol formation and maturity

The Kleinian analyst Hannah Segal asserted that 'all communication [was] made by means of symbols'. According to her, not only material objects but also words functioned as symbols. They were the means by which feelings and phantasies could be verbalised and communicated externally, but they were also the means by which thought was verbalised internally, as a way of understanding the self. She wrote of people who seemed to be 'well in touch with their unconscious', who were aware of their deeper impulses and feelings. In these individuals, she believed, there was a 'constant free symbol-formation', which allowed them to be aware of and in control of '*symbolic expressions*' of unconscious material (Segal, 1988, p. 169).

For Segal, the capacity to form and use symbols is affected by the degree of maturity an individual has reached: the degree of success in the use of symbols is related to the amount of *projection* involved. When it predominates, aspects of the self are projected into an object to such an extent that it *becomes* something else. The object then is not a true symbol but what she called a 'symbolic equation' (Segal, 1988, pp. 164–5).

Segal saw the need to protect the loved object from internal aggression, as experienced in the 'depressive position', as a powerful stimulus for the formation of symbols. Symbols *represent* the original object and displace aggression from it, thus lessening the guilt and fear of loss. True symbols help in negotiating loss by being internalised, as a way of repairing and preserving the original object symbolically; as acknowledged 'creations' of the subject, they can be used 'freely'. 'Symbolic equations', on the other hand, are delusional attempts at replacements; they *become* the lost object and are used to *deny* the loss. As a result, they do not aid renunciation, or future development (Segal, 1988, pp. 166–9).

Unlike Klein and Segal, who saw the creative use of symbols as driven by guilt and as an attempt to restore the damaged object, Wright (citing Winnicott) describes creativity as arising from an inner need due to something lacking in the mother/child interaction. There is a search for a 'form' which fits and symbolises the missing experience, an attempt to 'establish the integrity of the *self*' (Wright, 2009, p. 60).

There are parallels in these descriptions of the use of symbols and the use of religious symbols. The symbolic object used retains something of its own qualities, but contains and represents something of the presence of the renounced or missing object; in the same way, a religious symbol retains its own material attributes but also contains a sense of another ungraspable reality, which is evoked for the observer. The religious symbol and the reality it represents, like the psychoanalytic symbol and the remembered presence of the object, are brought into a close relation to each other. However, one does not *become* the other. If this distinction is lost, in the realm of religion, the object becomes an 'idol', or, in Segal's terms, a 'symbolic equation'.

The internalised 'combined object' and triangular structures

Segal's linking of the capacity for symbol formation with the move to 'depressive' functioning is pursued in the work of Britton. He stresses the importance of the formation of an internalised, parental, sexual couple, a 'combined object', for the capacity to think and symbolise. Like Klein, Britton writes of the child's need to accept the realities of the Oedipal situation: as the development of the 'depressive position' proceeds he has to come to terms with the fact that his parents are a sexual couple and that he is excluded from their relationship (Britton, 2004, pp. 84–5). As the child comes to accept this reality, the internalised 'combined object' is established. Britton emphasises that unless the infant has already established a 'securely based maternal object' (an internalised 'good-enough' mother), then the capacity to accept the Oedipal reality will be compromised. The ability to negotiate the hates, rivalries, and fears of abandonment of the Oedipal situation, and the development of the 'depressive position' will be adversely affected. He uses Bion's concept, the 'container/contained' relationship, to clarify the link between the establishment of a secure maternal internal object and success in negotiating the Oedipal situation. A good containing mother/child relationship in which the child feels understood and affirmed, and in which the mother's capacity to symbolise the child's feelings is internalised by the child, is a firm basis for the negotiation of the Oedipal situation. This negotiation is succeeded by the development of a good, creative, 'container/contained' internal, parental couple (Britton, 2004, pp. 85–9). Because its formation depends on the negotiation of Oedipal loves, hates and fears, the development of the combined object is witness to an ability to tolerate the tensions between these feelings, and it is out of these tensions that the capacity to think and symbolise develops.

If the child can accept his parents as a good sexual couple he finds himself in a new position. The link between the parents, and each parent's link with the child, form what Britton calls 'triangular space'. In this space, the child is able to observe the parents and can be observed as a separate subject. He can now relate, as 'a witness and not a participant'. This introduces the idea of being observed. It provides 'a capacity for seeing ourselves in interaction with others and for entertaining another point of view whilst retaining our own, for reflecting on ourselves whilst being ourselves'. The capacity to see the parents in a 'benign' relationship, Britton suggests, allows the development of a space of reflection and mental freedom. It is the 'basis for a belief in a secure and stable world' (Britton, 2004, pp. 85–7).

Harris Williams describes the poetic Muse as a 'symbol-making power', and as an internal object, similar to the combined object described above. It contains the emotional tension of contrary feelings and offers inspiration in creative work. She quotes Blake's use of 'marriage of contraries' and Milton's use of 'hateful siege of contraries' to describe their sources of inspiration (Williams, 2005, pp. 4–7). The poet is able to symbolise unconscious material so that it becomes conscious and can be thought about.

However, a good internal parental couple such as this does not always develop, and the symbolising capacity is then compromised. For instance, according to Bion, as described by Britton, a mother's failure to accept what the child projects is felt, not only as a failure but also as an attack on the child's link with her as a good object, and the only way the child can preserve the mother as good in these circumstances is to attribute the hostility to another source. It is then felt as coming from the father. In this situation, the idea of the parents' coming together inevitably reinstates the mother as a 'non-receptive, deadly mother', and this is experienced as an unbearable mental catastrophe (Britton, 2004, pp. 89–90). In addition, again drawing on Bion, Britton describes how, when containment fails, the child's primitive fears, instead of being mollified, become more terrifying. They manifest themselves as a sense of 'nameless dread' (Bion, 1967, p. 117): 'a fear of being overwhelmed by uncontained, untransformed, psychic elements or of living in the aftermath of their annihilation' (Britton, 1998, pp. 54–7). These two consequences are particularly important in understanding the states of mind of the Wesley brothers.

The processes described earlier are, of course, influenced by the child's constitution and temperament, especially the predominance of negative feelings such as hate and aggression, and also by external traumatic events. However, in favourable circumstances, he is able to 'think', reflect, and use symbols, including words, to make sense of his inner world, and to manage fragmented and disturbing experiences and feelings. Several authors quote Shakespeare, who expresses this exactly in *A Midsummer Night's Dream*:

> And as imagination bodies forth
> The form of things unknown, the poet's pen
> Turns them to shapes, and gives to airy nothing
> A local habitation and a name.
>
> (V.1. 14–17)

Here it is the poet's pen which can symbolise the 'things unknown', but it also describes the way the mother contains the child's fragmented experience and converts it to something which can be thought about and begins to have meaning. The poet, the mother, or the therapist, are all striving to provide 'A local habitation and a name' for these fragmented, chaotic and conflicting elements. A poet who succeeds in giving 'airy nothing / A local habitation and a name' can be seen as having a particular facility in accessing these deeper parts of the self, and giving them meaningful form. As in Anne Stevenson's poem 'How Poems Arrive':

> You say them as your undertongue declares,
> Then let them knock about your upper mind
> Until the shape of what they mean appears.
>
> (Stevenson, 2017, p. 29)

At the opposite extreme from the poet are individuals who were not well contained as infants, in whom the capacity to symbolise has not been internalised, and in whom their own symbolising capacity is therefore compromised; then uncomprehended, distressing affects and experiences must remain 'walled off' in the inner world, like a foreign body, and erupt into consciousness as a disturbing sense of 'nameless dread'.

Kristeva – the 'symbolic' and the 'semiotic'

Like the authors quoted above, Kristeva focuses on the capacity to verbalise and to use symbols as it develops in the child's very early relationships. She, too, stresses the importance of the love within the parental couple and the dynamics of their triangular relationship with the infant. However, in order to understand her thought it is necessary to appreciate that she often uses words in an idiosyncratic way.

She has adopted some of the concepts described by the French analyst Jacques Lacan, but she differs from him in many aspects. While adopting Lacan's use of the term *symbolic* to indicate a realm of laws, rules and words, Kristeva uses the term *semiotic* in her own idiosyncratic sense to describe the means by which a child relates to the world prior to the acquisition of language. At this early stage, the child responds to the sound and rhythm of words rather than their content. These 'semiotic' ways of relating and communicating precede those of the 'symbolic' realm but also coexist with it. The child gradually becomes increasingly dependent on more structured, organised, meaningful language, but 'semiotic' remnants persist in the *form* of language and in other sensory and bodily experiences. The 'semiotic' is the realm of the maternal, of the body and of devouring drives. According to Kristeva, as a child acquires language and moves into the realm of the 'symbolic', the 'semiotic' will continue to erupt into it in one way or another. This eruption occurs in literature, particularly poetry, and is expressed in the form, style or rhythm of language; in its silences, shifts, metaphors, ironies, paradoxes, illogicalities or slips of the tongue; and in the tone of voice of the speaker (Kristeva, 1986, pp. 90–123). It is not always clear whether she sees the relationship between the symbolic and the semiotic as 'dialectical' which suggests opposition, struggle and a striving for transcendence or as a 'dialogue' suggesting harmony and a relationship. Edelstein argues convincingly that for Kristeva the relationship is one of dialogue. Thus, Kristeva's *Stabat Mater* comprises 'symbolic' and 'semiotic' discourses on motherhood and on the Virgin Mary and shows an interlacing, mutually enriching form of relationship, rather than an oppositional one (Edelstein, 1992, pp. 31–3).

Kristeva describes the merged relation of the child with the mother, and she uses the term *chora* for this realm of the semiotic. She borrows this term from Plato, for whom the *chora* was 'an ancient, mobile, unstable receptacle, prior to the One, to the father, and even to the syllable, metaphorically suggesting something nourishing and maternal' (Kristeva, 1985, p. 5). She describes the 'prehistoric' mother/child relationship and the child's experience at the beginning of the separation. If the child is to enter the world of meaning (the realm of the 'symbolic') and have her own psychic space for thought and reflection, there has to be a separation from the mother. There must be a movement towards a paternal *function*. Drawing on Freud, Kristeva attributes this function to a 'third party'. She appropriates Freud's idea of a 'father in his own personal pre-history' and his description of a very primitive form of identification, prior to object love (Freud, 1923, p. 370, in Kristeva, 1983, p. 26). This 'imaginary father', or the 'father in individual pre-history', arises and acts *within* the mother/child symbiotic relationship (or dyad), rather than as an external agency that breaks up the dyad; this 'third party' is portrayed by Kristeva as a loving, reliable, calming father, to be distinguished from the prohibiting rival of the later Oedipus complex (Kristeva, 1983, pp. 42, 46, 374). The term 'imaginary father' describes, not an object but a paternal *function*, which is available for an 'idealising identification'; through this identification, the infant becomes *like* the 'non-object', the 'imaginary father'.

Kristeva points out that Freud's understanding of this archaic identification was of an 'oral assimilation', which included ideas of devouring and incorporating the other. For Kristeva, the 'being like' involves developing the capacity to verbalise. The physical urge to devour is sublimated in 'the joys of chewing, swallowing, nourishing oneself . . . with words. In being able to receive the other's words, to assimilate, repeat, and reproduce them, I become like him: One. A subject of enunciation. Through psychic osmosis/identification. Through love' (Kristeva, 1983, pp. 25–6).

Her description suggests maternal, paternal and infantile elements within a matrix, in which the infant has not yet become a discrete object. The maternal elements relate to skin contact, care of sphincters and feeding, while paternal aspects relate to symbols and verbalisation. She offers a reminder that the baby's first vocalisations are usually in interactions with the mother so that, while the use of words is seen as a 'paternal' function, it is initiated within the maternal matrix (Kristeva, 1983, p. 27).

Once a degree of separation from the mother has been achieved, the infant is struggling with feelings of loss and grief. There is a loss of omnipotence and she becomes aware of her internal emptiness and that she is merely '*like* someone else', only an imitation of her objects (Kristeva, 1980, p. 10). As we have seen, Segal believed that all communication and so the capacity to relate to others depended in the capacity to use symbols, including words. Similarly, Kristeva describes the emergence of the self in the context of language and she describes it in terms used of language: the 'symbolic' and the 'semiotic'. The child has to achieve some balance between the pull of the 'maternal *chora*' and the identification with the 'imaginary father', between the 'semiotic' and 'symbolic' (Kristeva, 1986, pp. 93–105). If this balance is achieved there emerges '*le sujet en procès*', not yet a subject, but the beginnings of the self (Kristeva, 1985, p. 9). To be in this place of balance but also of 'discomfort, unease' and 'dizziness' is likened to being suspended, unstable and fragile, a 'frightened body', on a thin net of words, symbols and rules over an empty void (Kristeva, 1980, pp. 9–11, 1983, p. 42). According to Kristeva, the supportive 'loving father' must also be capable of 'playing his part as Oedipal father in symbolic Law': there must be a 'harmonious blending of the two facets of fatherhood'. If this blend exists, it allows the development of speech which is linked to affective meaning and which has 'live meaning' in relationships with others (Kristeva, 1987, pp. 23–4). She goes on to describe an Oedipal situation, which, as for Klein, arises prior to that described by Freud and involves not just a 'paternal *function*' but the mother's desire for another, usually the father. A mother who does not have such a desire for another becomes what Kristeva describes as a 'clinging mother', whose demands on the child for love adversely affect the child's capacity for loving and the development of his psychic life. The mother's love in this case becomes a devouring kind of love. The child cannot 'hatch from such an egg' (Kristeva, 1983, p. 34). When the mother does desire another, the child is loved by the mother 'in respect of the other'. The child is discussed as 'he' in the discourse between mother and father, and this represents the beginnings of his becoming a separate object. Such a child is freed to love another because he has been loved in a way different from the fused, devouring love, which would have left him restricted only to searching for a maternal substitute, 'who would cling to his body like a poultice – a reassuring balm, asthmatogenic perhaps, but nevertheless a permanent wrapping'. It is the mother's desire for a third that remains important. According to Kristeva, the mother's desire for the paternal phallus is a 'godsend' for the child. It is this desire that assists the child in understanding that the mother's entire function is not consumed in responding to his needs. This 'godsend' is the mother's gift to the child, who identifies with it, with the 'father–mother conglomerate'. The importance of this for the child is the realisation that the mother is not complete, she *wants* something beyond the mother/child dyad. Kristeva refers back to Freud's famous question, 'What does woman want?' and she suggests that what the child must conclude is that at any rate the mother wants 'not I'. She writes, 'And it is out of this "not I" . . . that an Ego painfully attempts to come into being' (Kristeva, 1983, p. 41). The awareness that the mother's want is for 'not I', which initiates the child into the symbolic realm, is associated with feelings of pain, emptiness and loss, and the child is supported in managing these feelings by the identification with the 'imaginary father'. The emptiness is preserved and tolerated rather than magically abolished. The child is held over the emptiness and pain, 'in the sight of the third party', and is 'calmed' and turned into 'a producer of signs, representations and meanings'. It is in this situation, supported by the 'imaginary father' that the self begins to 'be' (Kristeva, 1983, pp. 42–3) The identification, the 'being like' the 'father in pre-history', is described as an 'amatory identification', a loving identification, which is 'loaded' with pre-verbal and 'drive-affected' elements. It brings together the symbolic and the semiotic. In the light of this, Kristeva describes the object (or strictly the not-yet-object) of this identification, as a 'metaphorical object of love', and the identification as 'metaphoric'. The 'metaphorical object', like a metaphor, attempts to bring meaning to what was incoherent, chaotic and loaded with drives, affect and physical sensation: '*Metaphor* should be understood as a movement towards the discernible, a journey towards the visible'. The 'imaginary father' offers a pull, a 'drawing', towards the realm of words, symbols and the making of meaning, but the identification with 'him' incorporates also the 'semiotic' so that there is no loss of heterogenicity in such a metaphoric identification (Kristeva, 1983, pp. 24–31). As in analysis, where there is an 'idealising identification' with the analyst, the subject is always changing, repeatedly losing her identity in response to changes in relationships. Kristeva's subject is always a '*sujet en procès*', a split subject, 'mortal and speaking' (Kristeva, 1985, pp. 7–9).

If the function of the 'father of pre-history' is inadequate, then the only paternal function remaining is that of the prohibitive Oedipal rival. To merge with the Oedipal father is to be dominated by the paternal law, where words are interpreted in a fixed, rigid way, or idolised. The attraction of a return to the maternal *chora* is strong but also felt as dangerous: a place of chaos, meaninglessness and madness.

It is to be avoided and is associated with ideas of filth, defilement and death. Kristeva describes it not as the object, but as the 'abject'. She sees 'all religious, moral, and ideological codes on which rest the sleep of individuals', as means of avoiding the abject (Kristeva, 1980, pp. 209–10). The 'abject' exists at the point of separation between mother and child. It is part of the struggle for individuation: it creates repulsion in the subject and hence is a protection from being pulled into meaningless madness:

> No, as in true theatre, without make-up or masks, refuse or corpses *show me* what I permanently thrust aside in order to live. These bodily fluids, this defilement, this shit are what life withstands, hardly and with difficulty on the part of death. There I am at the border of my condition as a living being. My body extricates itself, as being alive, from that border.
> (Kristeva, 1980, p. 3)

The abject incorporates blood, including menstrual blood, and has associations with blood loss at birth, the painful, traumatic separation of the child from the mother. It is linked with the maternal and with abhorrence of the maternal (Kristeva, 1980, pp. 71–9). Kristeva writes that it is this threatening abjection which 'motivates' Freud's incest dread, and that the prohibition associated with it is the basis of the development of a discrete self; it facilitates the entry into the symbolic realm and the social order (Kristeva, 1980, pp. 62–4). She sees many religious rituals as warding off these primitive fears of sinking back into the abject, of being irretrievably lost in the mother. Filth becomes 'defilement' in religious ritual, and rituals of defilement and purification are a means of dealing with this fear. It is a fear of losing the whole self in a realm of chaos, madness and meaninglessness, rather than of losing a part of the self, as in Freud's castration anxiety (Kristeva, 1980, pp. 63–4).

The function of the 'imaginary father' can be compared to the containing, symbolising function of the mother in the mother/child dyad, as described by Britton: it is a necessary preliminary if the child is to cope with the challenges of the Oedipal situation, or, in Kristeva's terms, with the mother's wanting 'not-I'. Her account is also reminiscent of the previous discussion of the development of an internalised combined object and the development of a 'third position' (Britton, 2004, pp. 87–9), a subjectivity developed in a triadic setting, a 'triadic subjectivity'.

When there is a failure of balance between the pull of the maternal *chora* and the imaginary father, there is, for Kristeva, an absence of 'psychic space', a condition which she suggests is found the *'new maladies of the soul'* (Kristeva, 2001, p. 135).

Through case histories she shows how in the absence of an adequate relationship with an 'imaginary father', the infant is unable to achieve a sense of autonomy and is likely to develop a variety of symptoms. In helping such sufferers, the therapist 'is summoned in place of the imaginary father'; it is the reliable loving transference which takes the place of the love of the 'imaginary father' (Kristeva, 1983, pp. 48–53).

How then, faced with the hazards and terrors of the 'abject', and the severity of the 'Law of the Father', is it possible to maintain the balance necessary to create one's own psychic space, to tolerate stoically the knowledge of the split self and the underlying emptiness and to resist collapsing into a dyad? Kristeva argues that it is important that culture should provide ways in which an idealisable 'imaginary father' can be symbolised in order to support an individual in the face of the 'abject': 'The speaking being is a wounded being', struggling with an 'aching for love', with incomprehensible urges to devour, and feelings of loss. Without an opportunity to symbolise an 'imaginary father', an individual who is drawn towards a dyad with the mother, a 'magnet of desire and hatred, fascination and disgust', suffers from an 'abolition of psychic space', a space which would only be provided in a triadic relationship (Kristeva, 1983, pp. 372–4).

Kristeva explores opportunities to symbolise archaic experience in literature, art, psychoanalysis, and religion. Because she is a non-believer, her views on whether religious symbols can elucidate unconscious desires and imaginings, and hence promote growth and change, are ambiguous and difficult to interpret. She provides brilliant expositions of how particular religious symbols, rituals or narratives would seem to function in a way that would promote integration, but these are undermined by her suspicion of theology and her dwelling on the defensiveness and limitations of religion, particularly what she sees as the dogmatism and 'logocentricity' of theology. She describes its defensive use in avoiding fears of mortality and of facing up to the dark side of the self. She suggests that in most forms of religion, rather than offering support in the acceptance of the self as divided, there remains an unsatisfactory choice between a search for transcendental symbols, which facilitate a denial of division and difference within, and an identification with the 'abject', which emerges in religion as persecution and oppression (Kristeva, 1980, pp. 88–9). She implies that contemporary forms of Christianity are inadequate for the required task and that only 'on the fringes of mysticism, or in rare moments of Christian life' does it fulfil an integrating function (Kristeva, 1980, p. 131).

Nevertheless, in our present era, which she sees as largely deprived of the Christian narrative of a loving God (this 'amatory discourse'), she suggests that, apart from psychoanalysis, we are left unsupported (Kristeva, 1983, pp. 376–81). She goes on to describe Christian narratives, and the use of symbols in ritual, in ways which do in fact appear to offer the required symbolisation. She demonstrates their resonance with a believer's painful experiences, both in early development and in later struggles to deal with the dark side of the self. Her descriptions of these resonances show her awareness and profound understanding of the ways in which believers can be helped at a deep level by their religious experience. She applauds the mystics' emphasis on 'affect', especially love ('the dynamics of amatory passion as a corporeal as much as spiritual passion') rather than rationality. She sees their form of religion as bringing together the 'symbolic' and the 'semiotic' in a healing way (Kristeva, 1983, p. 158).

Although she sees the Christian story and Christian dogma as 'illusions' and suggests that a successful psychoanalysis would enable a patient to understand them as such, she writes that at the end of his analysis fantasy could return, no longer in the form of dogma but as a 'source of energy for a kind of artifice, for the art of living' (Kristeva, 1985, p. 9). This different way of relating to religious symbols is reminiscent of Paul Ricoeur's use of the term *second naivete*, which describes a way of relating to religious symbol as metaphor (Ricoeur, 1967, p. 350).

Kristeva and religious symbolism

The following are examples in which Kristevan uses her theory to show how religious symbols can be seen as evoking early experience, and as bringing together the 'symbolic' and the 'semiotic' aspects of the self.

She writes of the New Testament meaning of *agape* as found in Paul's letter to the Romans; '*agape*' as the love of God, who 'loved us first'; as unconditional and unmerited; as 'gift, welcome and favour', 'a fatherhood that isn't stern but familial and enlightening'. The gift of God's love is accomplished through a death, Christ's passion, his 'oblation', and it is through this *passionate* love that the believer is able to live 'by grace and not by law' (Romans 6:14). The believer's response to God's *agape* is reminiscent of the child's 'idealising identification' with the loving, welcoming, 'imaginary' father in the archaic triangle. Kristeva asserts that there is no 'idealising identification' which is not experienced as involving a loss of the 'not-yet subject', which is experienced as a death and as the killing of the love object. It is this love as a 'death-sentence' which is symbolised in the 'agape of the cross'. The believer must identify with Christ, in his death and Resurrection; by the putting to death, not of his physical body, but of the 'lustful' body; he will be welcomed by God as 'pure spirit, as Name and not as body'. Kristeva writes that the actual killing of one's own body 'as a condition for ideal identification' is 'suspended by the evangelical narrative': 'It is at the same time crystallized, brought to the fore and immediately fastened to the experience of Christ and of him alone'. For the believer, it is the death of the lustful body on the 'path to agape', and the identification with an 'adoptive father' which allows the development of a 'psychic space': 'agape builds psychic space as the complex space of a subject'. Similarly, in the archaic triangle, the infant is in a situation in which she is assaulted by powerful feelings of loss, imagined death and murderous wishes to devour, struggling to resist the 'abject' and supported by her identification with the 'imaginary father'. The 'agape of the cross' provides a 'universal narrative' into which the believer's unique personal 'fantasy' can be 'unloaded' (Kristeva, 1983, pp. 36, 139–47).

Kristeva cites the suffering Christ as a figure with whom the split, wounded self, traumatically torn from the maternal *chora*, can identify. However, the believer is also rewarded like Christ with identification with God, with immortality and with the receiving of a name (language). She writes of the symbolism of Christ's passion, as bringing into play 'primitive layers of the psyche': the forsaken Christ shows God's participation in the condition of the sinner but also the child's melancholy separation from the mother, prior to the discovery of the 'other': 'now in the form of symbolic interlocutor rather than nutritive breast'. It is not surprising, she concludes, that the 'masses' believe (Kristeva, 1985, pp. 40–2).

Kristeva also explores the ways in which Christianity attempts to deal with the basic dreads and fears of the 'abject'. While in pagan rituals, the maternal is warded off in rites of defilement and purification, and in Judaism the 'abominable' remains external and is maintained on the outside by law and taboo, in the New Testament, the 'abject' is interiorised as 'sin' (Kristeva,1980, p. 17). The Christian verbalises the abject as sin and 'repents': 'Threatening, it is not cut off but reabsorbed into speech. Unacceptable, it endures through subjection to God of a speaking being who is innerly divided and, precisely through speech, does not cease from purging himself of it' (Kristeva, 1980, p. 113).

This notion of 'sin' leads to a 'superego spirituality' – it 'holds the keys that open the doors to Morality and Knowledge, and at the same time those of the Inquisition' (Kristeva, 1980, p. 122). However, she also gives a detailed account of how the Eucharist, to which the believer comes having confessed his 'sins', evokes archaic experience and brings together the 'symbolic' and the 'semiotic'.

She points out the emphasis on physical and spiritual hunger and the frequent repetition of the word *bread* in St. Mark's gospel (15:11); she links this with Jesus's later saying, 'This is my body', as he gives bread to his disciples, and which also occurs in the liturgy of the Eucharist. The two themes of 'devouring' and 'satiating' invoke the primal fantasy of a lust to devour and swallow up the other, and Kristeva describes them as 'surreptitiously mingled' in the narrative of the Eucharist as a way of 'taming cannibalism'. The divided being, mortal and speaking, 'flesh and spirit', who symbolises his 'abject' by internalising it, finds catharsis in the Eucharistic ritual, by acting out murderous, devouring impulses in the eating of Christ's body as bread. It is an acting out of a forbidden act, which takes the destructive guilt-inducing power out of impulses to devour. Kristeva describes the Eucharist as the 'material anchorage and logical node' of this primal fantasy, and as bringing together the 'semiotic' (eating and bread) and the 'symbolic' (through symbol and the words of the liturgy). Nevertheless, she concludes that because the 'abject' is completely 'subsumed' into the 'symbolic' realm (in words), the subject is 'reconciled' with it and is no longer a 'being of abjection but a lapsing subject' (Kristeva, 1980, pp. 114–20).

Here Kristeva sees Christian symbolism as inadequately identifying the true horror of the 'abject', as if the deep evils of humanity are somehow glossed over, minimised or avoided. This is unlike the way it is dealt with in Judaism, which she sees as facing up to and excluding the 'coarse and intolerable truth of man' (Kristeva, 1980, p. 129). In Christianity, it is either denied or becomes the 'very site of spiritualisation'. It becomes a form of *felix culpa*: in confessing, the subject is forgiven, purged and 'purified'. In this way, Kristeva suggests, the 'abject' is not fully symbolised; the subject is left with an unconscious, unsymbolised 'abject', a 'fearsome ineradicable evil, an "inexorable carnal remainder"' (Kristeva, 1980, p. 120). This relates to her belief that the split self can never be healed. For her, this Christian 'purification' is not 'trouble free': 'evil . . . will not cease tormenting him from within' (Kristeva, 1980, p. 116). For Kristeva, the 'flesh', or what might be termed in religious language 'original sin', or the 'serpent', remain: there is a *'coincidentia oppositorum'*. But for her, this divided self is not a cause for despair but for acceptance or even *'jouissance'*, a 'joying in the truth of self-division (abjection/sacred)' (Kristeva, 1980, pp. 88–9).

She allows that the use of religious narrative and symbol can promote harmony and stability, and provide the development of psychic space for thinking, reflecting and experiencing. However, she suggests that most religions do not adequately symbolise the split 'mortal/speaking' subject. There are some exceptions: as we have seen, she excludes the mystics, as exemplified by Bernard of Clairvaux, from this criticism. She also uses a story from the life of Christ to show an aspect of Christianity which does not lead to the 'doors of the Inquisition'. The story of the repentant woman who washed Christ's feet with her tears, dried them with her hair and anointed them with ointment (Luke 7:38) is an example of Christ's responding to 'impurity', not with condemnation but with an overflowing of feeling: 'Christ gives himself up to it, deluged with a kind of overflowing of an interior flux and its ambiguity bursts forth in that scene. Sin turned upside down into love'. Here sin is described as the reverse side of love; it is converted to holiness, beauty and *'jouissance'*, a taming of evil (Kristeva, 1980, p. 122–3). Christ's response evokes Williams's description of a relationship with a loving God in a believer's 'growth to goodness'. It is a relationship to a God of love, generosity and mercy as seen in Jesus, leading to joy and delight in the beauty of God, and of inadequacy and vulnerability, requiring a loving response.

These are far from the responses of condemnation, persecution, and punishment which Kristeva sees as the usual responses of the church to the putting of sin into words in confession (Kristeva, 1980, p. 131). For her, the failure of religion adequately to symbolise the 'abject' occurs when the emphasis is on sin as action and as a transgression of the law, which can be remitted, rather than on impurity or defilement; it occurs when religion is focused on the transcendent and, unlike the mystics, overlooks its affective and bodily aspects

Kristeva sees poetic writing, art and music as sources of experience which involve both the 'semiotic' and the 'symbolic', but she questions whether these will be able to 'bear the burden' without religion. She is concerned about those people she calls 'survivors of primary narcissism'; those in the present 'secular age', where there is less and less psychic space and an increasing turn to narcissistic alternatives such as drug abuse, 'entertainment' and consumerism. How can they continue as *'sujets en procès'*, open to growth and transformation? In the absence of religion, can it be through poetry, art, music or psychoanalysis (Kristeva, 1983, pp. 377–81)?

If it is through religion, what forms of religion are likely to preserve the psychic space, and which are likely to abolish it? Some of the instances in this chapter have shown how Christian sacraments and narratives provide opportunities for the bringing together of the symbolic and the semiotic, which Kristeva sees as essential for integration and growth. Subsequent chapters offer other examples of religious forms which appear to designate and *hold* the 'abject' rather than 'displace' or deny it. Crownfield writes that 'Christianity has long provided a public, interpersonal semiotic of identity and desire that has sustained and continues to sustain many lives' (using semiotic in the conventional sense). He believes that whether Christianity can continue to fulfil this function will depend, not on whether it involves illusions but on whether it exists in a form which offers 'triadic openness' or one which offers narcissistic alternatives (Crownfield, 1992, p. 63).

The psychoanalytic theory discussed suggests that if a subject has not achieved some balance between the 'symbolic' and the 'semiotic', he will have difficulty in relating to the symbols, liturgies, metaphors and narratives of Christianity in a way which allows for a 'sublimation' of unknown psychic material. He may embrace a religion but relate to the symbols involved as if they were idols, for instance, by interpreting the words of scripture in a literal and rigid fashion, and not as objects which provoke reflection or evoke something beyond themselves, or the symbols may come to be seen merely as meaningless and ineffective, and not as an opportunity for the expansion of awareness.

Kristeva's work on the importance of an infant's 'idealised identification' with the 'imaginary father' and its resonance with the believer's 'idealised identification' with the God of *agape*, raises the question as to whether Christian symbolism can offer a *replacement* for an inadequate archaic experience of the 'father of individual pre-history', or whether an individual must have had a 'good enough' early experience to be able to relate in a triadic way to such a symbol. If the latter is the case, an individual without such an early experience would tend to resort to dyadic alternatives.

Forsyth's '*Faith and Transformation*' (1997) compares human growth to maturity in theological and psychological (mainly developmental) terms. It addresses St. Thomas Aquinas's understanding of the reciprocal effect of nature and grace: not only does 'grace presuppose nature' (*gratia praesupponit naturam*), but grace also perfects nature (*gratia perficit naturam*; *Summa Theologicae*, I, q.2, art 2 and I, q,1, art 8 in Forsyth, 1997, pp. xv–xviii). Forsyth concludes that the 'faith experience can be described in terms of human growth' and draws many parallels between the two, thus implying his agreement with Aquinas's reciprocal effect (Forsyth, 1997, p. 200). Looked at from a psychoanalytic point of view, the situation is more complicated. If, as the theory in this chapter suggests, change and growth in a religious context depend on the capacity to use religious symbols as a means of 'sublimating' archaic material, and this, in turn, depends on a 'good-enough' early experience, then change through symbolisation can only occur in those lucky enough to have had such a solid early experience. According to this rationale, a religious experience of symbols could not *replace* the early experience: that is 'nature' could not be 'perfected'. This would suggest that only *gratia praesupponit naturam* is true, an outcome likely to be seen by believers as limiting the power God's grace (Forsyth, 1997, p. xvii). The examination of the childhood and upbringing of the Wesley brothers, particularly with regard to whether their early experience was 'good enough', might shed some light on this huge and probably impossible question.

References

Bion, W., 1967. A Theory of Thinking. In *Second Thoughts*. New York: Jacob Aronson.
Bollas, C., 1993. *Being a Character: Psychoanalysis and Self-Experience*. London/New York: Routledge.
Britton, R., 1998. *Belief and Imagination*. New York/London: Routledge.
Britton, R., 2004. The Missing Link: Parental Sexuality in the Oedipus Complex. In *The Oedipus Complex Today*. London/New York: Karnac.
Crownfield, D., 1992. The Sublimation of Narcissism in Christian Love and Faith. In ed. D. Crownfield, *Body/Text in Julia Kristeva*. Albany: State University of New York.
Edelstein, M., 1992. Metaphor, Meta-Narrative and Mater-Narrative in Kristeva's "Stabat Mater". In ed. D. Crownfield, *Body/Text in Julia Kristeva*. Albany: State University of New York.
Forsyth, J., 1997. *Faith and Human Transformation: A Dialogue Between Psychology and Religion*. Lanham/New York/London: University of America Press.
Freud, S., 1923. The Ego and the Id. In *On Metapsychology: The Theory of Psychoanalysis*. Harmondsworth: Penguin Books, vol. 11, 1984.
Kristeva, J., 1980. *Powers of Horror*. Translated by L. Roudiez. New York: Columbia University Press, 1982.
Kristeva, J., 1983. *Tales of Love*. Translated by L. Roudiez. New York: Columbia University Press, 1987.
Kristeva, J., 1985. *In the Beginning Was Love: Psychoanalysis and Faith*. Translated by A. Goldhammer. New York: Columbia University Press, 1997.
Kristeva, J., 1986. Revolution in Poetic Language. In ed. T. Moi, *The Kristeva Reader*. Oxford: Blackwell.
Kristeva, J., 1987. *Black Sun*. Translated by L. Roudiez. New York: Columbia University Press, 1989.
Kristeva, J., 2001. *Melanie Klein*. New York: Columbia University Press.
Ricoeur, P., 1967. *The Symbolism of Evil*. Translated by E. Buchanan. Boston: Beacon Press.
Segal, H., 1988. Notes on Symbol Formation. In ed. E. Bott Spillius, *Melanie Klein Today: Mainly Theory*. London and New York: Routledge.
Stevenson, A. 2017. How Poems Arrive (to Dana Gioia). *The Hudson Review*, 70(1).
Williams, M., 2005. *The Vale of Soulmaking: The Post-Kleinian Model of the Mind and Its Poetic Origins*. London/New York: Karnac.
Winnicott, D., 1971. *Playing and Reality*. Harmondsworth: Penguin Books.
Winnicott, D., 1990. *The Maturational Process and the Facilitating Environment*. London: Karnac.
Wright, K., 2009. *Mirroring and Attunement*. Hove: Routledge.

Chapter 5

Resonances
Psychic space in a religious context

Before turning to the Wesleys' early relationships and their vicissitudes, and the likely effects on their developing personalities, this chapter considers what opportunities for growth and change might also have been available to them through their religious beliefs and practices: the ways in which religious beliefs and practice might increase awareness of the deep aspects of the self and so promote integration. What were the possibilities for relating to 'transformational objects' and for 'triadic relating'? Were there places of balance where the 'symbolic' and the 'semiotic' were in dialogue? Were there Christian figures, narratives, doctrines, rituals or sacraments which were able to symbolise unconscious material?

In exploring these questions, the word *resonance*, from the Latin *resonantio*, meaning an 'echo' or a 'resounding', is used repeatedly. It is the most appropriate word to describe the ways in which the theological and psychoanalytic concepts relate to each other. It suggests a complex connection between the archaic human experience evoked in religious contexts and the stimuli that evoke it, implying a 'metaphoric' relationship, rather than one described in terms of exact or literal parallels or analogies.

Transformational objects

As described above, the child's earliest relationship with a 'transformational object' and the choice of subsequent 'transformational objects' (including religious objects) are often associated with a sense of something familiar, or uncanny, or even sacred; a feeling thought to be due to their evoking the early transforming experience with the mother (Bollas, C., 1987, pp. 14–17). St. Augustine's fourth-century account of 'finding God' epitomises this theory. It was a '*re*discovery of God, the return to a truth already somehow known, to a knowledge already somehow present within the searching self' (Turner, 1995, pp. 58–61). It was a '*re*cognition'. He felt as if he had come home.

God as transformational object?

There are many variable and wide-ranging experiences in which God is believed to be a transformational object. I will look at two different groups, for both of whom this is the case. In both groups, powerful emotion and a degree of 'regression' are usual, so it is necessary to think about what is meant by the term *regression*. It is an unfashionable word in psychoanalysis (Britton, 1998, p. 72), but Bollas uses it to describe a form of dependency on the therapist as a 'transformational object'; he describes an 'ordinary' rather than a dramatic phenomenon, which facilitates the patient's getting in touch with early experience (Bollas, 1987, pp. 269–70). Michael Balint's description of the types of regression occurring in the transference relationship also remains valuable. He asserted that regression could act either as resistance or as a therapeutic tool (Balint, 1968). In the latter case, he described the return in the transference to a new beginning, where a re-experiencing of ways of relating could lead to a change in the way the subject related to those close to him. The patient was allowed to experience a relationship which involved a 'harmonious interpenetrating mix-up' evocative of very early pre-verbal experience, with a 'pliable' but 'indestructible' therapist; this encouraged a new beginning. Balint called it 'regression for the sake of progression' or 'benign regression' (Balint, 1968, pp. 132–6).

He distinguished this 'benign regression', which is similar to that described by Bollas, from a more problematic regression, which is difficult to manage and which he described as 'malignant'. This second form involves an insatiable, intractable urge for gratification in the subject, with a seeking for an external object to satisfy his instinctual needs. There is a passionate hope that the therapist will act to satisfy these needs. Such regression demands understanding and tolerance but not gratifying action on the part of the therapist. Balint described this as a 'regression aimed at gratification', in contrast with the benign form which was 'regression aimed at recognition'.

In the benign form, the patient uses the relationship with the therapist to 'reach' herself, to be recognised and to recognise herself. The associated weakening of ego functioning is merely temporary, so that the patient can think, reflect, and recognise what is happening in her inner world. In malignant regression, the wish is to gain gratification and to repeat any gratifying experiences in an addictive way; there is a mood of desperation and passionate clinging to the object, with an 'unending spiral of demands and needs', and pressure on the therapist to gratify them (Balint, 1968, p. 144–6). It involves the wish to repeat and replace an earlier experience rather than to change internally. These are qualities of a merged dyadic relationship reminiscent of Kohut's 'object hunger' referred to earlier.

Where there is a degree of regression in religious experience, it is of interest to understand whether the regression involved is of a kind which would be expected to promote growth. The characteristics of the regression, which hinder or promote change in therapy, are likely to have a similar effect when regression occurs in a religious context, so that the type of regression will have an influence on whether or not the experience is transformative. Does the experience represent a search for a replacement for previous lost or unmet needs, or does it involve a relationship with a 'transforming object' which can allow a new beginning?

In the following two groups, the believers would see a relationship with God as potentially transforming. Their differences illustrate not only the ways in which growth and change might be facilitated but also ways in which they are more likely to be inhibited.

God as transformational object in peak experiences

The first group is one in which 'peak experiences' occur. As Turner has suggested, these experiences are misleadingly called 'mystical' by some: in the mediaeval tradition, the term 'mysticism' described 'moments of negativity' which were intrinsic to the whole practice of the Christian life. Subsequently, it came to describe a more 'anti-intellectualist, experientialist, "voluntarism"', a transient experience (Turner, 1995, p. 272). However, the presence of 'experience', in the positive sense, has been and remains widespread. It has a central place in many religious contexts. Many different phenomena occur, sometimes evoking a sense of the ineffable and/or an enhanced sense of self. Some are extraordinary, florid forms such as visions, auditory and tactile hallucinations, which may be associated with intense feelings and bodily sensations, such as those of St. Theresa of Avila. Others are similar to Rudolph Otto's powerful experience of the numinous (*mysterium tremendum et fascinans*; Otto, 1917). There are experiences of intense loving feelings towards God in the 'religion of the heart' (experienced by the Pietist movement in Germany, the Moravians, and the early Methodists). There are emotional responses, such as joy or remorse, occurring in explicitly religious settings. There are similar responses to quotidian or symbolic events occurring outside a specifically religious setting but which can be interpreted as being of religious significance. Some of these 'peak experiences' are associated with the psychological shifts which occur in conversion experiences, and many are reminiscent of those found in the writings of early Methodists.

For William James such experiences were the core of religion. He judged experiences not by their particular contents but by their 'fruits', the lasting effects on the lives of the believers (James, 1902, p. 237). The transformative experiences he described occurred mainly in those he called 'sick souls'. These were individuals who had a sense of their own dividedness. Their search for wholeness was through suffering, self-knowledge and struggle, until they experienced a final surrender to something beyond the conscious self. According to James, this could be expressed, either theologically, as owing to the 'direct operations of the Deity', or psychologically, as a consequence of an interaction between the conscious and the 'subconscious' parts of the personality (James, 1902, pp. 210–11).

The experiences follow a familiar sequence: after some kind of internal or external crisis, there is a feeling of being broken up, a strong sense of sinfulness, humiliation, helplessness and a need for grace. It involves a 'bringing to brokenness', which is then transformed into a joyful sense of God's love, forgiveness and power. The relief of giving up the struggle, of ceasing to wrestle with conflicts, results in feelings of joy, of contentment and of things 'falling into place'. There is a release of energy and a sense of empowerment and hope (Rambo, 1993, pp. 130–6). The affective element of these experiences is described as different in quality from ordinary, everyday emotional responses. They are felt as having deeply personal and religious significance and as coming from beyond the self. The supernatural erupts into the natural. There is a sense of the ineffable and often a sense of union with a loving, forgiving presence. They have a noietic, revelatory quality, and the extent to which the subject feels overwhelmed is variable.

In this form of religious experience, although there is a sense of fusion, which suggests regression to an infantile state, there is no loss of the sense of identity; on the contrary, the sense of stability and integration is increased. Meissner compares it to a passionate sexual relationship. The crossing of boundaries and emptying out of the self in 'the loving embrace of the object', he claims, need not be regressive (Meissner, 1984, pp. 151–2). I would argue that it does indeed evoke earlier experiences of merging but that the regression is of a 'benign' rather than 'malignant' type: a regression 'in the service of the ego'. There is a temporary letting go of ego functioning, with a suspension of its observing capacity but a rapid resumption of reflection, and an examination of the experience in the light of reason. There is an openness to unconscious phenomena and to emotional and bodily reactions, in other words, to the 'semiotic', and individuals who undergo such experiences can be seen as sufficiently secure of their ego function to relax it temporarily.

There are countless examples in both Roman Catholic and Protestant, particularly Puritan, religious lives, which repeat the same themes, although the language used varies. Feelings of union, peace, contentment, acceptance and forgiveness are common, but there is also a recognition of the 'dark side' of the self and of the world, as typified by James's 'sick souls'. Sinfulness and inner badness are known about and attended to, or 'suffered'. These are often associated with feelings of guilt, hopelessness and unworthiness. Pleasurable feelings occur, associated with feelings of union, and although these are suggestive of a regression to an early experience of blissful fusion with the archaic mother, there is no compulsive urge repeatedly to seek out the experience itself, in order to meet a need or replace a lost object. The experiences are usually short-lived, provoked by a random stimulus and cannot be deliberately self-induced. The processes involved are examined psychoanalytically in more detail in the next chapter; it becomes clear that the emphasis is on transformation rather than gratification.

God as transformational object in the fundamentalist, revivalist tradition

The contemporary religious scene includes a wide range of groups who adhere to fundamentalist beliefs and who accept or reject 'charismatic' elements. In examining these, I have chosen to use Martyn Percy's work on John Wimber, who in the 1980s founded the Vineyard movement in the United States and whose influence continues to be felt in many denominations throughout the world (Percy, 1996, pp. 13–16). In the previous group, the emphasis was on God's love, acceptance and forgiveness. In this second group, power is central, and Percy interprets

Wimber's ideas and practices as based on the economics of 'power': the power of God, the power of the leaders and the 'empowerment' of believers.

Percy examines the distribution of power within the system and the practices which support it. These include a frequent conflation of the power and fatherhood of the leader with the power and Fatherhood of God, with the expectation that this authority will be accepted without question; a belief in the inerrancy of Biblical text; and an expectation that only through acceptance of these authorities, will the believer be filled with God's power. To question the authority of the leader is to question the authority of God (Percy, 1996, pp. 26–7, 37–9). Percy points to many features in this form of worship which, I would suggest, are likely to reduce its potential to facilitate change. They include missed opportunities for bringing Kristeva's 'symbolic' and 'semiotic' into dialogue.

First, his observations of the worship practices lead him to conclude that emotional states of 'passivity' and 'passion' are aroused in the congregation by the use of repetitive songs. These songs include metaphors which tend to be infantilising, primitive and magical, and which stress intimacy and identification with an idealised, powerful God. There are feelings of bodily bliss, of surrender, of specialness, of being merged and filled up and of empowerment. 'Sin' and human weakness as persisting problems are virtually absent from the songs; if they do appear the sufferer is seen as the victim of evil forces, rather than as personally responsible. If the believer 'surrenders' passively to God's love and power, then any pain, grief or misery will be quickly resolved, as the 'victim' receives God's empowerment and love (Percy, 1996, pp. 61–6, 80). There is a relentless emphasis on human dependence and on an almost magical, powerful, instantaneous transformation from weakness to wholeness (Percy, 1996, pp. 124–5). There is no real acknowledgement of inner dividedness and ambiguity. The 'magical' switch from 'sin to purity' and 'weakness to strength' can be seen, in Kristevan terms, as an example of religion which fails adequately to elaborate the 'abject'.

Second, the emotional state induced, together with a discouragement of questioning and dialogue, tend to undermine separateness and reduce the capacity for initiative, critical thought and the taking of responsibility. The interactions encouraged have features characteristic of dyadic relationships. On one hand, they may be reminiscent of fusion with the 'maternal *chora*' (non-verbal, affective, physical): the use of words and music induces the emotional state, described earlier, which transports the believer away from the messy business of sinfulness and the realities and particularities of daily life. Inducing this state regularly results in an expectation of the same experience at each service. If the experience is felt as rewarding, then it can be sought out repeatedly. These 'merged' experiences can be overwhelming so that there is no sense of the persistence of a functioning, observing, reflecting ego; they are labelled and repeated, rather than reflected on and examined. These features, and the subject's expectation and hope of the experience being repeated, would be attractive to those seeking to recover a lost experience. On the other hand, the rigid adherence to dogma and rules, mainly designed to keep purity within and weakness and difference without, expresses an identification with the Word and Law of the Father. There is little evidence of a triadic space for recognition, reflection and change. Primitive defences, such as splitting and projection, predominate, with the polarisation of good and evil, an identification with an idealised object and a projection outward of what is felt as 'bad'.

Third, the perception of Christ tends to emphasise power rather than love. There is an emphasis on the majesty and power of Christ and the omnipotence of God. Throughout, there is difficulty with paradox but particularly with the paradox central to the doctrine of the Incarnation: 'strength made perfect in weakness' (Percy, 1996, 128–9). In addition, a dyadic rather than triadic emphasis is apparent in the lack of prominence given to the Trinitarian nature of the divine. This results in a loss of emphasis on the concept that 'distinctiveness of identity' can coexist with 'mutuality and relationship', as symbolised by the Trinity: this is reflected in the hierarchical structure of the community, which is aimed at retaining the leader's power, rather than at 'interdependence, equality and openness' (Percy, 1996, pp. 61, 88). There is also little use of sacrament, or symbol; these are seen as undermining the power of words, which are paramount (Percy, 1996, p. 16).

An interesting evolution has occurred in Wimber's movement, and in other fundamentalist and revivalist churches: it comprises a gradual change from an emphasis on experiences of 'joy, celebration and love', which involve bodily expressions of emotion, to a concentration on holiness. Percy sees this as a necessary transition. If the power of the church is to be maintained, its members must be seen as pure, strong and successful, demonstrating God's power (Percy, 1996, pp. 113–14). The frequent association of ecstatic and physical experiences, on the one hand, and rigid rules (particularly about sexual matters), on the other, could be interpreted differently: in Kristevan terms, it suggests a flicking between a dyadic experience of the 'maternal *chora*' and a dyadic adherence to the paternal text and law. It is as if the second develops as a protection from the first, felt as too exciting and dangerous, as if there is a retreat to the 'Law of the Father' rather than a balance or dialogue between the 'semiotic' and the 'symbolic'. Percy writes that 'it is ironic that movements that often begin by embodying joy, celebration and love in community life, end up with disembodiment and legalism' (Percy, 1996, p. 114).

The techniques used can be seen as capitalising on an individual's needs to use religious beliefs and experiences defensively, which would lead to a prediction that they would be more likely to maintain a form of stability, or to stultify, rather than to promote growth, though it is not clear to what extent this is the conscious intent of its leaders.

These two groups ('peak experiences', and the revivalist and fundamentalist traditions) have been presented in this way as a means of clarifying the elements which tend to predominate within them, but this is an artificial separation. All individuals respond differently, and the groups are not distinct, either in their practices, in the responses of believers or in their effects. For instance, many of the 'revivalist' characteristics would have occurred in early Methodism, and 'peak' and 'conversion' experiences, *not* limited to an increased sense of empowerment, will occur in a revivalist/fundamentalist setting. The relative importance of all the features drawn out by Percy, but especially the Trinity, paradox, symbolism, and 'mystical' experience, will emerge as crucially different in the religious lives of the Wesley brothers. Their individual responses should shed light on the prediction that the practices of the second group would tend to hinder rather than promote growth.

Other transforming objects

Objects of beauty

Most religious believers would see their main source of transformation and growth as their relationship with God as seen through Christ, but certain objects of beauty, both in nature and in works of drama, art, poetry or music, have the capacity to evoke a sense of the ineffable, which resonates with something internal that is deep and archaic. They have a capacity to disturb, which is associated with resonances with the past, with the eruption of the 'semiotic' into the 'symbolic', and they can be an important element in transformation, either within a specifically religious context or outside it. Bollas describes the experience of an unbeliever, on conversion to Christ, who feels suddenly enclosed by a 'sacred presence'. He feels held by the object and as if the environment had changed from ordinary to sacred. He compares it with a similar interaction with an aesthetic object, 'when a person is shaken by an experience into absolute certainty that he has been cradled by, and dwelled with, the spirit of the object, a rendezvous of mute recognition that defies representation'. Such experiences are usually unexpected, non-cognitive and 'wordless'; there is a 'density' of feeling and a deep sense of gratitude (Bollas, 1987, pp. 30–1). They are followed by a change in the subject's sense of himself and his world.

Monti writes of an engagement with a transforming object, for instance, a piece of music or a picture, in slightly different terms. He compares the need for a 'detachment' necessary for an aesthetic experience with the 'detachment' of religious experience. It involves a letting go of quotidian distractions, with an achievement of 'stasis' or 'stillness', and a capacity to view the world *sub specie aeternitatis*, a feeling centred not in the self but in the Other. It is similar to Kohut's 'cosmic narcissism'.[1] This, however, is a temporary state of affairs which is followed by a regaining of a sense of an 'enhanced' self. The self is enhanced by a sense of delight, 'felt freedom', knowledge, clarity and of an acquaintance with reality and truth. *Clarity* is used here to mean a recognition of the almost startling 'particularity' of an object, attention to which confronts the observer with a sense of the mystery of existence. For Monti such experiences point to a divine presence, and he gives many examples of people who, in contemplating art or music, have had a powerful sense of God in everything. He stresses that 'delight' is used to mean not merely pleasure but to refer to a sense of knowing something clearly and with certainty. However, it involves more than logical inference: it requires what he calls an 'intuitive apprehension'. It can be gained from finding new meaning from a tragic drama, as well as from a beautiful picture (Monti, 2002, pp. 118–24).

'Ordinary objects'

The philosopher and theologian Schleiermacher believed that it was not only through objects of beauty that an individual could experience and know God, but through a particular contemplative response to 'ordinary' objects:

> The contemplation of pious men is only the immediate consciousness of the universal being of all finite things in and through the infinite, of all temporal things in and through the eternal. To seek and to find this infinite and eternal factor in all that lives and moves, in all growth and change, in all action and passion, and to have and to know life itself only in immediate feeling – that is religion.
> (Schleiermacher, 1821, p. 79)

The religious consciousness he describes depends on a response to an object in the world, by means of what he describes as 'perspectivity' (*Anschauung*, literally a 'looking at') and feeling. He describes these two faculties coming together when an object is first attended to. The subject is temporarily and briefly identified with the object, and the process of 'beholding' and 'feeling' come together briefly as an experience, an experience of 'the universal being of all finite things in and through the infinite'. These experiences, though vital and meaningful, are transient, and constantly fade and return. For Schleiermacher, 'perspectivity' and 'feeling' are in constant 'interplay', as a person interacts with the environment, constantly coming together and separating. He is not describing a peak experience but an ongoing religious responsiveness to the created world (Schleiermacher, 1821, pp. 87–8).

While the experience Schleiermacher describes is not an overwhelming emotional response, neither is it entirely intellectual. As Sykes points out, Schleiermacher describes attempts to express belief in God in terms of systematic theories and moral activities, as involving an active *grasping after* the being of God; Schleiermacher's form of contemplative religion emphasises 'receptivity' rather than 'activity' and an experience of being *grasped by* God (Sykes, 1971, pp. 25–9). The bringing together of 'perspectivity' and 'feeling' is reminiscent of the bringing together of Kristeva's 'symbolic' and 'semiotic' in the apprehension of meaning. Schleiermacher disparaged a *grasping after* God (which would be interpreted in Kristevan terms as relying only on the 'symbolic'), while he advocated receptivity (which involves both).

It is clear from all the preceding examples of interactions with potentially transforming objects, that although the believers would expect to 'grow to goodness' as a result of their relationship with their chosen objects, it is unlikely that this will invariably happen. It is most likely to occur when the 'oceanic' feelings experienced are temporary and transient, when the sense of self is not overwhelmed but feels enhanced and where there is a continued awareness of reality and of separateness from the object. That is, when the object is not sought in a 'hungry' way as a replacement for a lost object but the sense of reality and of the self are preserved so that the awareness of the 'dark side' is maintained or increased and the struggle with it continues. In other words, the 'abject' is elaborated and not displaced, denied or 'magicked' away.

A dialogue: the interaction between the 'symbolic' and the 'semiotic'

'Spaces' appear in religious contexts, similar to Kristeva's place of balance, where the 'semiotic' and the 'symbolic' coexist or intersect. As we have seen, Kristeva stresses the limitations of religion but makes an exception for twelfth-century mystics, admiring Bernard of Clairvaux's preservation of the heterogeneity of flesh and spirit (Kristeva, 1983, p. 169). However, she describes her own writing on him as a 'museum page', suggesting that she thinks it would be of interest only to a few.

Early mystical theologians describe two modes of striving towards God (the apophatic and the cataphatic) and the interaction between the two. In their descriptions, there is a noticeable emphasis on 'wrestling' and 'struggling'. The cataphatic struggle, which can be seen as being in the realm of Kristeva's 'symbolic', involves a stretching of the intellect to its limit in trying to comprehend the nature of God. The apophatic struggle, which can be seen as being in the realm of Kristeva's 'semiotic', is beyond words and the intellect and is one of tolerating unknowing without despair.

In his study of four writers, Augustine, Denys the Areopagite, the author of the Cloud of Unknowing, and John of the Cross, Turner describes them as 'mystical theologians'. He distinguishes this use of the term *mystical* from its later use, where it comes to be associated with certain kinds of religious *experience*, where there is emphasis on the affective aspects and the esoteric nature of the experience (Turner, 1995, pp. 252–73). In the earlier authors, 'mysticism' is seen as intrinsic to the whole of their Christian practice, and their journey towards God retains intellectual struggle and a Platonic dialectic. It is at first cataphatic: it uses words, which can never be adequate, to name God so that affirmations are made but have to be denied. Eventually the denials too are inadequate and, in turn, must be denied. This denial of the denial leads to an opening out beyond logical thought, to something new: an example used by Turner is the affirmation that 'God is light'. This is inadequate and must be denied, so therefore, 'God is darkness'. But finally, the negation between darkness and light must be negated, becoming 'God is a brilliant darkness', metaphorically transcending both previous metaphors (Turner, 1995, pp. 22, 38). As he suggests, this is not merely an artful form of language. It is deliberately paradoxical, a collapse of affirmation and denial into 'self-subverting' and disordered language, which is disturbing and leads to an apophatic silence beyond the limits of language. The 'cataphatic' struggle with words gives way to what Turner calls 'this characteristically apophatic self-subverting utterance' (Turner, 1995, p. 45).

A similar process is expressed in different terms by Michael de Certeau. In describing the texts of the Gospels, he suggests that they point to a 'movement of transcendence' which is produced by the way the stories are organised. The dialogues are not based on binary structures. The logic involved is not 'the one or the other', nor is it 'the one and the other', but it is often 'neither the one nor the other': 'neither Jewish nor heathen; neither circumcised nor uncircumcised, but spiritually circumcised; neither clean nor unclean, but pure in heart' (de Certeau, 1997, p. 154). This, de Certeau explains, creates a new, open, unfixed hypothesis. It is not dogma or law, but permits spiritual action based on the believer's individual response to the text. There is an openness about it: it involves risk because the outcome is uncertain, but it also involves an aliveness. It is similar to the 'self-subverting language' of the cataphatic, which also involves risk, as it is not known where the second order 'negation of the negation' will lead.

The 'apophatic' is a realm of loss, beyond the limit of language, where bewilderment has to be accepted, ideas given up, and 'possessive' desire, the desire to own or use, has to be relinquished (Turner, 1995, p. 184). Such a description mirrors Bion's analytic stance, and it is not surprising that he borrowed some of the mystics' terminology to describe processes which are difficult to describe in psychoanalytic terms. The description of persistence in the face of risk and uncertainty is reminiscent of Bion's concept of 'faith', which he regarded as necessary in analysis for the symbolising function. The characteristics of the 'apophatic' also evoke his ideas on the difference between 'pain' and 'suffering'. In therapy, as outlined by Harris Williams, the therapist's 'pain', in a situation of uncertainty, results in symptoms which press towards an active response; if the pressure to act is resisted, the therapist may experience severe anxiety which can feel 'catastrophic' and almost unbearable. If this pain can be 'suffered' (i.e. contemplated rather than acted upon), then meaning will emerge; but in order to bear the pain, there must be 'an act of faith' which involves the denial of memory and desire (Williams, 2005, pp. 192–3).

In the early mystics, the cataphatic intellectual struggle gives way to or intersects with apophatic uncertainty. Turner's study leads him to conclude that the apophatic cannot be conceptualised or experienced: 'The apophatic . . . is intelligible only as being a moment of negativity within an overall theological strategy which is at once and at every moment both apophatic and cataphatic' (Turner, 1995, p. 265). An interaction with the apophatic in the religious journey is to be distinguished from a 'peak' experience; it is embedded in religious practice, in liturgy and sacrament. However, although the apophatic moment involves loss, tension, unknowing, and anxiety, 'brilliant darkness' suggests an intensity and the possibility of celebration.

Kristeva describes two possible responses to being in a similar place of not knowing, between the 'symbolic' and the 'semiotic', suspended over an abyss, where contradictions can never be reconciled and one's own dividedness has to be faced. One involves resorting to dyadic alternatives. The other is celebration or *jouissance*. Tillich's theology includes a description very similar to Kristeva's second response. Citing Seneca, he describes joy as the response to the 'affirmation of one's essential being in spite of desires and anxieties': it is not a joy resulting from fulfilled desires but 'real joy is a "severe matter"; it is the happiness of a soul which is "lifted above every circumstance"' (Tillich, 1952, p. 25).

The early mystics' description of the 'apophatic' has similarities with the realm of the semiotic. The apophatic is described as 'not experienced': it is a place beyond words, beyond thinking, of uncertainty, of boundlessness, of potential, of risk and of 'aliveness'. It can only be apprehended through a continuous interweaving of apophatic and cataphatic. Such interweaving is apparent within the Christian narrative; there is often a disturbance of ordinary logic, which leads to a sense of uncertainty, unknowing and risk, and thus to an opening of the mind to new experience and to the possibility of change. For instance, in the Eucharist many intersections of the existential and the essential occur. 'Kairos', a moment of significance, meaning and integration, intersects with 'chronos', the continuation of ordinary temporal experience. The immanent, the elements taken into the body, intersect with the transcendent, the body and blood of the risen Christ. What Duns Scotus calls the *Haecceitas*, the thisness, the particular individuating, unique properties of the bread and the wine, intersect with the universal (Eco, 1988, p. 206). In addition, the material and physical, the eating and drinking of the bread and wine, are embedded in the language of the liturgy, which adds 'symbolic' meaning to the 'semiotic'.

The reading of biblical texts, religious poetry and liturgy and the singing of hymns are further opportunities for the intersection of the 'semiotic' and the 'symbolic'. Poetry particularly can evoke pre-verbal, 'archaic' experience, by disrupting logic and rationality. Silence can also have the same effect, when the limits of language have been reached.

All these instances which may occur in religious worship, can be seen as offering, through the disruption of the 'symbolic' by the 'semiotic', a 'psychic space', a place of healing. If the believer can 'suffer' the apparent contradictions, conflicting feelings, paradoxes and illogicalities, excluding 'memory and desire' and avoiding a *grasping* after knowledge, and if he can remain, like the mystic at the intersection of the 'apophatic' and the 'cataphatic', a place of unknowing and risk, there is a possibility of growth. According to Kristeva, they are opportunities in which the believer can enter 'a discourse where his own "emptiness" and her own "out-of-placeness" become essential elements, indispensable "characters" if you will, of a *work in progress*' (Kristeva, 1983, p. 380).

Symbolising the semiotic

In psychoanalytic theory, symbols, including words, are seen as the basis of communication and the means through which emotion and phantasy become available for thought. Symbols are potentially transformative when they resonate with previously 'unknown' material from archaic experience which could not previously be thought about. This 'unknown' is from a time before words, and includes chaotic feelings and sensations and destructive and murderous impulses, which become 'unthinkable', but may be brought to awareness by symbol or narrative or be the subject of catharsis in a ritual. In the last chapter, we saw the ways in which Kristeva envisaged religious symbols as evoking early experience and as bringing together the 'symbolic' and the 'semiotic': the 'imaginary father' symbolised by the God of *agape* in the archaic triangle, the catharsis of primitive impulses in the Eucharist and the ways in which Christianity deals with the abject. Public or private Christian worship may offer a space to interact with symbols in this way.

These ways of interpreting symbols, as referring back to early experience, have been described by Paul Ricoeur as 'regressive or archaeological'. However, when symbols are examined by theologians, it is with collective Christian symbols that they are usually concerned: those in which a material object, figure, dogma, text or sacrament is perceived as disclosing something beyond itself, something of the divine. These 'theological' ways of interpreting symbols, those which 'anticipate our spiritual adventure', Ricoeur called 'progressive or teleological'. He believed that the richness of symbols relied on a 'dialectic' between two functions (archaeological and teleological), which were 'thought to be opposed to one another but which symbols coordinate in a concrete unity' (Ricoeur, 1970, p. 496). We will return to this view after two brief diversions: first, to look at the way in which two theologians, Tillich and Ward, have examined religious symbolism in ways which are not limited to 'progressive' interpretations but which show their capacity to approach 'unthinkable', deeper aspects of the self; and second, after examining some functions of triadic images in Christianity.

Tillich saw symbols as a central part of Christian faith and the source of human knowledge of the divine. For him, both symbols and signs pointed to something beyond themselves. Symbols, however, were 'natural', in that they participated in the reality they represented, while signs were arbitrary, depending on convention, and could be changed according to the 'demands of expediency' (Tillich, 1951, pp. 265–8). He saw symbols as unlocking other dimensions of reality both beyond and within the believer, and stressed their 'experiential' nature. It was the personal response of the believer to the multivalent, ambiguous, reconciling nature of symbols which led to an opening up of the depths of the personality, and to an intuiting of the transcendent. He saw symbols as dynamic and changing, and suggested that they could become irrelevant or meaningless, or die, unless there was a continuous lively interaction with them (Tillich, 1957, p. 190).

Although Tillich insisted on the close relationship between the symbol and that which was symbolised, he insisted that one was not to be identified with the other. If the symbol was perceived as the same as the reality it symbolised, where there was a failure to 'deliteralise' or 'break' the symbol, its role changed from that of a symbol to that of an idol (Tillich, 1957, p. 190). When symbols were not 'deliteralised', faith was tipped into idolatry, for instance when ecclesial authority was identified with the divine or when the sacraments were presented as having a form of 'magical' power. He saw the latter as manipulating the believer, accessing the unconscious without the believer's conscious knowledge, a violation rather than a means of transformation (Dourley, 1981, pp. 92–3). This picture of an 'unbroken' symbol recalls Segal's description of a 'symbolic equation', which was so full of the observer's projections that it *became* the thing it represented. 'Unbroken' symbols and 'symbolic equations' provide certainty but cannot be used freely and do not promote growth.

Tillich saw 'Jesus as the Christ', the Cross, and the Resurrection as the central symbols of Christianity. He stressed Jesus's participation in the 'negativities' of existence: 'serious temptation, real struggle, [and] tragic involvement in the ambiguities of life' (Tillich, 1957, pp. 154–5). Christian salvation was interpreted as a healing process. Christ symbolised the holding together of the opposites, of which life, in Tillich's view, was made up. Through a 'participation' in Christ, an identification, there could be a reuniting or healing of the splits 'between God and man, man and his world, man and himself' (Tillich, 1957, pp. 192–3).

The Cross symbolised Christ's subjection to existence, while the Resurrection symbolised his conquest of it, and for Tillich each symbol was meaningless without the other (Tillich, 1957, pp. 176–7). God's self-surrendering love, as shown by the Cross, awakened a loving response in the believer, but it was a message about divine justice as well as divine love. For Tillich, this was not in terms of a 'substitutary atonement', but involved God's taking the self-destructive consequences of 'estranged existence' upon himself. There was a removal of guilt and punishment, but not as 'an act of overlooking the reality and depth' of the ambiguities of existence. The Cross was the manifestation of divine participation in human life, and atonement involved man's participation in Christ's suffering: 'God takes the suffering of the world upon himself by participating in existential estrangement'. Tillich compared the suffering involved in the believer's participation in Christ, with processes in psychotherapy. The believer had a consciousness of guilt and a sense of deserving punishment, but it was accompanied by a knowledge that there was a release from guilt and punishment through God's love. For the patient, the 'torment of existential insight into his being' had to be suffered before healing was possible (Tillich, 1957, p. 199).

The believer in the world estranged from God, healed through participating in Christ, met by God's agapeic love, resonates with Kristeva's understanding of the child's separation from the mother and the identification with the 'imaginary father', as she struggles towards meaning and the formation of her identity. Kristeva writes, 'Christ abandoned, Christ in hell, is, of course, a sign that God shares the condition of the sinner' and suggests that the Christian narrative evokes the human story of the acquisition of language and the capacity to symbolise (Kristeva, 1985, p. 41). Graham Ward elaborates this link by looking at the resonance between the infant's melancholic period before the acquisition of language as described by Kristeva, and God's kenosis, initiated by the pouring out of his love in the Incarnation, the Word made flesh. God is manifest as a human slave, whose earthly life ended in death on the cross: he describes it as a narrative of dispossession (Ward, 1998, pp. 236–9). In Ward's exegesis of Philippians 2:5–11, God is a maker of 'forms' and 'representations'. Christ is incarnated in the '*form* of a slave'; man is created in the '*image* of God'. If God is a maker of representations, then man as 'in the image of God' is similarly a maker of representations (*homo symbolicus*), and the human condition is one of dispossession and resemblances. Ward cites the Swiss theologian Urs von Balthazar: the kenotic narrative continues through the human world of 'resemblances' and 'representations', through the crucifixion to silence and death, in which 'representation experiences its crisis'. Finally, it is only on the 'far side of death' through the Resurrection, that Christ receives the 'name which is above every name'. It is only through suffering and death, and after Christ returns and participates in the love of the Trinity, and is identified with it, that he achieves his true identity. Through his passion, his suffering and love, comes a name, that is, identity and meaning, and not a confusion of resemblances.

Christ as a man symbolises the human condition as a 'crucified' condition, 'as constantly abiding in a state of dispossession and resemblances'. Through God's grace, the believer, a 'maker of images' who identifies with Christ in his suffering and dispossession, comes to 'see and know differently'. The kenotic process is the means through which a meaningful understanding of confusing 'resemblances' is gained (Ward, 1998, pp. 239–43). We saw 'through a glass, darkly; but now face to face'.

Kristeva's, too, is a kenotic narrative: the loving mother's allowing a painful separation, in which her love suffers; the pain and suffering of the child, abandoned in a place of emptiness, experiencing himself as only an imitation of his objects; the depression and mourning prior to the acquisition of language; the supportive 'metaphoric' identification with the 'imaginary father'; and the participation in the parental love which leads to an ability to signify what was previously unrepresentable and to speak meaningfully. The resonances are clear.

This interpretation of the kenotic narrative, and the resonances evoked, show how the Christian narrative can engage with the semiotic. While Tillich's 'participation in Christ's suffering' *implies* an evocation of archaic images of loss, separation and violence, Ward makes Kristeva's link more explicit. Like Kristeva he presents the narrative of the Incarnation, the Crucifixion and the Resurrection of Christ not as an analogy but as an 'allegory of love' (*allegoria amoris*). He suggests that through the kenotic narrative, the believer is 'caught up not in a knowledge of God but a knowing of God, a revelation of God about God, that issues from the movement of His intra-Trinitarian love' (Ward, 1998, pp. 251–3). That this is a kind of knowledge which is beyond words and logic, and which engages the believer at a deep level, is supported by the resonances with the archaic experiences described by Kristeva. In Ricoeur's terms, by coordination of 'regressive' and 'progressive' interpretations, there is a richer experience of the symbolism.

Triadic symbolism

Moltmann has emphasised that the Trinity is not a 'self-contained group in heaven', Father, Son, and Holy Spirit, but a *process* involving the three persons, 'a shorter version of the passion narrative'; it 'keeps believers at the cross' and brings God down to earth. It is a narrative depicting God's love and grief in delivering up his son to death, Christ's love in his willing surrender to death on the cross, their mutual love and God's unconditional love, as 'he takes on himself grief at the contradiction in men and does not angrily suppress this contradiction'. His love is shown in the power of the spirit for the loveless, the unloved and even for enemies: 'a folly and scandal in this world' (Moltmann, 2001, pp. 253–8), the *allegoria amoris*. We have already seen the resonances between this kenotic narrative and Kristeva's understanding of the infant's early experience.

Christian symbolism offers 'triadic' experience. This is most obvious in the symbolism of the Trinity, what Kristeva calls the 'crown jewel of theological sophistication', and which she sees as incorporating all aspects of psychic life, the affective and non-verbal, as well as the 'symbolic' (Kristeva, 1985, p. 43). It is central to Ward's elucidation of kenosis. A failure to understand God as the Trinity has serious sociological consequences, as described by Percy.

St. Augustine's thinking about the human mind in relation to the Trinity is reflected in his description of the soul. As Turner outlines it, admitting that he is paraphrasing rich and complicated Augustinian ideas, the believer knows himself to be 'in the image of the Trinity'. An analogy is drawn between the interior powers of the mind (memory, intellect and will), and the Father, Son, and Holy Spirit. Memory is the source of pre-reflective (pre-verbal) self-knowledge, and the intellect has the power to reflect on (and verbalise) what memory generates. There is a mutual seeking out of memory and intellect, a mutual loving, and it is the 'will' which constitutes this relationship. 'In the same way does the Father love the Son and the Son the Father. And the mutual love is the Holy Spirit' (Turner, 1995, pp. 94–6). The implication is that the mind itself has a 'trinitarian' or triadic structure, in which the 'will' or Spirit has a loving, unifying function. It implies that the 'triadic' is of 'natural' and profound significance for human beings.

The triadic structure of the Trinity, as understood by Tillich, can be paralleled with that formed in the archaic situation as described by Kristeva. Tillich describes the Trinity as comprising a unity in which the unnamable God of the Abyss and the Son are linked by the Spirit, the essence of their relationship. The Godhead gives 'the power of being to everything that is'; the Son (the *logos*, which 'has been called the mirror of the divine depth') articulates meaning and gives form to God's creativity; the polarities of 'power' and 'meaning' are united by the Spirit (Tillich, 1951, pp. 276–9). In the archaic triangle, the infant is balanced between the forces of attraction and repulsion of the maternal *chora*, on one hand, and the supportive, affirming love of the 'imaginary' father, on the other; the entry into the 'symbolic' realm is facilitated by identification with the mother's love for the father, for the 'not-I'. Similarly, the Christian believer relates in a triadic way to both the God of the Abyss, in 'awe and wonder', or fear and fascination, and is affirmed by the forgiving, accepting agapeic love as revealed in Christ, the Word. The believer is 'indwelt' by the Holy Spirit, the love between Father and Son, just as the infant identifies with the mother's love for the 'not-I'. In the same way as the infant learns to speak and develops his identity, the believer who 'participates' in Christ's separation, suffering and death, through the power of the Spirit, is rewarded with a 'name' (an identity) and finds true meaning. Both are triangles where kenotic and agapeic love circulate. Both the Trinity and the archaic triangle embody the unnameable 'semiotic' as well as the nameable 'symbolic'. They both incorporate the role of separation and loss in the search for meaning. The relationships in both are triadic rather than dyadic, allowing space for thought and reflection, the possibility of identity and individuality as well as mutuality.

This understanding of the Trinity is also reminiscent of the psychoanalytic theory of inner triadic space and creativity discussed previously. Just as the internal 'combined object' acts as a muse in artistic creativity, or in more quotidian life as an inspiration for reflection, symbolisation and creative thinking, the Christian sees the Holy Spirit (the essence of the loving relationship between un-nameable Father and the incarnate Son (logos), as 'dwelling within him' and similarly inspiring creative thinking and living.[2]

In these triadic spaces, there are resonances with Kristeva's description of the infant painfully torn away from the union with the maternal, uncomfortably balancing over a void, resisting the powerful regressive pull to a dyadic relationship with either maternal or paternal objects, but tolerating the consequent anxiety and uncertainty. This 'place of balance' also recalls Tillich's description of courage and the need for self-affirmation in the face of anxiety over the threats of fate or death, meaninglessness and doubt, condemnation and punishment (Tillich, 1952, pp. 171–6). For Tillich, the capacity to affirm oneself in the face of anxiety is seen as arising from divine grace. In Kristevan terms, the infant is supported over emptiness by the 'father of pre-history' and the believer by his successor, the God of *agape*.

It is helpful to see Christian symbols in the context of Paul Ricoeur's understanding of the two different ways of interpreting them: 'regressive' or 'progressive' hermeneutics. 'Regressive' symbols were seen as manifesting archaic meanings belonging to the 'infancy of mankind' (Ricoeur particularly concentrated on Freud's antagonism to religion with its interpretation of religious belief in terms of primitive fantasy), while 'progressive' symbols looked toward something beyond the self, toward something of the divine. One he associated with a repetition of childhood experience, and the other, with adult life and experience. But he believed that they could come together; symbols could 'realize the identity between the progression of figures of spirit and mind and the regression to the key signifiers of the unconscious' (Ricoeur, 1970, pp. 496–7).

Ricoeur believed that the *force* and richness of religious symbols could be attributed to the inseparability of the two forms of interpretation and to the 'recapturing of primal fantasies'. He described these fantasies as speaking of loss and of the 'lack inherent in desire' and felt it was the resulting sense of emptiness which inspired the 'endless movement' of interpretation (Ricoeur, 1970, p. 540). Advancement of meaning, Ricoeur stated,

> occurs only in the sphere of projection of desire, of the derivatives of the unconscious, of the revivals of archaism. We nourish our least carnal symbols

with desires that have been checked, deviated, transformed. We represent our ideals with images issuing from cleansed desire.

(Ricoeur, 1970, p. 497)

This suggests an integrating process, but while he saw traditional religious symbols as having multiple meanings and as serving as vehicles for new understanding, requiring an effort of mind in order to understand and extend their meaning, more regressive 'dream' symbols were described as mere 'vestiges': fragmented, stereotyped and worn out (Ricoeur, 1970, p. 505). They had to be 'rescued' and 'cleansed'. Ricoeur would see a 'glimpse of the transcendent' as a 'progressive' interpretation, to be integrated with 'regressive' but *cleansed* interpretations relating to infancy. For him the 'revivals of archaism' contributed an enriching or 'nourishing' quality, his descriptions suggested a degree of opposition between the two hermeneutics; he described the relationship as 'dialectical' (Ricoeur, 1970, pp. 496–8). This may be compared with the 'dialogue' Kristeva advocates between the 'symbolic' and the 'semiotic'. For her a 'dialogue', unlike a dialectic, is not bound by logic; it is 'relational' and strives for harmony, rather than opposition (Kristeva, 1986, p. 58).

Nevertheless, Ricoeur's awareness of the 'archaic' and 'teleological' aspects of symbols and of the self is reminiscent of Kristeva's 'split-self', and for him, it is the awareness of the 'dark side', of the 'sin of the just man', that discourages self-righteousness (Ricoeur, 1970, pp. 548–9). Although Ricoeur is concerned with the new meaning to be gained from symbols, through the nourishment of 'progressive' interpretations by 'regressive' understandings, it is possible that his privileging of the 'progressive' function risks a displacement or avoidance, rather than an elaboration of the 'abject'. In the work of Klein and her followers, and in Kristeva, both kinds of function of a symbol or ritual, and a dialogue between them, are necessary for transformation. Without this the 'abject' is not symbolised and remains to be experienced as 'nameless dread'. Kenosis as interpreted by Ward would indeed incorporate 'archaic' as well as 'teleological' aspects, and Tillich's emphasis on the need to 'accept acceptance', though being unacceptable as the basis for the 'courage of confidence', implies God's holding of the *coincidentia oppositorum* in his agapeic love (Tillich, 1952, pp. 161–2). Both give full value to 'regressive' as well as 'progressive' interpretations.

Both Kristeva and Tillich stress the need for an awareness of the 'dark side'. Kristeva would advocate not just a toleration of it but *jouissance*, a 'joying in the truth of self-division' (Kristeva, 1980, pp. 88–9). Tillich would advocate the need for courage to *bear* the darkness within but would see this as being possible only through God's grace. They would both agree that the sacred is to be glimpsed in the ambiguity and suffering of human existence. It is in the acceptance and toleration of the 'shadow', 'the dark side' that liveliness and energy exist. When it is denied, there is a sense of deadness and unreality. It is this 'entering into' the dark side, which is part of psychoanalysis but which is also found in Tillich and in Ward's interpretation of kenosis, that Kristeva suggests is missing from contemporary religions.

The examples given suggest that by providing spaces in which there are opportunities for relating to symbols and other transformational objects, for triadic relating, for an opening up of self to the unknown, there is a possibility of change. This change can come about through an encounter of the terrifying aspects of the psyche with forgiving love. Distressing psychic contents can be illuminated and given more manageable meaning, so that they can be accepted and even loved, rather than experienced as 'nameless dread'. Part II discusses to what extent John and Charles Wesley were able to come to trust in the agapeic love of God, to feel accepted and loved and to confront their deep and troubling feelings.

Notes

1 Chapter 3, p. 37.
2 Triangularity is also present in the paralleling of the Oedipal triangle with the triangle created by God; Mary, the mother of Jesus; and Jesus himself. The suffering Christ, with whom the believer can identify, represents suffering humanity. Unfortunately, as Crownfield writes, in Christian communities which have patriarchal structures, the Father/God in this triangle would represent the phallic, Oedipal, prohibiting Father, while the female would be 'abjected'. This would 'reactivate the original terror and rage in the form of the abjection of mother', rather than tending to ameliorate archaic experience'. If, however, the Father can be understood as the loving, forgiving ('imaginary') Father, and Mary as *Virgin* and Mother, then these figures can provide (and have provided) a stabilising structure for many, in spite of what Kristeva would see as a defensive use of Mary (Crownfield, 1992, p. 60).

References

Balint, M., 1968. *The Basic Fault: Therapeutic Aspects of Regression*. London/New York: Tavistock Publications.
Bollas, C., 1987. *The Shadow of the Object*. London: Free Association Books.
Britton, R., 1998. *Belief and Imagination*. London/New York: Routledge.
Crownfield, D., 1992. The Sublimation of Narcissism in Christian Love and Faith. In ed. D. Crownfield, *Body/Text in Julia Kristeva*. Albany: State University of New York Press.
de Certeau, M., 1997. How Is Christianity Thinkable Today? In ed. G. Ward, *The Post-Modern God*. Oxford: Blackwell.
Dourley, J. P., 1981. *The Psyche as Sacrament: A Comparative Study of C.G. Jung and Paul Tillich*. Toronto: Inner City Books.
Eco, U., 1988. *The Aesthetics of Thomas Aquinas*. Cambridge, MA: Harvard University Press.
James, W., 1902. *The Varieties of Religious Experience: A Study in Human Nature*. London/New York: Penguin Classics, 1985.
Kristeva, J., 1980. *Powers of Horror*. Translated by L. Roudiez. New York: Columbia University Press, 1982.
Kristeva, J., 1983. *Tales of Love*. Translated by L. Roudiez. New York: Columbia University Press, 1987.
Kristeva, J., 1985. *In the Beginning Was Love: Psychoanalysis and Faith*. Translated by A. Goldhammer. New York: Columbia University Press, 1997.
Kristeva, J., 1986. Word, Dialogue and Novel. In ed. T. Moi, *The Kristeva Reader*. Oxford: Blackwells.

Meissner, W., 1984. *Psychoanalysis and Religious Experience*. New Haven/London: Yale University Press.

Moltmann, J., 1974. *The Crucified God: The Cross as the Foundation and Criticism of Christian Theology*. London: SCM Press, 2001.

Monti, A., 2002. 'Types and Symbols of Eternity' How Art Points to Divinity. *Theology*, 105(824), pp. 118–26.

Otto, R., 1917. *The Idea of the Holy*. London: Oxford University Press, 1923.

Percy, M., 1996. *Words, Powers and Wonders: Understanding Contemporary Christian Fundamentalism and Revivalism*. London: SPCK.

Rambo, L., 1993. *Understanding Religion and Conversion*. New Haven/London: Yale University Press.

Ricoeur, P., 1970. *Freud and Philosophy: An Essay in Interpretation*. New Haven/London: Yale University Press.

Schleiermacher, F., 1821. *On Religion: Speeches to Its Cultured Despisers*. Translated by T. Tice. Richmond: John Knox Press, 1969.

Sykes, S., 1971. *Friedrich Schleiermacher*. Bath: Lonsdale and Bartholomew.

Tillich, P., 1951. *Systematic Theology I*. London: Nisbet & Co Ltd.

Tillich, P. 1952. *The Courage to Be*. London/Glasgow: Collins, 1963.

Tillich, P., 1957. *Systematic Theology II*. London: Nisbet & Co Ltd.

Turner, D., 1995. *The Darkness of God: Negativity in Christian Mysticism*. Cambridge: Cambridge University Press.

Ward, G., 1998. Kenosis and Naming. In ed. P. Heelas, *Religion, Modernity and Postmodernity*. Oxford: Blackwell.

Williams, M., 2005. *The Vale of Soul-Making: The Post-Kleinian Model of the Mind and Its Poetic Origins*. London/New York: Karnac.

Part II

John and Charles Wesley

Figure 6.1 Susanna Wesley

Figure 6.2 Samuel Wesley Snr

Chapter 6
Evangelical nurture

The second part of the book examines the lived experiences of the Wesley brothers. The first part has examined the processes involved in growth and development theoretically; this part considers the ways in which these processes were played out in the brothers' personal and religious lives, and the differences between them. This chapter examines their family of origin and the religious, cultural and historical influences they shared.

Puritan background and family culture

Puritanism was a very strong influence on both sides of the Wesley family. Their paternal grandfather, John Wesley Snr. (1636–70), was the Incumbent of Whitchurch, Dorset, from 1658, although he seems never to have been ordained as a priest. Even during the last days of the Commonwealth, concerns were raised about his authority to hold office, and he was 'upbraided' by the Bishop of Bristol for supporting Parliament against the king until the 'last gasp'. He was accused of irregular preaching, neglecting the prayer book and disagreeing with the liturgy. He was imprisoned in Blandford prison, although subsequently he was briefly allowed to continue in his living; after the Act of Uniformity, he continued to preach, usually in secret, but he refused to take the oath at the time of the Five Mile Act. As a result, he had to leave his family and go into hiding. On his return, in spite of preaching at 'prudent' meetings only, he was often arrested and served three more prison sentences (Clarke, 1823, pp. 23–47).

The Wesleys' maternal grandfather, Dr Samuel Annesley (1620–96), was a major figure in Puritan London. He was a Presbyterian minister, one of the Puritan preachers approved by the Long Parliament. He was nominated by Richard Cromwell to St. Giles, Cripplegate, but was ejected under the Act of Uniformity in 1662. He continued to preach in spite of convictions and fines. He was seen as a 'patriarch of Dissent' until his death (Schmidt, I, 1953–66, p. 43). It is thought that his second wife, Mary White, was the daughter of the Puritan lawyer John 'Century' White, a scourge of idle Church of England clergymen. They had many children, possibly as many as twenty-four, of whom two boys and seven girls survived into adulthood (Young, 1985, p. 54). One of the surviving girls was Susanna Annesley (1669–1742), the mother of John and Charles Wesley; it has been argued that Susanna had a special relationship with her father and that, through her, Samuel Annesley's Puritanism became an important strand in the origin of Methodism (Newton, 1968). There is little information about Susanna's relationship with her mother.

Samuel Annesley is said to have belonged to the group of Presbyterians who held orthodox views (Bolam, 1968, p. 105), but his sermons are an important source of information about his precise beliefs on reprobation, morality and the limiting of atonement to the elect (John Wesley published some of them in his Christian Library). One of his sermons, preached at the funeral of the Reverend Thomas Brand (Annesley, 1692), demonstrates the aphorism that 'Puritans were Calvinists in the study, but Arminians in the pulpit'. It is an example of Annesley using complicated logic to offer hope of salvation to all, and particularly to those in despair, without quite contradicting the doctrine to which he was required to subscribe (Newton, 1985, pp. 42–4). Here he was closer to his grandsons' views on universal redemption than might have been anticipated.

Another of Annesley's sermons also calls into question the description of Annesley as a traditional 'high Calvinist' (Annesley, 1674, pp. 1–46). It demonstrates his beliefs and his expectations of himself and others, which would have permeated Susanna's early life. Its text is: 'Jesus said unto him, Thou shalt love the Lord thy God with all thy heart, and with all thy soul and with all Thy mind. This is the first and great commandment' (Matthew 22:37–8). The sermon addresses, in a logical, detailed and analytic way, what it means to love God. It is a 'branching' sermon, full of lists, categories and practical advice. There are four exhortations, which are the 'wheels of Christ's Chariot that's paved with love, to bring his beloved to Glory': be watchful for sins; keep one's temper; love God out of duty, when one cannot out of grace; and study Christ ('Pray and strive to know what it is to feel that Christ be all in all'). He emphasises the role of the will and the importance of striving, being watchful, and persevering, particularly in times of doubt. He takes the Calvinist view that grace is the source of the capacity to love God, but in the absence of a feeling of an assurance of loving God, he is not judgemental but urges increasing duty and effort, not quite as a way of earning salvation but with a strong suggestion that grace and assurance will follow. He relies heavily on reason and strongly encourages his listeners to use their reason and intellect, even in the absence of the 'appropriate' feelings or a sense of rightness.

He demands absolute commitment and recommends the most intense introspection and self-examination. It is not sufficient to search out sin but to be especially vigilant against the most loved sin – the 'darling sin' – and to be particularly watchful for spiritual sloth, brilliantly described as: 'the soft moth of our spiritual wardrobe; a corroding rust in our Spiritual Armory; an enfeebling consumption in the very vitals of Religion'. But, having conquered sloth, the dangers have not been overcome; it is then necessary to guard against spiritual pride. The introspection must never stop; there can be no relaxation. Every success brings another hazard. There is a similar absence of relaxation, and also a lack of acceptance of any sad, angry or rebellious feelings, in his attitude to suffering; he urges a stoical toleration of it. Afflictions are like nasty medicine given to a sick child.

Despite the emphasis on struggling towards inner holiness and perfection and the need for 'good works', he remains within the Calvinist tradition, warning against 'inherent grace'. He stresses that 'good works are the *genuine fruits*, though not the meritorious causes of justification'. But for all his insistent demands for watchfulness, and ceaseless striving for inner holiness, he also offers hope to people who are struggling. He refers to his text as this 'most difficult commandment', but he reassures his listeners. Although its demand 'includes the highest perfection possibly attainable in this life; yet let not this difficulty fright you, for through Christ our *sincere* love (though weak) is accepted; and our *imperfect* love (because growing) shall not be despised'. Annesley shows himself to be aware of human frailty: he understands that only 'tolerable perfection' is attainable in this life. At the same time, he describes intense and even ecstatic feelings involved in the experience of devotion: 'This divine love, 'tis the *unspeakable enlargement* of the heart *towards* God; 'tis the *exstasie* and *ravishment* of the heart *in* God; 'tis the Soul's *losing* its self in God'. In this he exemplifies the thesis put forward by Gordon Rupp, that there is a continuity of emphasis on 'devotion of the heart' (devout meditation and prayer, and a concentration on the sacred humanity of Christ) in the context of an austere life, which runs from mediaeval Benedictine and Cistercian origins to the fourteenth-century 'Nuns of Helfta' in Saxony to Luther and the German mystics. While not claiming any direct link with the seventeenth-century Puritans, Rupp points out a strong affinity between the two traditions (Rupp, 1977, p. 119).

Annesley's powerful and passionate preaching appeals to the emotions, and particularly to deep psychological yearnings to merge with an object in a blissful and fulfilled state. The reference to the soul '*losing* its self in God' is at the beginning of the sermon; it continues as an intense, attractive experience of devotion. However, he quickly resorts to his 'homely' metaphors, such as the 'moth', which keep the ideas accessible, and then to lists and categories, which provide a framework. Both the emotions and the intellect are engaged, and there is a containment provided by the form taken by the sermon. There are unrelenting demands, which reflect Annesley's demands on himself, but there is also a strong sense of a man of feeling with an awareness of human frailty, and the need for and the possibility of forgiveness. In Kristevan terms, Annesley's sermon on the love of God shows a capacity to balance the 'semiotic' ('devotion of rapture', rhetorical language, passionate feelings, bodily metaphors) and the 'symbolic' (logical, analytical prose, rules for living, obsessional attention to detail) and, by the use of this balance, to create a psychic space for reflection and thought.

Each of the grandfathers gave his faith absolute priority, and each, by his preaching and example, stressed the need to examine contentious issues carefully. Having reached an opinion, it was imperative to act in its defence. This lack of compromise was necessary whatever the consequent suffering to themselves or their families; these traits persisted through the generations.

Early experience

Susanna and Samuel Wesley

Samuel Annesley entrusted his private papers and manuscripts to Susanna, and it is on this basis that she has been seen as his favourite child (SW, p. 5). There is no special mention of Susanna in Annesley's will, and no direct evidence regarding his feelings towards her, so it is not possible to conclude that she was his favourite with any certainty, but to have been chosen as the recipient of his papers, the containers of his thoughts, his intellectual and spiritual struggles and his deepest beliefs, and the guardian of his reputation, would have made her feel especially valued. Her position as a woman at that time, and his selection of her in preference to her brothers, would have been particularly affirming. His respect for her intellect may well have been related to her decision shortly before the age of thirteen, to leave the dissenters and join the Church of England. This decision was supported by detailed arguments, setting forth her reasons and outlining the principal controversies between the dissenters and the established church (SW, p. 71). Her research must have required a great effort even for a clever twelve-year-old, and her decision would have been an enormously challenging one for the daughter of such an eminent and knowledgeable father. It is striking that Dr Annesley gave serious attention to her document and respected her decision, in spite of his own unhappy experience of having to leave the Church of England. His response would have demonstrated his appreciation of her intellectual capacities and her worth as an individual; she would have felt profoundly valued and even special.

In November 1688, shortly before she was twenty, Susanna married Samuel Wesley. He too had 'dissented from dissent'. He had been educated in a dissenting college, but after the death of his father, his family struggled financially. He had left home to continue his education as a member of the Church of England and 'servitor' at Exeter College, Oxford (Clarke, 1823, p. 65). He took Holy Orders (deacon 1688, priest 1689) and in 1690 was appointed Rector of South Ormsby. Six years later, the crown living of Epworth was conferred on him by Queen Mary; both positions were in remote Lincolnshire.

When he and Susanna married he was seen by his contemporaries as a promising academic and literary figure. Clarke tells of his rapid and prolific writing: he seldom polished or refined his work, and his '*pen* was seldom idle'. He had serious literary ambitions, but the quality of his poetry was judged to be uneven (Clarke, 1823, pp. 74–9). Julian described his work as 'tedious and prosaic', and Pope and Swift were of the same mind (Julian, 1892, p. 1256). However, he showed evidence of enthusiasm, industry, liveliness of mind and a sense of humour, which would have appealed to Susanna's own eager mind. The evidence of Samuel's later life shows him to have been a man unwavering in his principles and far from reticent in expressing his convictions. This would quickly have become apparent to Susanna, and his passionate religious conviction would have mirrored her own. His qualities were attractive in themselves, and many of them pointed to a similarity to her reliable father, which would have drawn her to him. Reliability, however, was not one of Samuel's characteristics, and the vicissitudes of family life brought into focus the obverse side of many of his qualities. From the beginning of their marriage, they were poverty-stricken; throughout it, they remained poor and were often in debt.

Early in their marriage, Susanna allowed herself to be guided by Samuel's firm opinions, as when she was brought back from a brief attraction to Unitarianism. Later, as she became more secure in her own views, they were often at odds. As she wrote to John Wesley in 1724: ''tis an unhappiness almost peculiar to our family that your father and I seldom think alike' (SW, p. 106). Here the disagreement was over the relative importance of 'practical divinity' and 'critical learning', but there had been more serious and long-lasting disputes. In 1701 or 1702 Susanna refused as a 'non-Juror' to say 'Amen' to a prayer for William III, on the grounds that she had already sworn allegiance to the deposed James II. Samuel refused to touch her or to 'come into bed' with her, until she 'asked God's pardon and his': 'if we have *two* kings we must have *two beds*' (Clarke, 1823, p. 94). Neither party relented, and he left home for several months, threatening to go to sea as a chaplain, leaving Susanna and six children facing destitution (SW, pp. 35–7).

His passionate convictions and his impatience with those who held other views irritated the dissenters: he had left them after having benefited from an education in a dissenting academy and had written a paper criticising their educational methods. This was published in 1693, almost ten years after it was written, without their consent or his knowledge and led to a bitter dispute (Clarke, 1823, pp. 82–5). His tendency to stir up trouble was not limited to his controversy with the dissenters. It became local and political in 1705, when he openly supported the Tory candidate in a local election in Lincoln, believing that their opponents were planning to 'raise up Presbyterianism over the Church' (Clarke, 1823, p. 103). As a result, his family was subjected to a great deal of harassment: there were two fires at the Epworth Rectory, which were likely to have been caused by his enemies; cows were stabbed; and crops on their small-holding were burned. In a letter to the Archbishop of York (May 1705), he described a tragic event: while he was in Lincoln for the election, outside his house in Epworth there had been drumming, shouting and the firing of guns, and the small children playing in the garden had been threatened by the mob. Susanna had already lost eight children and had just given birth to her fifteenth child. The nurse, exhausted by the noise, had fallen asleep and '*overlaid*' the baby. The servants thrust it 'cold and dead' into Susanna's arms almost before she was awake. Samuel wrote, 'She composed herself as well as she could and that day got it buried'. The letter ends, 'All this thank God does not in the least sink my wife's spirits. For my *own*, I feel them disturbed and disordered: but for all that I am going on with my reply to Palmer', referring to his dispute with the dissenters (Clarke, 1823, pp. 104–5). Soon after this he was imprisoned for debt in Lincoln Castle. A further letter to the Archbishop dated 25 June 1705 showed some concern about having to leave his 'poor lambs in the midst of so many wolves'. However, he was quickly diverted from this anxiety, knowing that the 'great Shepherd' would protect them, adding, 'My wife bears it with that courage which becomes her, and which I expect from her'. He continued with his plans to do good among his 'fellow jayl-birds' (Clarke, 1823, p. 106).

However unbearable the circumstances, he appeared to take at face value Susanna's outward appearance of being in control, of being able to manage to make ends meet and to take care of the children. He could not allow himself to consider the degree to which his actions affected her, though as will be seen from her writings, she was at times driven almost to despair. Such behaviour was, of course, not exclusive to Samuel, and it has to be viewed in the context of the customary treatment of wives by their husbands at the time.

It is surprising, in view of their domestic trials and the serious differences and battles between them, that a strong and loving bond endured between them until Samuel's death. Susanna retained a sense of his essential goodness throughout, attributing his failures to higher motives. Any faults were explained by his being too good, too honest, too generous, too compassionate. Writing to her son Samuel in 1710, she compared herself unfavourably with her husband. She commended him as an example, one who had always served God, while she herself was 'too bad' to be imitated (although she acknowledged the value for Samuel of her constant prayers and a 'little good advice'; SW, p. 75).

Susanna always deferred, or appeared to defer, to Samuel's academic ability. Although she answered John Wesley's letters with his theological queries in ways which demonstrated her own theological sophistication and formidable powers of reasoning, she would never omit the suggestion that if he were not satisfied with her efforts, he should consult his father, whom she saw as a better 'casuist' than herself (SW, p. 112).

It is not certain how many children Susanna gave birth to; it was probably nineteen in twenty years (Baker, 1988, pp. 161–2). Most of that time she would either have been pregnant or nursing a young baby, so it might be thought that she would have welcomed a rest from this when she and Samuel were apart. Naturally, she did not write openly about their sexual relationship, but a letter, written when they were apart, suggests that she valued it: 'But I am inexpressibly miserable, for I can see no possibility of reconciling these differences, though I would submit to anything or do anything in the world to oblige him to live in the house with me' (SW, p. 36). The language used is that of a passionate lover, but at the same time, her intellect tells her there is no possibility that the differences can be resolved. The acknowledgement of this has an Annesley ring to it: she needs to feel 'a conscience devoid of offence'. The financial anxieties at the time could have contributed to the 'passion' in the letter, but its tone suggests Susanna's intense wish to have Samuel with her. Her repeated pregnancies confirm that they were sexually active for many years, but it is not possible to be definite about whether this was out of wifely duty or in response to a need for sexual contact, which she found gratifying and comforting. If it were the latter, her passionate sexual nature was an aspect of herself which she would have had to accommodate psychologically and spiritually, and their sexual relationship would have been an important aspect of their close bond.

Susanna Wesley's role

Having been the daughter of a moderately prosperous and eminent London clergyman, it would have been a huge shock for Susanna to find herself as the wife of a poor rector in an obscure corner of Lincolnshire. A young, intelligent woman, with an assured sense of her own 'special' intellectual capacities, she had to find a role that felt worthwhile, compatible with her religious aspirations and, if possible, 'special'. Her writings were central to the development of such a role.

In the seventeenth century, the traditions which emphasised the authority of the Holy Spirit (as opposed to those relying mainly on scripture), such as the Puritan tradition, offered to women a chance of extending their sphere of influence beyond their traditional roles. When the spirit or the 'Inner Light' could be invoked as a guide, it could be used as a way of challenging the patriarchy inherent in biblical teaching (Irwin, 1979, pp. xvi, xxvii–xxx). Susanna valued conscience, reason, and religious experience, all of which she saw as dependent on the work of the Holy Spirit, so that she could follow her own conscience and extend her role beyond the traditional one of a woman of her time (Wallace, Jnr., 1984, pp. 171–2). In addition to her writing, it involved her contemplative life, her presiding over acts of worship outside the church, and the education of her children, which she felt as a special trust and responsibility. She made this extension of her role explicit in a letter to her absent husband, telling him that although she was not a man she would 'do somewhat more', beginning with her children's education (SW, p. 80).

A great deal of the content of Susanna's letters and journals is concerned with intellectual analysis and argument, but sometimes she is carried away by her own rhetoric. When she writes about the benefits of quietness and withdrawal, her style becomes more fervent and emotional:

> When you condescend, Lord, to manifest yourself, all pain and want and care, all sense of misery vanishes in a moment, no unkindness or loss of friends, no contempt, reproach of enemies, no evil of any kind does afflict any longer. The noblest wine, the most generous of cordial doth not so much exhilarate and cheer the spirit as the least perception of your favour through Jesus Christ doth refresh and glad the soul, when ready to faint under the weight of its corrupt nature and tired with an unsuccessful pursuit of happiness in the enjoyment of what the world calls good. 'Tis these blessed lucid intervals when the soul by contemplation holds you in view that we say with the apostle, 'Master, it is good for us to be here'. Supreme eternal being! Fountain of life

and happiness! Vouchsafe to be ever present to the inward sense of my mind. I offer you my heart – take possession by thy Holy Spirit for the sake of Jesus Christ. Amen. Amen.

(SW, p. 333)

The language is passionate and evocative of the language used by her father in his sermons. Susanna could relinquish some of her control and lose herself in a blissful sense of merging in the contemplation of God's presence, and she would usually emerge from her periods of withdrawal with a new sense of purpose and direction. But she was suspicious of 'too much spiritual elation' (Wallace, Jnr., 1984, p. 169). Her letters and journals show that most of her waking life was tightly ordered and controlled; her self-discipline and the discipline involved in bringing up and teaching her children were also reminiscent of her father.

Educating children

She believed deeply that the work of educating children was the same as that of saving their souls. Central to the struggle to save their souls was her belief in original sin: through pride and sensuality, Adam and Eve had suffered a corruption of the will, and the subjection of the appetites of the body to the superior qualities of the mind had been lost. In this unregenerate state, bodily desires and selfishness predominated. The education of children was a battle to retrieve this situation, to work towards a subjection of the child's will, first to the will of the parents, and later, when understanding allowed, to the will of God. This mirrored her own struggle to control her own desires and appetites, to discover God's will and be obedient to it. The intensity and urgency of her account suggest a fear that these worldly impulses would overwhelm her good efforts and that she would be at their mercy.

Her beliefs and the methods she used to break the child's will have been the subject of much interest and criticism. They were set out in a letter to her son John at his request (24 July 1732) and later published (SW, pp. 369–73). The child's will should be broken as soon as possible, however painful the process, even before he could run or speak properly. She believed that an indulgent parent was doing the devil's work and was damning the child, soul and body, for ever. It is clear that she did not intend to be cruel. She believed that parents who did not set out to impose their will on their children from the beginning were mistaken and that their misplaced kindness was, in the end, more cruel. Unless an early start was made, it was almost impossible to control self-will at a later stage. She did indeed begin early and the control was firm and consistent; if a child was rebellious, and not controlled by instruction and reprimand, she did not flinch from corporal punishment. A child from one year old should be 'taught to fear the rod and cry softly'.

Her expectations of the children's educational progress were extraordinarily high but were usually fulfilled. The children appear to have managed to concentrate for hours on end, as was expected of them. The girls' education was taken as seriously as the boys', although they did not go away to school: no girl was taught to sew before she could read perfectly (Susanna saw the early teaching of sewing as the reason that the reading of many women was 'not fit to be heard'). Her usual method was to start teaching a child to read when he or she reached the age of five. The day before, the house was prepared and everyone warned not to enter the appointed teaching room between 9 and 12 a.m. and 2 and 5 p.m. She allowed one day for the child to learn his or her letters, and only two of the children took a day and a half (until she had experience of other children's abilities, she thought these two were slow learners). Her eldest son Samuel took only a few hours to learn the alphabet and then began to read using the first chapter of Genesis. He was reading the whole chapter within a few weeks. The other children followed a similar pattern. When they had learned their letters, they learned to spell and then to read, at first a line and then a verse. They were not allowed to stop until they could do their set task satisfactorily, however long it took.

Susanna saw education as giving the children access to a knowledge of God through his revelation in scripture, and through other works that offered spiritual guidance, so it was crucial for saving their souls. Her belief was that through discipline and worship in the home, they learned how to control their bodily appetites and selfish instincts and how to respect others; they developed a pattern for life, which provided regular opportunities to experience the presence of God. They would learn to be constantly aware of their own sinfulness but also of God's love, justice and mercy, and they would be strengthened against temptation.

Such a regime sounds oppressive in the extreme and, as such, would be expected to have resulted in some of the children showing some kind of disturbance, or, at least, that some might have become rebellious or found it impossible to learn. There is no evidence of this in her writings. The children seem to have been able to concentrate and to learn quickly, and they maintained their intellectual curiosity and read widely throughout their lives (Clarke, 1823, pp. 362f).

While Susanna talked of the need to break the children's will, she seems not to have broken their spirit, and there were several factors which were likely to have mitigated her apparently oppressive methods. First, she was aware of the need for praise. Here, Susanna was ahead of her time: while she did use verbal and physical punishment if necessary, she did not neglect praise, and this was not given only when the children achieved success. In quite an advanced way, she gave a reward for effort. If a child was obedient or tried to please, even if he did not succeed, his intention should be recognised, and he should be helped 'with sweetness' to do better next time. Second, her method was consistent. There was no feeling of unpredictability or unfairness; the children knew where they were and what to expect. The rules she imposed recognised their wishes, feelings, likely hurts and need for respect, and they were a means of ensuring that these were taken into account on a daily basis. A child who confessed a fault was not beaten (this was aimed at abolishing the temptation to lie), and no child was ever punished twice for the same fault. A child's right to his property was respected, even if it had only the value of 'a farthing, or a pin'. It must never be taken from him, particularly without consent. Promises were to be strictly observed and a gift once given could not be 'resumed', unless it had been given conditionally (SW, pp. 372–3). Third, she was able to think about each child's individual needs, treating each one separately as he learned to read, and taking age into account. She writes that, in her youngest child Kezia's case, she was persuaded against her plan to wait till a child was aged five before teaching her to read, and as a result the child took longer (SW, p. 371). She also set aside time to talk with each child on its own, 'on something that relates to its principal concerns'. These opportunities occurred only weekly, but it is notable that the conversation was child-centred, based on *its* principal concern (SW, p. 80).

Finally, Susanna was a warm woman. She permitted humour and teasing, though it is not clear whether she encouraged it. The children's reactions to her suggest that she gave them much more than a 'method'. Her own sense of being a valued and important individual, which came from her father (and possibly also from her mother), would have allowed her to bring a similar gift to her children. There was certainly a great warmth in the way she addressed them in her letters, and she conveyed a sense that they were constantly held in her mind, not only as children but as adolescents and adults. She wrote to Charles Wesley, at the time of his brother Samuel's death in 1739, that perhaps she had loved him 'too well' and that she had worried that she would not survive his loss, 'but none knows what they can bear till they are tried' (SW, p. 179). The children would have been aware of such strong, loving feelings, even in the context of severe discipline. Her writings convey an enthusiasm, conviction and sense of urgency about her beliefs, and this, too, would have been obvious to the children, even when they were very young. Her precepts included the need for good manners, and she became perturbed by the children's 'clownish accent', 'songs' and 'rude ways' after a period during which they lived with local families after a rectory fire in 1709 (SW, p. 372). However, there does not seem to have been an absence of humour. Clarke gives an account of the children's teasing of their younger sister, Martha, who was 'distinguished for deep thoughtfulness, for grave and serious deportment, and for an equanimity, of evenness of temper, which nothing could discompose'. His account does not portray a dour or sober household (Clarke, 1823, pp. 511–12).

'Evangelical nurture'

In a study of temperament in Protestants in eighteenth-century America, Greven was interested in their personal and religious experience, their feelings, and perceptions and the effects of unconscious elements, as well as their rational thought and theology and their child-rearing practices. He discerned three types of Protestant temperament: the 'Evangelical group' who believed in original sin, in 'inner depravity' and in the 'corrupt body' and whose children were governed by 'love and fear'. They relied on a sudden conversion experience in which they were 'born again' from a 'state of nature and of sin to a state of grace and ultimate salvation'. The 'Moderate' group did not embrace the idea of the total and ineradicable depravity of humanity. The children were governed by 'love and duty'. A gradual 'growth in grace' and the 'development of habits of virtue' could lead towards salvation. They were 'authoritative', rather than 'authoritarian'. The 'Genteel group' based their methods on 'fond affection' rather than 'conscientious discipline'; their methods were based on 'love and reverence' (Greven, 1977, pp. 17–18, 192–9, 265).

Greven anticipated that the children who experienced the most repressive forms of child-rearing ('evangelical nurture'), who felt threatened by the withdrawal of love, would have difficulty in establishing basic trust and autonomy, and that they would be likely to show evidence of pervasive and persistent guilt and shame from an early age (Greven, 1977, pp. 54–5). He located Susanna Wesley's child-rearing practices in the 'Evangelical' (the most repressive) group (Greven, 1977, p. 160). However, on reading her own account, it is not easy to place them firmly in either of the first two groups; they demonstrate features of both. The children were governed by both 'love and fear' and 'love and duty'.

Nevertheless, her belief that their bodies were the seat of corruption and that it was necessary to break their will, her strict discipline and the use of corporal punishment, all suggest that her practices were situated towards the more repressive end of Greven's classification. For the children, the guilt and shame induced by not reaching the required standards, the anger, rage and aggression stimulated by being controlled, restricted and beaten, and the lack of acceptable outlets for such feelings, must have led to a level of repressed passion that was difficult to manage, even allowing for the effect of mitigating factors. Susanna herself was also a product of 'evangelical nurture', and at times, her obsessional rumination, constant self-examination, self-blame, and harsh routines brought her to the point of exhaustion. She often despaired that she would not be able to persevere to the end: 'How shall I be assured that "the world, the flesh nor the devil", shall never be too hard for me?' (SW, p. 306).

Although she believed in forgiveness for others, she had difficulty accepting that it could extend to herself. It was only towards the end of her life, as she was taking communion, that she actually *felt* herself receiving forgiveness. Her experience is recorded in John Wesley's journal of 3 September 1739. She said that she had never before dared to ask for her own forgiveness, but when she heard the words of the liturgy, as she was offered the wine, she knew that 'God for Christ's sake had forgiven *me* all *my* sins' (BEJ, 19, p. 93). But her doubts and self-chastisement returned even after this: 'Oh, how inexcusable is that person who has knowledge of these things, and yet remains poor and low in faith and love. I speak as one guilty in this matter' (SW, p. 181).

There was a lifelong struggle to maintain the supremacy of love over hate in Susanna's inner world. Her own 'evangelical nurture' resulted in her seeing desires and bodily appetites as dangerous (the world, the flesh and the devil). They had to be subdued if depression and despair were to be fended off. For most of the time she achieved this by obsessional discipline in thought and action, which gave her a sense of being in control and therefore not liable to be swept away by overwhelming passions, and by the use of retreats from the world, in which she could feel her goodness reinforced by identification with a God of goodness, forgiveness and love. The struggle was exhausting and intense, and relied on her holding on to her understanding of the nature of God, of fallen humanity and of the means of redemption through Jesus Christ. Her need for this framework, which helped her to live with the dark side of herself, explains the passion with which she held on to her beliefs, the importance of her faith in her life and her desperate wish that her children's souls should be saved by sharing it. Her sense of desperation, of a life and death struggle, of belief being vital for survival, was no doubt a crucial element in her children's subsequent attitudes to religion.

Haartman (2004) writing in psychoanalytic terms specifically about eighteenth-century Methodism, has described Christian 'conversion' as a possible solution for the sequelae of authoritarian parenting such as those described above. He suggests that many of those listening to the preaching of John and Charles Wesley, and the Wesleys themselves, would have been subjected to similar early experiences (Haartman, 2004, p. 15). He describes a marked form of defensive splitting in the inner world of such individuals, which tends to result in a polarisation of love and hate and a similar split image of the parents. The children's rage and guilt resulting from the powerlessness, fear and humiliation caused by harsh discipline and corporal punishment, have to be isolated from the positive feelings towards the idealised parents who, though feared, have to be preserved as all good in the child's mind. Their images of God reflect this split; God is seen either as harsh and punitive or as all loving and gratifying (Haartman, 2004, pp. 2, 7–8). There is a constant battle to eliminate unacceptable sexual and aggressive instincts, to subdue bodily passions and to placate the punitive Father/God; it is so exhausting that the sufferer seeks relief. Haartman sees Wesleyan conversion as potentially resolving this split state, through a four-stage process which was described by John Wesley and to which Charles Wesley would also have subscribed (Haartman, 2004, p. 38).

There is first a 'desolation crisis' induced in the believer by the preaching of 'the Law'. This re-creates the infantile experience, in which fear, shame, self-blame and a desperate need for help predominate. Second, through the preaching of the Gospel of salvation, a solution to the previous distress is found. This manifests itself as a 'jubilant awakening', with a sense of 'unitive ecstasy' of the believer with a loving, forgiving God. The sinner is 'justified' and feels accepted and assured of forgiveness. The image of God changes from a demanding, punitive God to that of the God of *agape*. In the third stage, doubts, failures and fears return, but the believer is sustained by the memory of the 'unitive ecstasy'. Finally 'sanctification' is achieved in the longer fourth phase. This final phase requires the believer to 'watch and pray', that is to practise self-examination, to resist temptation, and to engage in the 'practice of the presence of God' (to bring to mind consciously the experience of 'unitive ecstasy'). It is this memory which is crucial to sustaining and supporting the believer in the struggle to face rage, rather than act on it, and to believe that it is possible for a bond with a loving parent to be maintained. The image of the loving parent survives the hate and aggression which is directed at it (Haartman, 2004, pp. 40–7). For this shift and integration to occur, trust in God as a non-abandoning 'good object' has to be achieved. When the influence of the individual's unconscious 'bad' objects is very powerful, there is great difficulty in letting them go and trusting in God as a constant, loving, forgiving object; the spectre of the punitive parent persists, and there remains a fear that the 'good' object will revert to 'bad' (Haartman, 2004, p. 67). In the absence of this trust, unconscious contents remain too dangerous to access. In Kristevan terms, the 'abject' is too threatening, and the subject retreats to a dyadic relationship with the Oedipal father.

Haartman suggests that repressed conflicts due to infantile trauma are expressed in religious symbolism during this process: ambivalence to parents, as enmity to God; rage, as innate corruption and rebellion; parental punishment, as God's wrath; loss and actual bereavement, as 'alienation, deadness and mourning after God'. This use of symbolism 'magnetises unconscious memories, feelings and fantasies'. Both the unconscious contents and the symbols are brought together in consciousness and can be thought about and reflected upon. But a facing up to internal ambivalence and fear of punishment is possible only under the safety offered through the formation of a 'conscious therapeutic alliance with a merciful deity'. A forgiving God loves in spite of the believer's sinfulness (Haartman, 2004, pp. 81–7). Haartman asserts that conversion facilitates internal *change*, by promoting integration, rather than merely *managing* conflict or neurosis (Haartman, 2004, p. 210). It is a shift which would correspond to a shift from Klein's paranoid-schizoid position to the depressive position, with the establishing of a good (loving, accepting, forgiving) internal object.

The same symbolism can also be seen, in Kristevan terms, as a focus for unconscious remnants relating to even more 'primitive' experience, that of the 'archaic triangle': the erosion of ego function and consciousness of weakness and sin in the 'desolation crisis', evoking the sense of loneliness, abandonment, and anxiety in the early stages of mother/child separation; the experience of 'unitive ecstasy' as evoking the metaphoric identification with an idealised 'imaginary' father; the process of 'watching and praying' as the evoking of the memory of this identification with the loving, forgiving father as a support as the infant achieves a triadic balance, avoiding dyadic merging with either the mother (and sinking into the 'abject'), or with the Oedipal father.

Haartman concludes that the persistence of bad objects in the inner world limits the possibilities for transformation. The good object may be glimpsed, but because love and hate are not fused, it is distorted by aggression. While the restored image of the unconditionally loving father is offered, the critical, punitive father is never far off. The sufferer is impelled to continue by his own efforts to placate his wrathful Father/God (2004, pp. 216–18). Haartman quotes John Wesley's descriptions of his own improved ability to handle situations which provoked lust and aggression, resulting from some change in himself (Haartman, 2004, p. 194). These claims cannot always be taken at face value, as we shall see.

Does eighteenth-century Methodism offer a *uniquely* effective opportunity for transformation and growth, as Haartman claims? He suggests that its effectiveness was owing to John Wesley's insistence that self-examination was to be carried out only after a 'unitive' experience had occurred, just as a patient needs to be held in a trusting relationship in therapy before she is able to address painful material. This, Haartman suggests, demonstrates Wesley's 'psychological genius': that he had an 'implicit understanding of the unconscious' and that he 'anticipated psychoanalytic theory' (Haartman, 2004, p. 4, 47, 190–1). The idea that Wesley was a psychoanalyst *avant la lettre* is hard to credit; nevertheless, as will become clear, he did have an extraordinary capacity to see his own needs in others. In some circumstances, he was able, almost 'instinctively', to offer them the help they needed.

It is probable that the Puritan background, and the 'evangelical' culture of the Wesley family, would have had certain adverse consequences for the children's development, and Haartman offers 'conversion' as a possible 'cure' for these sequelae. The following chapters explore whether the *actual* experiences of the Wesley brothers fit with these suppositions. Were the predicted consequences of their early experience realised? And if so, were they ameliorated by their conversion experiences? And how did they differ?

References

Annesley, S., 1674. *A Supplement to the Morning-Exercise at Cripplegate or Several More Cases of Conscience Practically Resolved by Sundry Ministers*. London: Cockerill.

Annesley, S., 1692. *The Life and Funeral Sermon of Reverend Thomas Brand*. London: Printed for Dunton.

Baker, F., 1988. Investigating the Wesley Family Traditions. *Methodist History*, 26(3), pp. 154–62.

Bolam, C., Goring, J., Short, H. L., and Thomas, R., 1968. *The English Presbyterians*. London: Allen and Unwin.

Clarke, A., 1823. *Memoirs of the Wesley Family*. London: Printed by J. and T. Clarke.

Greven, P., 1977. *The Protestant Temperament: Patterns of Child-rearing, Religious Experience, and the Self in Early America*. Chicago: University of Chicago Press.

Haartman, K., 2004. *Watching and Praying: Personality Transformation in Eighteenth-Century British Methodism*. Amsterdam/New York: Rodopi.

Irwin, J., ed., 1979. *Womanhood in Radical Protestantism: 1525–1675*. New York/Toronto: Edwin Mellen Press.

Julian, J., 1892. *A Dictionary of Hymnology*. London: John Murray.

Newton, J., 1968. *Susanna Wesley and the Puritan Tradition in Methodism*. London: Epworth Press.

Newton, J., 1985. Samuel Annesley (1620–1696). *Proceedings of the Wesley Historical Society London*, 45(2), pp. 29–45.
Rupp, G., 1977. A Devotion of Rapture. In ed. R. Buick Knox, *Reformation, Conformity and Dissent: Essays in Honour of Geoffrey Nuttall*. London: Epworth Press.
Schmidt, M., 1953–66. *John Wesley: A Theological Biography*, three volumes. Translated by Norman Goldhawk et al. London: Epworth Press, 1962–73.
Wallace Jnr, C., 1984. Susanna Wesley's Spirituality: The Freedom of a Christian Woman. *Methodist History*, 22(3), pp. 159–73.
Young, B., 1985. Sources for the Annesley Family. *Proceedings of the Wesley Historical Society London*, 45(2), pp. 47–57.

Figure 7.1 John Wesley

Chapter 7

John Wesley (1703–91)

'His countenance as well as his conversation, expressed an habitual gayety of heart, which nothing but conscious virtue and innocence could have bestowed. He was, in truth, the most perfect specimen of moral happiness which I ever saw'. So wrote the Irish theologian Alexander Knox of John Wesley, who had greatly influenced him as a young man (Knox, 1828, vol. II, p. 344).

Early biographies of John Wesley vary between triumphalist, hagiographic accounts, on the one hand, and critical or even denigrating ones, on the other. Sometimes this reflected the position of the authors, but it was also related to the complex and conflicting characteristics of Wesley himself. The titles of two important biographies highlight these aspects: Richard P. Heitzenrater's *The Elusive Mr. Wesley* and Henry Rack's *Reasonable Enthusiast*. Heitzenrater (2003, p. 32) points to the frequent use of such epithets as 'radical conservative', 'romantic realist' or 'quiet revolutionary', while Rack (2002, p. xiv) chose the title of his book to emphasise the paradoxical aspects in Wesley's life. He saw Wesley as an enigmatic figure and stressed the difficulty in interpreting the many legends and biographies created by his followers and the 'smokescreen' left by Wesley himself in his journals and other writings.

The 'paradoxical' nature of Wesley appears to have become something of a legend in itself, suggesting that there was a mystery about him, something incomprehensible. This chapter seeks to understand the contradictions psychoanalytically, rather than to respond to them as mysterious: his original writings have been used, drawing largely on the very comprehensive Bicentennial Edition of his works. The exploration is limited, as far as possible, to those written without an eye to publication, as these are likely to be the most reliable sources through which to understand his inner experience. The main part of this chapter is an account of Wesley's interactions with his faith and with other people; it is followed by an attempt to make sense of them psychoanalytically.

Wesley's account of his pre-conversion religious life

We saw in the last chapter that conversion has been suggested as a possible remedy for the adverse effects of 'evangelical nurture'. From his own account, prior to his conversion, John Wesley felt very dissatisfied with himself. In his journal for 24 May 1738 (the day of his 'conversion') he wrote an outline of what he then saw as his spiritual progress up to that time. It was preceded by a quotation from a letter to a friend expressing his present despair. He feared that he would never find salvation: 'Let the dead bury their dead! But wilt thou send the dead to raise the dead?' (BEJ, 18, pp. 241–2).

It is therefore interesting to start with his own history of his religious life at that stage and to consider his hopes and expectations of conversion (BEJ, 18, pp. 242–5). He wrote that up to the age of ten, he believed that he remained sinless because he had been washed by the Holy Ghost at his baptism. Because of his strict education, he understood rules and commandments but said he had no understanding of 'inner obedience or holiness'. At school, during the next six or seven years, there were fewer external rules, and he felt guilty for neglecting his duties, but he recognised that most people would not have regarded his breaches as serious. His hopes of salvation then lay in doing better than others, having a friendly attitude to religion and continuing with his religious practices (prayer, reading and church attendance). During his early years at Oxford, he proceeded in much the same way. His hope of being saved from his lapses was through brief periods that he had learned from his teachers to call 'repentance'.

He was ordained as a deacon in 1725 and a priest in 1728. His account described a change in his religious life in 1725. He was studying 'Christian Pattern' in Thomas à Kempis's *The Imitation of Christ* and came to realise that religious laws concerned inner thoughts as well as deeds and words, and that the heart was the seat of religion. In addition to attending Holy Communion weekly, he set aside one or two hours daily for religious retirement, including rigorous self-examination, and resolved to meet with only 'serious' people; he exhorted others to follow his example. Having read William Law's *A Practical Treatise on Christian Perfection* and *Serious Call to a Devout and Holy Life*, he became convinced of the wide extent of God's law and said he found his soul enlightened so that everything appeared new. He decided that he must strive for absolute obedience, and at that point believed that if he could keep strictly to God's law, in his inner being as well as in his speech and actions, God would accept him, and he would be saved. He launched into a vigorous programme of good works, which included visiting the poor, the sick and those in prison. He denied himself all luxuries and even some necessities, practising self-denial, including fasting, until, as he wrote, 'I apprehended myself to be near death'. This was the time when he, his brother Charles and others were part of the 'Holy Club'. Their aim was to achieve 'inward holiness' and to attain the 'image of God'. However, in spite of his adherence to a regime that seems to have outstripped even his mother's practices in strictness (at least so far as dangerous fasting was concerned) John failed to find any comfort or assurance. He was influenced by a 'contemplative man', whom he visited for the first time in 1732, who convinced him that 'outward works were nothing'; this was probably William Law (BEJ, 18, pp. 245–6, n.46). Wesley said he accepted

Law's advice as coming from God but subsequently could only 'drag on heavily' with outward works, relying on his own efforts until he sailed for Georgia in 1735 (BEJ, 18, p. 246).

On board the ship he met the Moravians and was impressed by their fervent faith. He recorded that they tried to show him a 'more excellent way', salvation by faith, which he failed to understand. In retrospect, he said he thought he had known better than the Moravians and had thought their beliefs were 'foolishness'. In Georgia, he was 'still under the law', but he found himself still 'carnal, sold under sin' (BEJ, 18, pp. 26–7). Returning to England in 1738, in a despairing state ('In this vile, abject state of bondage to sin') and with a sense of something missing, he attributed his uneasiness and distress to his lack of belief. It was in this state that he met the Moravian preacher Peter Böhler. Böhler told him that true faith was attended by the conquering of sin and by forgiveness and peace, and that it was a free gift of God bestowed upon all who strove to find it. To Wesley, this appeared like a 'new Gospel'. He resolved to renounce his dependence on his own works and righteousness and to strive by every means for salvation by faith: a belief that Christ had died for him, and that he could trust Him to forgive his sin, to sanctify and redeem him (BEJ, 18, pp. 247–9).

The conversion and its aftermath

Having given this account of his earlier experience, Wesley described how he continued to seek for this saving faith, though he often felt indifferent, dull or cold, with 'unusually deep lapses into sin', until Wednesday, 24 May 1738. As was his custom in the mornings, he opened the Bible at random and found encouraging texts suggesting that God's promises would be fulfilled and that the Kingdom of God might not be far off. He went to St Paul's Cathedral, where the anthem was 'Out of the depths I have called unto Thee', which spoke of the mercy of God and of redemption (Psalm 130: 1–4, 7–8). Finally, in the evening, he went 'very unwillingly to Aldersgate Street', where he heard Luther's Preface to the Romans, which described 'the change which God works in the heart through faith in Christ'. He described a sense of his own heart being 'strangely warmed' and a feeling of being saved: 'I felt I did trust in Christ, Christ alone for salvation, and an assurance was given to me that he had taken away *my* sins, even *mine, and* saved *me* from the law of sin and death' (Romans 8:2). However, he went on to describe his almost immediate doubts (which the 'enemy' suggested to him), an absence of the anticipated joy of conversion and his 'heaviness, because of manifold temptations'. He described being 'buffetted' by doubts and temptations over the following days, but by the following Sunday, he was preaching on salvation by faith (BEJ, 18, pp. 249–53). This conflict between 'works righteousness' and 'salvation by faith' reflected his inner struggles and preoccupied him from 1738 for the rest of his life. Wesley's early image of God was of a demanding, unforgiving, awful God who imposed strict laws. In 1738, and through the Moravians, he glimpsed an alternative: a forgiving, loving accepting father. He had a brief sense of this alternative father in his experience at Aldersgate Street, but he could never quite hold on to it. His struggles continued.

These were apparent in four areas of his life. First, he accepted with great sadness that he could not *experience* what he preached, and he had persisting feelings of emptiness, deadness and a fear of 'falling into nothing'. Second, he remained rigidly severe in his self-examination for evidence of sin and fastidious about his personal appearance; he also had to be strenuously and constantly active up to the time of his death. Third, although he was celebrated as a saviour of the souls and pastor to thousands, he was sometimes lacking in empathy, concern and care, especially for those close to him. Finally, his relationships with women could only be described as disastrous.

'More light than warmth'

In his introduction to the first volume of the Bicentennial Edition of Wesley's letters (BEL, 25, pp. 7–8), Frank Baker insists on Wesley's loving nature. He says that Wesley 'loved people', and he remarks on the warmth which is apparent in the letters, with words such as *affectionate* and *love* occurring on almost every page. He also quotes Alexander Knox on Wesley's 'predilection for the female character', and on his 'peculiar effluence of thought and frankness of communication' to his women correspondents (Knox, 1828, vol. II, p. 340). Baker refers to a letter from John Wesley to Knox, in which he professed that the longer he knew him, the more he loved him; in it he quoted his brother Charles, who said that he (John), once he loved somebody, would love them through 'thick and thin' (Knox, 1828, vol. II, p. 358). Clearly, Wesley saw himself (as did Baker) as loving and constant.

However, Baker also refers to a letter from Wesley to Sarah Crosby (12 June 1766). In this letter, Wesley quoted an observer, who had said that Wesley appeared to be almost unaffected by things that would have made him (the observer) 'run mad' (BEL, 25, pp. 8–9). This character trait was attributed by the observer, and by Wesley himself, to 'God's doing', in giving him a temperament which would allow him to carry out his 'peculiar work' and to maintain his authority. A letter written when Wesley was aged eighty-three, to Elizabeth Ritchie (24 February 1786), said that he did not remember having heard of other people having an experience like his. For as long as he remembered, he had been 'led in a peculiar way. I go on in an even line, being very little raised at one time or depressed in another' (BEL, 25, p. 9). Baker concludes that this even temper, and his belief in divine providence, led to the 'remarkable serenity' of Wesley's letters.

Apart from the instances quoted earlier, where he explained his imperturbability as a useful attribute for his work, he more usually found it a trial to have more 'light than warmth'. In the same letter to Elizabeth Ritchie he went on to say that he was usually influenced by reason or scripture rather than 'impressions'. He 'saw' more than he 'felt' and wanted to experience more 'love and zeal for God' (Telford, VII, p. 319). In his 'abundance of seeing', he had a sense of something missing.

Such references to a lack of feeling are not uncommon in Wesley's writings. His journal of 14 October 1738, five months after his Aldersgate experience, records that he could not find the 'love of God or Christ' within him. He felt dead, and his thoughts wandered in prayer meetings; he complained that he usually had only 'cold attention' at the Eucharist: 'hence when I hear the highest instance of God's love, my heart is still senseless and unaffected. Yea, at this moment, I feel no more love to him than to one I had never heard of' (BEJ, 19, p. 18). A month later he wrote to a Moravian friend, Richard Viney, about the beginnings of a revival: 'The Spirit of the Lord hath already shaken the dry bones, and some of them stand up and live. But I am still dead and cold, having peace indeed, but no love or joy in the Holy Ghost' (BEL, 25, pp. 583–4). Almost twenty years later he wrote to Charles Wesley on 27 October 1766, expressing his doubts and lack of 'direct witness' or experience of God, his only 'proof' being from 'such as fairly shines from reason's glimmering ray' (Telford, V, p. 16).

In spite of, or perhaps because of, this sense of something lacking, he noticed an increase in 'zeal for the whole work of God', which he found inexplicable:

> I am *'borne along'*. I know not how, that I can't stand still. I want the world to come to *'what I do not know'*. Neither am I impelled to this by fear of any kind. I have no more fear than love. Or if I have [any fear, it is not that of falling] into hell but of falling into nothing.
>
> (Telford, V, p. 16)

He was unable to keep still; he had to keep active to fend off some unpleasant affect which he was unable to name or actually feel but which was experienced as deadness or coldness. Of his friend John Fletcher, he wrote in 1785, 'I grudge him sitting still; but who can help it? I love ease as well as he does; but I dare not take it while there is another world' (Telford, VII, p. 272).

There is some evidence that the coldness and deadness were associated with depression. This is evident in three letters John wrote after the end of a relationship, when he was angry with the recipients (1749–50). He had difficulty in expressing his feelings directly. In one letter, he wrote, 'For I am a sinner. Therefore, it is just if I go heavily all my days' (BEL, 26, p. 394); and in another was clearly so despondent and tired that he admitted to wishing that he could die (BEL, 26, p. 408). His anger emerged in the guilt-inducing effects of his letters on those he felt had treated him unfairly, and his distress also leaked out in a wish to be released from his struggle.

Any impulses toward suicide would, of course, have been morally repugnant to him and could not have been acknowledged. However, it is of interest that in a letter he wrote to the Prime Minister, William Pitt, in May 1784, he was uncompromising in his urging the prosecution of 'self-murderers'. He recalled how the bodies of the 'Spartan matrons', amongst whom there was a 'rage for self-murder', were dragged through the streets naked. This he said, put a stop to the practice at once, and that hanging every self-murderer in chains would have the same effect in England (Telford, VII, p. 236). The virulence of this letter raises the possibility of an inner pressure from self-destructive impulses in himself. Freud used the term *disavowal* to describe a process in which disturbing unconscious wishes could be dealt with by 'turning a blind eye' to them. They could be somehow known but not known at the same time (Freud and Breuer, 1893–5, p. 181, n.1). As described by Britton, this defence can include the development of 'counter-beliefs', which may be held with violent intensity, driven by the anxiety defended against (Britton, 1998, pp. 15–16). Wesley's reaction is suggestive of such a defence; self-righteousness replaced his anxiety when he could attribute his self-destructive wishes to the Spartan matrons.

While Wesley was unable to understand the feeling of deadness he described, and preferred to avoid it, the way he addressed his correspondents in some of his letters suggests that he was addressing a part of himself. On 25 March 1772, he replied to Ann Bolton, who had written to him about 'emptiness'. This had reminded him of the 'Mystic writers':

> They are perpetually talking of 'self-emptiness, self-inanition, self-annihilation' and the like: all very near akin to 'self-contradiction'.... And I am many times ready to tremble *lest you* should slide into it again, and lest I myself should lead you into it while I tell you (as my manner is) just the thought that rises in my heart.
>
> (Telford, V, p. 313)

His writings convey a constant struggle with feelings of deadness and coldness and his fear, not of hell, but of 'falling into nothing'. Powerful feelings of anger, grief, greed or destructiveness would have been intolerable to him, and so they would have to have been kept out of consciousness. As a result, not only would these feelings be inaccessible, but so would his loving feelings as well. How this felt and perhaps something of what lay behind it, is movingly shown in an exchange of letters with his mother. A letter from Susanna of 21 February 1732 described what the Eucharist meant to her. It is one of those letters in which she was 'led away' by the 'vast subject' of Christ's Incarnation and Passion, the wonder and incomprehensibility of the Atonement and the mystery of the Divine Institution of the Eucharist. It is an emotional torrent, full of exclamation marks and worthy of Dr Annesley (SW, pp. 148–50). Wesley replied, agreeing with her account, but added that though his brother and a Mr. Morgan were moved by it and that he agreed intellectually, his heart did not feel it (BEL, 25, pp. 327–30). He went on to speculate why this might be and listed all the religious practices he had used to try to induce the feeling he sought and to ask her advice. From his childhood, he told her, she had 'renounced the world', and he concluded that perhaps a similar renunciation would also help him. He then touchingly asked her to pray for him, to hold him in her mind before God: 'If you can spare me only that little part of Thursday evening which you formerly bestowed upon me in another manner'. He believed that her early attention to him had formed his judgement, but it was his heart that now needed correction. The letter ended by taking his mother to task for saying she had loved him too well and would try to love him less. Susanna had said this because she thought she was soon to die and had felt she must let go of worldly attachments. Wesley agreed but asserted that he was not merely a perishable worldly thing: that if she thought him 'sick unto death', she should love him more and pray for his healing more ardently. He ended by looking to the future and wondering whether he would survive in her absence, suggesting that if she died, his death would soon follow.

This was a cry from the heart. He had identified that, for his heart to be 'correct', she would have had to attend to him individually, and his only memory of this was the Thursday evening session as a child with her. He was also aware that his early experience of her had formed his 'judgement' and not his 'heart'. He was asking for attention in 'another manner', not just because he was now an adult but also in a manner that attended to the heart and not merely to the judgement. He reproached her for putting doctrine, the need to abandon worldly attachments in order to approach God, before her love for him. His relating this back to his early experience suggests that it was an old and familiar pattern. He clearly identified it with his 'something missing' which he later called 'coldness' or 'deadness'. The anguish shown in these accounts is far removed from the 'gayety of heart' described by Alexander Knox.

Appearance and self-discipline

In spite of his small stature (he was five feet three inches tall), Wesley commanded respect. According to Abelove, he used his 'gentility' to exact deference. He took great pains with his hair: unlike many men of his time, he did not wear a wig, but his hair was long, smooth, and slightly curled at the ends. There were reports that he looked 'angelic'. Horace Walpole is said to have commented on the 'little soupçon' of curl in his hair. In addition to his gown, cassock and bands, he wore silk gloves, a gold stickpin at his breast and large silver buckles on his shoes. He is said to have set himself apart from his preachers by giving advice about their dress, which was to be different from his own. It is also suggested that Wesley used his gentility to encourage love from the poor in a variety of ways: he allowed them to get unexpectedly close to him and often stayed in their homes rather than with the gentry; he studied 'physick' and dispensed remedies; he gave away all the money he earned, except that spent on travelling. He dispensed not only 'physick' and money, but 'free grace' to all. The picture is of an elegant and ascetic figure mixing with all social groups, dispensing help for physical and spiritual needs, and preaching outside to crowds of thousands (Abelove, 1990, pp. 7–15). It gives weight to one assertion that in this 'providential role', which confirmed his personal and professional identity, there was some sense of himself as a Christ-like figure (Moore, 1974, pp. 47–9).

During Wesley's time at Oxford, the asceticism, self-examination and religious observations of the Holy Club were extreme. Even Susanna Wesley questioned the lengths to which John and Charles were prepared to go. She was worried that Charles would develop consumption: he could not eat a full meal without vomiting. She wrote to John (25 October 1732), urging them to take better care of their health, though with little hope that they would heed her advice. The letter ended,

> I must tell ye, Mr. John Wesley, fellow of Lincoln, and Mr. Charles Wesley, Student of Christ Church, that ye are two scrubby travellers, and sink your characters strangely by eating nothing on the road, . . . ,[1] to save charges. I wonder you are not ashamed of yourselves. Surely if you but give yourselves leave to think a little, ye will return to a better mind.
>
> (SW, pp. 151–3)

In spite of the failure of their rigorous measures to deliver the feelings of assurance of acceptance by God, and John Wesley's deeper realisation of the meaning of justification by faith in 1738, he was never able to relax his efforts to work towards salvation. His efforts became less extreme, but he continued to encourage himself and others to constant good works, self-examination, frequent use of the means of grace and periods of religious meditation. Like his grandfather, Wesley described this as 'faith working through love', rather than salvation by works, but there remained an insistent, obsessional quality about his own practice which suggested a motivation through fear more than through love. This quality is evident in many of his letters. In one to Sarah Ryan (14 December 1757), following a barrage of questions about her thoughts and prayers and a list of insistent demands as to how she should behave, he warns of the dreadful consequences if she should fall short (BEL, 27, pp. 108–9). This was the third of three letters written within a month, all in the same vein. Fear was prominent, as were thoughts of falling into destruction; it is as if he were addressing his own fears.

He continued to advocate the preaching of both 'faith' and 'works', but there is evidence of an increasing stress on works as he grew older. On 4 November 1772, he wrote to Charles Wesley about Gospel preaching on the sufferings of Christ or salvation by faith, which he said could be 'the most useless, if not the most mischievous' unless accompanied by the strong inculcation of 'holiness' (Telford, V, p. 345). A month later, he wrote,

> I often cry out, *Vitae me redde priori*. Let me again be an Oxford Methodist! I am often in doubt whether it would not be for the best for me to resume all my Oxford rules, great and small. I did then closely walk with God and redeem the time. But what have I been doing these thirty years?
>
> (Telford, VI, p. 6)

His struggle to feel accepted by God continued into old age. Like his mother, he understood the theology of salvation by faith and preached it to others, but for much of the time there is evidence that he was not able to accept that it applied to him.

Saviour of souls but exasperating brother

Thousands came to hear Wesley preach; they felt their faith deepened and they committed themselves to the life and faith he advocated. He was endlessly energetic, travelling, according to Hampson, more than 200,000 miles and preaching more than 40,000 sermons (Hampson, 1791, pp. 190f in Rack, 2002, p. 535). There is a well-established legend that Wesley saw this work as part of his 'special' destiny, following the rectory fire in February 1709, when he was five years old. His own account, in which he modified his mother's memory of the event, was published in the first issue of the *Arminian Magazine* of 1778 and reprinted by Heitzenrater (2003, pp. 43–4). He recalls being trapped in his room by the fire and being rescued through a window only after the rest of the family had been taken to safety and just before the roof collapsed. Heitzenrater (2003, pp. 44–5) also quotes Wesley from the *Gentleman's Magazine* of 1784, in which he denied the connection between the fire and his providential role, writing that this was an 'ingenious' idea but was 'in truth a castle in the air'. However, Wesley's journal records events at a watch-night service on 9 February 1750, when he suddenly remembered that this was exactly the time forty years before when he had been rescued from the fire: 'I stopped and gave a short account of that wonderful account of providence. The voice of praise and thanksgiving went on high, and great was our rejoicing before the Lord' (BEJ, 20, p. 320). After the fire, his mother saw him as having been mercifully preserved. On 17 May 1711, she wrote that she now intended to give his soul 'particular' care. She promised herself she would do her utmost to promote his religious and moral education (SW, p. 235). And so it appears that both Wesley and his mother saw his life and work in providential terms. He described himself as 'a brand plucked out of the fire' (Zechariah 3:2) on several occasions when he felt he had narrowly escaped danger.

Wesley insisted that personal contact was the best way to help people, and he visited the sick, the dying and those in prison. For those he was unable to reach, he produced 'tracts' suitable for particular situations. He had a vast correspondence and a great capacity for remembering the details of peoples' lives and those of their families. He did not disguise his preference for spending time with the poor rather than with the 'genteel' (Rack, 2002, p. 363), and he set up an efficient system of pastoral care within his movement, where people met in groups, the 'class meetings'. Their pastoral and spiritual needs were supplied by class leaders; they were encouraged to share their fears and failings with each other.

Wesley's power to influence people may well have been related to the deference he created, but it was also inextricable from the social situation of the time. Poverty and debt were rife, unemployment was high and there was much drunkenness and crime. Disease and mortality levels were also high (Langford, 1992, pp. 146–55). This was fertile ground for Wesley's message. His advice to the Methodists was that they should care for 'the hungry, the naked and sick' and 'exhort and reprove those they had dealings with'; rules were laid out regarding appropriate behaviour, urging frugality, self-denial and kindness to the poor; and he offered advice about marriage and drink (Rack, 2002, p. 442). His message of 'free grace for all', with its hope of a better life in Christ than the earthly one, must have been very welcome. However, Methodism appealed not only to the poor but also to the new middle classes of the mining and manufacturing industries, without whose support it is unlikely to have flourished as it did (Langford, 1992, p. 253).

That Wesley was so loved and powerful in his interactions with the Methodist people, and the intensity of their response, suggests that there were yet other forces at work connected with his personality. It has been difficult for scholars who have looked at Wesley as a pastor to avoid seeing his frequent insensitivity and occasional cruelty when dealing with people in trouble. Schmidt did his best to rationalise such behaviour, but even he had to acknowledge its existence. He gave examples which he hoped would show that Wesley prioritised his concern for the other's feelings over doctrinal divisions (Schmidt, II, 1953–66, pp. 129–31). He suggested that in Wesley, the 'severity and gentleness [were] one and indivisible'. He linked this to another letter giving advice on preaching, in which Wesley warned against offering hearers the 'love of God in Jesus Christ over-hastily'. One must first preach the Law with the utmost stringency, so that it 'searched the inmost recesses of the heart with inquisitorial power':

> 'Tis true that God alone in Christ *feeds* his children. But even they are to be *guided* as well as fed. Yea, and often *physicked* too. And the bulk of our hearers must be *purged* before they are fed. Else we feed only the disease. Beware of *all honey*. 'Tis the best extreme; but it is an extreme. O keep close to the Bible!
>
> (BEL, 26, p. 418)

Consciously, Wesley linked this theme of the requirement to preach both the Law and the Gospel to his fear of Antinomianism and his disapproval of Moravian preaching, but more personally, the Gospel without the Law, felt like a dangerous addiction. He knew intellectually that for wounds to be healed, the 'inmost recesses' had to be engaged with, and the believer had to trust in the forgiveness of a loving God. He could advocate these for others but struggled with both himself. In 1751, he wrote suggesting that 'so called' preachers of the Gospel corrupt the appetites of their hearers by offering them nothing but sweetmeats: they become so used to sweetmeats that they cannot appreciate the 'genuine wine of the kingdom'. They are given 'cordial upon cordial', which makes them temporarily full of 'life and spirit', but 'meantime their appetite is destroyed, so that they can neither retain or digest the pure milk of the Word'. Once the effect of the 'cordial' has worn off they feel lifeless, powerless and weak and are very hard to 'recover', as they can only call out for more cordial (BEL, 26, pp. 487–8). There could not be a better description of Kohut's 'object hunger', in which the 'Gospel' is sought as a replacement for an archaic object.[2]

As if speaking of himself, in a letter, to an 'anonymous Evangelical layman', he argued that the more people were convinced of their sin, the more it was permissible to include more of the gospel. However, there remained dangers in omitting the law: 'many of our hearers are still unconvinced' and 'many who are convinced will heal their wounds only slightly' (BEL, 26, p. 483).

In spite of his difficulty in getting in touch with his own deep feelings, he seemed capable in some situations of reaching others in a deep way. An account of his interactions with prisoners shows the kind of circumstances in which this capacity was apparent, unlike other occasions when he was far from empathic. His tract *A Word to a Condemned Malefactor* vividly demonstrates the way he worked in such a situation (Heitzenrater, 2003, pp. 149–52). It is a very powerful document, and while it might be viewed as a typical 'dangling over the pit' of a hell-fire preacher, it is more than that. It shows a capacity to meet the prisoner exactly where he is, pointing out that he is locked away behind bars, without hope, facing death (which meant losing all those he loved, as well his own body) and having to face his maker, when he is as far from 'holiness' as 'darkness from light'. There follows a terrifying list of the prisoner's 'sins' and failings, which are so wicked 'that even the world cannot bear you; the world itself spews you out'. Having relentlessly identified the prisoner's fears of imprisonment, his fear of death and his despair about his inner badness, he goes on to urge repentance, offering the hope of escape from damnation and urging the need for belief in salvation through Christ. He describes the offer of the saving love of God, which enables power over sin. By loving and trusting only in God, he would be led to the 'Kingdom' and would finally receive the words of Christ, spoken to the penitent thief at the Crucifixion: 'This day shalt thou be with me in paradise'.

Part of the power of this document, and no doubt of his daily visits, lay in Wesley's ability to give the prisoner his whole attention and total concern. This enabled him to detail the prisoner's inner badness without mincing his words; nothing was glossed over. He described exactly what the other was experiencing. It was an 'abject' state of affairs: he identified that part of the prisoner which he could not acknowledge in his own depths. Once the prisoner experienced himself as accurately known, he could accept the offer of hope from the now trusted figure. There was a sense of urgency about Wesley's message, a life-or-death feeling, which put pressure on the other to respond. This same feeling of a life-or-death struggle recalls that described in Susanna Wesley's struggle to deal with unacceptable feelings. The same sense of dread, with a desperate need to avoid falling into a place of destruction, existed in Wesley. Through others he was indirectly addressing his own inner 'badness'.

There is, however, considerable evidence that in many of Wesley's interactions with others, he had little awareness of the effect he had on them. While he appeared concerned, and 'saved souls' on a large scale, he often had difficulty empathising with people on a personal level, unable to imagine the hurtful effects of his words. He saw 'reproof' as a necessary part of the process of salvation, but he lost patience when people did not conform to his preconceived pattern. As Rack puts it, he was most gracious to those who were 'either submissive to his guidance or were in various ways inferior to him' (Rack, 2002, p. 542). In addition, he tended to idealise those to whom he formed an attachment. He was accused by some in his lifetime of not keeping friends who disagreed with him. He denied this in his letters (BEL, 27, p. 355), but they also show that there was often a cooling of the correspondence and a lack of contact after a disagreement (Telford, V, pp. 25–7).

Wesley's lack of empathy with people close to him is shown most starkly in his response to bereavement. He would, of course, not have seen it as such; he would have seen his words as 'reproofs', necessary for the spiritual good of the bereaved. Intense or prolonged grief was regarded as evidence of too great an attachment to the things of the world, of 'inordinate affection'. His usual pattern on these occasions was a brief acknowledgement of the loss, followed by a reminder that 'the Lord giveth and the Lord taketh away'. The most striking example is in a letter to his sister Martha of 17 November 1742 (BEL, 26, p. 90). She had married a clergyman, Westley Hall, who had been unfaithful to her before and after the marriage, and she had lost nine out of ten children (Clarke, 1823, p. 527). In the first brief paragraph he writes,

> I believe the death of your children is a great instance of God's goodness to you. You have often mentioned to me how much of your time they took up. Now that time is restored to you, and you have nothing to do but to serve our Lord without carefulness and without distraction, till you are sanctified in body, soul and spirit.

The second paragraph is concerned with her husband's undesirable association with the 'still brethren', and the third with concern for the desolate state of the Church of England. He ends, confirming that her husband had paid him for his books, adding that he wants only love from her, not money.

The effect of Wesley's letters can be seen, not in Martha's response (which is not available), but in a letter from another sister, Emily (24 November 1738), which demonstrates the degree of anger and exasperation that his blindness to others' pain could cause. Emily was struggling with severe poverty, debt and constant ill health, in need of 'common necessaries' and selling clothes for bread. She wrote thanking her brother for thinking of her but letting him know that his letter was of little comfort to her:

> For God's sake tell me how a distressed woman who expects daily to have her bed taken from under her for rent can consider the state of the churches in Germany. I am ready to give up the ghost with grief.

She listed her afflictions at length, mentioned that her brothers, Samuel and Charles '(God bless 'em)' had helped her financially over previous months and asked that he should remember his love for her and not 'forsake' her. 'Love to your sister in trouble is more pleasing in the sight of God than preaching to a thousand where you have no business'. She claimed that he had married her to her husband but then lost interest. She went so far as to suggest that if she killed herself, her '*damnation*' would be 'justly laid at [his] door' (BEL, 25, p. 589).

Such a response to worldly troubles, particularly bereavement and especially the loss of a child, has to be seen in the context of the eighteenth-century view of providence. The idea that 'the Lord giveth and the Lord taketh away' was offered as an explanation, with the hope of providing some comfort at a time of high infant mortality. Wesley found this in the life of Jean-Baptiste de Renty (1611–49). He remembered the story of de Renty's reaction to his wife's death, after which, 'he knew such a strange "holy unconcern" at this most severe of human losses that it could only be a demonstration of divine power' (Schmidt, I, 1953–66, p. 215). Not long before Wesley's death (3 January 1791), when his friend Adam Clarke had lost a child, Wesley reminded him of de Renty and added, 'But you startle me when you talk of grieving so much for the death of an infant. This is certainly a proof of inordinate affection; and if you love them thus all your children will die' (Telford, VIII, p. 253).

Wesley's responses to people in prison, in large crowds, and in his personal life, suggest that in certain situations which reflected his own needs in some way, he could accurately and powerfully identify a need and address it. This occurred when he was preaching: here people were looking up to him as if to be fed, and *en masse* they lost their own characteristics as individual people; they became ready containers into which could be projected his own need. As a result, his words would have been powerfully affecting. Similarly, people perceived as dependent, 'weaker' or 'inferior' were predisposed to receive his projected needy aspects. In these situations, he accurately and helpfully described his own state and offered the cure which he so desperately sought for himself. However, in situations where the other person asserted a separateness from him by disagreeing with him, or by describing an experience with which he could not identify, he had to resort to 'doctrinal' responses, such as 'providence', 'inordinate affection' or 'holy unconcern'. These responses were so out of tune with the experience of the other person that they were often felt as cruel and insensitive, as indeed they were. When he preached, he saw other people having the experience he wished for, and this gave him reassurance that what he preached about salvation was actually possible. His preaching not only brought hope of salvation to his listeners but to himself through them as well.

Relationships with women

In *An Account of an Amour of John Wesley*, Wesley included a summary of his views on marriage, in an attempt to clarify his thoughts (Wesley, 1749 in Heitzenrater, 2003, pp. 172–4). His first objection to marriage from the time he was six or seven years old was, 'Because I should never find such a woman as my father had'. However, this first objection was quickly removed, by his finding 'some, though very few women, whom I could not but allow to be the equal to my mother, both in knowledge and piety'.

In his subsequent relationships with women, he ran into all kinds of problems. Writers on both his life and his theology have struggled to reconcile their ideas about his spirituality and the morality he advocated, with his behaviour towards women. It is easy for a researcher to become confused when exploring the underlying sexual aspects of Wesley's relationships, between a legitimate, unbiased and straightforward examination of his reactions and a sense that one might be selecting out salacious material, which can then feel prurient or even sacrilegious. It is as if it is necessary to be one of two things: a follower of the loved and saintly man or one of the gossips who accused him of gross moral turpitude. It is not easy to be objective, but this should not prevent an attempt to understand the sexual pressures on him.

The following three extracts reflect this difficulty. In a short biography of Wesley, Waller writes of his letters, 'there were no sexual overtones either stated or intended in the letters to these women within the Methodist movement' (Waller, 2003, p. 101). Similarly, Rack, writing of the accusations of sexual misconduct which were sometimes levelled against Wesley and his preachers, acknowledges that his conduct made him an 'easy target': 'There is no reason to believe Wesley guilty of anything of this sort: his hesitant approach even to marriage, would of itself make it implausible'. His relationships with female correspondents were 'delicate and innocent', and there was nothing 'of erotic mysticism in Wesley's language'. It was his 'naive optimism' about the possibility of the 'regeneration of dubious characters' and his 'affectionate spiritual correspondence with godly women' which fuelled the suspicion of his critics (Rack, 2002, pp. 267–9). Schmidt writes of Wesley's relationship with Ann Bolton, one of his long-term correspondents, as if to exclude any sexual element: 'The austere old man became quite tender towards her' (Schmidt, II, 1953–66, p. 146).

Abelove believes that one reason for Wesley's separation from the Moravians was that he saw them as having too positive a view of sex. Wesley quoted their leader, Count Nikolaus von Zinzendorf, as claiming that 'Jesus had been incarnated man, so that the "Male member" might be sanctified, and born of a woman, so that the female genitals might be made equally "honourable"'. Wesley responded with horror: 'Were ever such words put together from the foundation of the world?' (Wesley, 1755, pp. 27–8 in Abelove, 1990, p. 54). Abelove links this attitude to sex with his condemnation of masturbation, his preference for celibacy, and his separation of men from women in indoor services and class meetings. He also dramatically suggests that by unconscious attempts to deny his parents' marriage, Wesley 'all but claimed for himself a virgin birth'. He attributes this theory to the following: Wesley's sending a copy of his mother's portrait at her death to every member of the London meetings and his arranging a big public funeral for her; his committing her body to be with her father's, without mentioning her husband, as was usual; and his inscribing the tombstone, 'Susanna Wesley, the Youngest and Last surviving daughter of Dr. Samuel Annesley', again omitting any reference to her husband. But his unconscious attempts to exclude his father did not quite succeed; when he bought the burial plot, he mistakenly inserted his father's name where his own should have been (Abelove, 1990, pp. 54–9). All this hardly amounts to his claiming a virgin birth for himself, but there is a suggestion that he had difficulty in thinking of his parents as a sexual couple.

The 'Cotswold Set'

His first contact with women outside his family was as a young man at Oxford. After his first degree, he was studying for his MA and came to know some well-connected clerical and military families in the Cotswolds, particularly the daughters. Between 1725 and 1734, he wrote letters to them and spent holidays with them (his brother Charles was a member of the same group). The letters and diaries suggest that he had a sense of being merged with idealised images of these women, who were almost interchangeable in his mind. They are seen as full of goodness and devoid of imperfection but exciting at the same time. It is not surprising that Rack writes of Wesley's discovering sex, at this time, as the 'serpent in his Eden' (Rack, 2002, p. 78).

Wesley may have proposed marriage to one of this group, Sally Kirkham, but only one of her letters is extant. Information about their relationship is available only from his frequent references to her in his letters to the other women and from his mother's and sister Emily's comments. It is known that after Sally's marriage their relationship continued for some time. The surviving letters are to Mary Pendarves (née Granville, a widow who later became known as an artist, Mary Delaney) and her sister Ann. They are full of youthful exuberance, recalling idyllic days spent in each other's company. They suggest mutual love and idealisation, and aspirations towards self-improvement, increased goodness and holiness. They addressed each other using romantic names from classical literature or nicknames (Sally was referred to as 'Varanese' and John as 'Cyrus' or 'Primitive Christianity'). The letters were at times parodies of conventional love letters, written in the third person, with flowery, rhetorical language and the playful use of names. There was an assumption that they were part of a very select and holy group.

Sally Kirkham (Varanese) married a Mr. Chapone in 1725. Five years later, Wesley wrote to Mary Pendarves bewailing his loss. He also described the 'soft emotion' with which he 'glowed' while corresponding with her (BEL, 25, p. 247). However, in this and subsequent letters, he made it clear that Mary was valued because she was associated with 'Varanese', and in eloquent language (but very tactlessly), he made plain the similarity of his feelings for both of them (BEL, 25, pp. 251, 262). He used one woman to replace another, without disguising the fact that she was a substitute. He seems to have been oblivious to the likely effects of this kind of comparison on the women involved. Initially Mary Pendarves went along with his requests, but, not surprisingly, she eventually lost interest and stopped answering his letters (BEL, 25, p. 389 n.1).

Ostensibly his motivation was to help these women to become better people. In a letter of 5 April 1731, having contrasted the spiritual state of his correspondents favourably with the 'bulk of mankind', he expressed his wish that his mind could unite with theirs 'in a single instance of humility' (BEL, 25, p. 275). A letter in September 1731 showed how he would become particularly excited and enthusiastic if they reported to him any good works they had performed (BEL, 25, 315). However, there were times when Wesley was aware that he had other motives in addition to wanting to 'improve' his women correspondents. In December 1731 he wrote, 'I perceive another principle is interwoven, a desire of recommending myself to their esteem. And if this be a fault I am much to blame' (BEL, 25, p. 262).

In his early diaries printed in Heitzenrater (2003, p. 56), he described his relationship with Varanese following her marriage. The entry for 14 October 1726 described several walks with her and her sister, Betty, and in it he quotes Varanese on their relationship. She expressed her reluctance to end it because she felt he preserved her from complacency: she argued that the acquaintance predisposed her to virtue, and (on 17 October) that the relationship was special: it would be 'almost a sin to prostitute those expressions of tenderness to others which I have at any time applied to you'. She would not end their relationship unless her husband resented it, and she was sure that would never happen. Wesley wrote that he 'sat with Varanese and Betty till eleven. Leaned on Varanese's breast and kept both her hands within mine. She said very many obliging things. Betty looked tenderly. Thank God; long-suffering'.

While the participants convinced themselves of the goodness and purity of their relationships, Susanna Wesley had reservations. In a letter of 31 January 1727, she warned,

> I have many thoughts on the friendship between Varanese and thee, and the more I think of it, the less I approve it. The tree is known by its fruits, but not always by its blossoms; what blooms beautifully sometimes bears a bitter fruit.

She also warned that the reason many do not attain to the kingdom of heaven is because 'there is some Delilah, some one beloved vice, they will not part with' (SW, p. 132). She used the words *darling sin*, quoting her father.

John's sister Emily could also be relied upon to get to the nub of the matter. Wesley had written accusing her of being too worldly. On 13 August 1735, she replied agreeing that God's will should take precedence over worldly desires but adding that God had given us bodies and desires and never intended to deprive us of creaturely love. She insisted that had he not lost his Mrs. Chapone (Varanese), his love would have been less 'spiritualised'. She said she hoped that then his love would have been fixed on heaven but suspected that some would have remained with his earthly love. Having lost all hope of happiness in the world: 'the mind, which is an active principle, losing its aim here, has fixed on its Maker; for happiness will ever be the end that all rational beings will aim at, and disappointed in one thing will soon fix on another' (BEL, 25, p. 431). She appears to have been suggesting that Wesley's disappointment in love was influential in his subsequent strenuous striving for holiness and possibly in his decision to become ordained. It is not clear whether this was the case, but the possibility is raised by the fact that he was ordained later in the same year in which his hopes relating to Varanese had been dashed. Whether his disappointment was a factor in his decision or not, Emily was pointing out that John was failing to consider that his actions could be affected by human love or loss: that love for God can easily be confused or conflated with feelings stirred up by human relationships.

These 'Cotswold' relationships were probably not unlike those in many other little coteries which appeared in middle-class society in the eighteenth century, where women held court and were flattered by young men and where they experimented with intellectual ideas. However, the effect on Wesley was significant. When he was part of this group, he was searching for a deeper faith; his grandfather Annesley had preached on the 'devotion of the heart', and he would have heard that theme repeated in his mother's teaching. In the Holy Club, he was beginning his determined struggle towards inward and outward purity, so that he might feel accepted by God. But any associated *feeling* of acceptance was absent, and although at this stage he did not use the words he came to use later, *coldness* and *deadness*, the lack of feeling he reported to his mother in his letters expressed the same sense of something lacking.

With the Cotswold women, it was different. In this situation, he did indeed feel *something*. The women were idealised: that is, he projected his own goodness into them and into his absolutely good God, whom he saw as 'Author of friendship's sacred tie' (BEL, 25, p. 256). The talk was of human and divine love so that he felt merged in a loving union with the women and God. That he could feel *something* made him feel more alive and even exhilarated. Through this merging, he could partake of its goodness and feel accepted; he was on the side of the angels and not the 'bulk of mankind'. This almost intoxicated state felt *so* good that the fact that he was breaking marital boundaries and putting himself in compromising positions was barely noticeable; it felt entirely full of goodness and God, rather than transgressive. The more full of goodness the women seemed (as when they reported their good works), the more full of goodness and the more alive he felt, hence his excitement. The erotic nature of the discourse suggests that what he felt was sexual. This state of affairs could only continue while he could convince himself that the sexual feeling was something other than it was. While it is difficult to imagine that he did not at some level recognise his excitement as having a sexual element, he had constantly to persuade himself that the relationships were based on the pure love of friendship. In a letter to Mary Pendarves (5 April 1731), he was addressing himself, as he examined his own feelings on reading her letters, 'When thy heart burns within thee at her words, is it not the warmth of life, of virtue? Do they not inspire some degree of the purity and softness of the heart from which they came?' (BEL, 25, p. 274).

As the relationships cooled he felt angry, let down and more separate. This is shown in his reply to Mary Pendarves, when she wrote to him in July 1734, after failing to respond to many of his previous letters. Wesley's letter is a bitter one, though couched in terms of his sorrow that he was unable to help her (BEL, 25, p. 390). While being solicitous, he let her know that he found her wanting, possibly beyond help, and not full of love as he had hoped; he made no effort to continue the correspondence. The anger and disillusionment resulted in his feeling more separate from her, no longer merged with her; she was now denigrated rather than idealised. Once this had happened the relationship could be viewed more objectively. The sexual feelings would no longer have been disguised as loving friendship and would be seen for what they were; in terms of his later response to the Moravians on the subject of sex, they would be full of 'horror'. When left to his own devices again, the deadness and coldness returned. When he left for Georgia in 1735, one of his motives was to escape from women. By then, he was denigrating them and seeing them as a dangerous threat. Many features of his interactions with the Cotswold women were to reappear in his subsequent relationships.

Sophy Hopkey

From 1725 onwards, Wesley had written in his diary about 'unclean thoughts' and his means of avoiding them (by shunning 'idleness, freedom with women and high-seasoned meats'; Heitzenrater, 2003, p. 53). On leaving Oxford for Georgia in October 1735, he wrote to John Burton that his main motive for going was to save his own soul, towards which end he hoped to remove himself from temptation. Wesley hoped he was going to an uncorrupted and primitive land, where he would remain celibate and devote himself entirely to preaching to the 'simple' heathen. He imagined them as noble savages who would be unable to 'construe away the text'; they would have 'no vain philosophy to corrupt it'; there would be 'no sensuous, covetous, ambitious expounders to soften its unpleasing truths'. They would be willing to learn and, in their simple way, would be able to judge whether what he preached was of God. By this means, he would learn the purity of faith and be converted himself so that God would then employ him to preach 'that the very ends of the earth may see the salvation of our God' (BEL, 25, pp. 439–42).

What awaited him was quite different. He found himself ministering not to the Indians but to the colonial community in Savannah. This was during the Trusteeship period, prior to Georgia's becoming a Crown colony in 1752: the community consisted of settlers from England or the Carolinas (Rack, 2002, p. 107). In addition, although his intent was to eschew women, he soon found himself on intimate terms with a seventeen-year-old woman, Sophy Hopkey, the daughter of a Savannah shopkeeper. Her story has often been told and is too long and complicated to repeat in detail here, but there are two aspects which appear to have been ignored or played down in previous accounts, including Wesley's own, which are important to highlight. The first is the gross disparity between Wesley's actions and his words, when seen from Sophy Hopkey's perspective; the second is the likely effect of this disparity. The focus previously has understandably been on Wesley: particularly on what he said and on how this affected his view of himself in relation to God. For Sophy, the contradiction between the intentions and feelings conveyed verbally and those conveyed through non-verbal behaviour must have been very confusing, and caused her to question her own judgement.

There was a vast difference in their positions. Wesley was older and superior to Sophy Hopkey in intellect and status. His role was that of her pastor and teacher. From his own account, while beginning with an intention to have 'no intimacy with any woman in America', on 13 March 1736, a few weeks after his arrival, he found himself talking to Sophy Hopkey about 'inward holiness', as part of a plan to speak to every communicant weekly. He claimed to have disliked her reserved manner at first, but said he was persuaded by others to help her with her problems over a previous relationship with a 'notorious villain'. He was deeply affected by her tearful distress and began to see her every two to three days. He wrote that he was careful to 'speak only on things pertaining to God', but one day at the end of July, after talking for some time 'I took her hand and, before we parted, kissed her'. He wrote, 'And from this time I fear there was a mixture in my intention, though I was not so sensible of it' (BEJ, 18, pp. 365–7).

Two weeks later, his account indicates that others were urging him to spend time with Sophy because of her distress about her former suitor and because, in her words, nobody but he could comfort her. He agreed and told her he believed that God had committed her to his charge. He told her that he would now treat her as he did his sisters in all his interactions with her, and devote himself to encouraging her to commit herself to God. He said he was pleased with her sensible, pious and gracious response. Having previously kissed her, he was trying to turn the relationship back into one between siblings, giving her a list of religious books and explaining their contents. However, at the same time he was letting her know how important she was to him. He had had a fever, and she suggested that if the fever returned on the following day, he should ask for her. He accepted her offer and sent for her. She came and sat with him and 'read several prayers and prepared whatever I wanted with a diligence, care and tenderness not to be expressed'. She had said that 'if Mr. Wesley dies, I shall lose the only friend I ever had in the world' (BEJ, 18, pp. 408–9).

It is not surprising that from this time, as the evidence in Wesley's account shows, she wanted a different relationship from that of teacher and pupil. If he was absent, she became 'scarce a shadow' of her former self (BEJ, 18, p. 430), and she provoked him to declare himself in various ways. For instance, on one occasion, she told him she could no longer struggle to fulfil his religious expectations of her. He wrote that all her religious resolutions had disappeared, and she planned to return to England, which would have been disastrous for her. He read to her from Law's *Serious Call* and Milton's *Paradise Lost* (leaving out the 'love parts' because they might 'hurt her mind') and begged her to pray, but all without success. It was only when he 'pressed her on the head of friendship' that she responded. She burst into tears and said, 'Now my resolutions begin to stagger' (BEJ, 18, pp. 431–3). By threatening to leave, she had managed to elicit some evidence of his feelings for her.

This pattern repeated itself throughout the year of their relationship. It was particularly evident in Wesley's account of the week-long boat journey they made together from Frederica to Savannah in October 1736. Wesley rationalised his decision to travel with her by noting that James Oglethorpe, the governor of Georgia, had suggested it. He also felt protected by his own plans to be celibate and by Sophy Hopkey's intention to live singly (she had once announced that if she could not marry her previous suitor, she would not marry at all; BEJ, 18, p. 435). A boat crew was with them, but they spent four nights in the open air, sleeping on the ground beside a fire where, as Wesley put it, 'none but the All-seeing Eye observed us'; 'To him alone be praise that we both withheld from anything that the world counts as evil'. But he had doubts about these sentiments and quoted St. Cyprian, resorting to Latin: '*Certe ipse complexus, ipsa confabulatio et osculatio, quantum dedecoris et criminis confitetur!*' (Assuredly the fact of lying together, embracing and kissing, constitutes a confession of unseemly misbehaviour!). The following day, he asked, as they were crossing the Doby Sound, in a high wind on a rough sea, whether she was afraid to die. 'No I don't desire to live any longer. O that God would let me go now! Then I should be at rest. In this world I expect nothing but misery' (BEJ, 18, p. 436). This has been interpreted as her suffering from severe depression (Schmidt, I, 1953–66, p. 197) but sounds more like an angry outburst from a confused, exasperated and possibly seasick adolescent. Her mood quickly changed, and Wesley described her subsequent behaviour. He was 'amazed' by her perfect demeanour, her patient suffering of discomfort and, particularly, the mixture in her of 'seriousness and sweetness'. This last was one of his favourite attributes in a woman. The calm did not last long: when he asked her how far she considered herself engaged to her previous suitor, she answered provocatively that she had promised that if she did not marry him, she would marry nobody else. Wesley, as the 'expression of a sudden wish', said, 'Miss Sophy, I should think myself happy if I was to spend my life with you'. Bursting into tears, she suggested they should avoid talking about marriage, and he agreed (BEJ, 18, p. 438).

Having described the return to Savannah, the journal continues with a long account of Sophy's idealised qualities: there is no guile in her; she is all stillness and attention; she is content with bread and water, patient of heat or cold, and is mild, gentle, long suffering, sympathetic, tender, compassionate, and possessed of every other possible virtue. At this point he began to be fearful and unsure how long he could sustain his intention to be celibate. Nevertheless, he continued to spend long periods with her, teaching her French and discussing religious matters. Sometimes he could 'not avoid using some familiarity or other which was not needful'. 'Sometimes I put my arm around her waist, sometimes took her by the hand, and sometimes kissed her'. In order to stop this, he told her he was worried that his behaviour might lead her to doubt his sincerity and that he would now speak to her, not as a lover, but a friend, and that he would never touch her again. This resolution lasted for ten days (BEJ, 18, pp. 439–42). This cycle of spending time with her, showing physical affection, responding to provocation to express his feelings, and then resolving to have a platonic relationship, occurred repeatedly. He wrote that, at times, he 'hinted at a desire for marriage', but did not make a proposal, and then told her that if he were to marry at all, it would not be until after he had completed his ministry among the Indians (BEJ, 18, pp. 467–72).

It is not surprising that eventually, he learned that she was about to be married, to a Mr. Williamson. Even then she gave him an opportunity to intervene: 'Sir, I have given my consent – unless you have anything to object'. Wesley wondered whether he was being provoked again, whether this 'was not artifice, merely designed to quicken me'. Although he was miserable at the thought of her marrying somebody else, he found that he could not prevent it by marrying her himself. He continued to seek her out repeatedly: they cried together, and she gave numerous hints of her feelings for him and opportunities for him to declare himself. He described his state of turmoil:

> 'Tis hard to describe the complication of passion and tumult of thought which I then felt. Fear of her approaching misery and tender pity; grief at my own loss; love shooting through all the recesses of my soul, and sharpening every thought and passion. Underneath was a faint desire to do and suffer the will of God; which joined to my doubt that the proposal would not be accepted, was strong enough to prevent my saying (what I wonder to this hour I did not say), Miss Sophy will you marry me?
>
> (BEJ, 18, pp. 484–5)

On one occasion, they were interrupted just before he said more than he should. Once reprieved, he wrote that he felt he was once more 'snatched as a brand out of the fire' (BEJ, 18, p. 482). Williamson, the man she planned to marry, eventually put a stop to the meetings, telling Wesley that after he and Sophy had met previously, she was in such a state that she had cried and would eat nothing and say nothing for two hours (BEJ, 18, p. 487).

On 9 March 1737, when it became clear that Sophie was to marry Williamson, Wesley described several hours of agitation and distress. He wrote that he had never previously had such a feeling: 'God let loose my inordinate affection upon me, and the poison thereof drank up my spirit. I was as stupid as if but half awake, and yet in the sharpest pain I ever felt'. He was tired of life and of the world. He tried to pray but was unable to:

> Then indeed the snares of death were about me; the pains of hell overtook me. Yet I struggled for life, and though I had neither words nor thoughts, I lifted my eyes to the Prince that is highly exalted, and supplied the place

of them, as I could, στεναγμοις αλαλητοις [with groanings, which cannot be uttered; Rom 8:26]. And about four o'clock he so far took the cup from me that I drank so deeply of it no more.

(BEJ, 18, p. 486)

On 10 April, Wesley heard that Sophy had been associating with Williamson for some months before she announced her intention to marry (BEJ, 18, pp. 497–8). He was angry: he felt that he had been deceived and that she had acted without consulting him. For these failings, for failing to attend communion over a period and, finally, for failing to inform him when she did plan to attend, he turned her away from Holy Communion on 7 August (BEJ, 18, pp. 534–5). Prior to this, however, he had remonstrated with her about her behaviour; she had been angry and protested her innocence. He also wrote her what he described as a 'mild and friendly' letter but which was, in fact, harsh: 'O how fallen! How changed! Surely there was a time when in Miss Sophy's lips there was no guile' (BEJ, 18, pp. 522–4). Four days later she had a miscarriage. This was attributed by her aunt to the 'chiding' she had received and to the 'unkind letter'. Wesley reported the miscarriage in his journal but made no further comment (BEJ, 18, p. 526).

As with the Cotswold group, Wesley here was involved in a relationship in which he felt merged with an idealised good object, where the content of the conversation was the love and goodness of God; he encouraged Sophy Hopkey to grow and become more perfect through his teaching. She was receptive to his teaching, struggled to fulfil his expectations and let him know that he was indispensable to her. She claimed that he had been her friend at a time when she could have expected only pity (BEJ, 18, p. 477). As before, such was the sense of partaking, through his merged state, of intermingled human and divine love, that he felt full of goodness and, at the same time, enlivened by his sexual feelings. As a result of this intoxicating mix, he again disregarded the proprieties and put himself in compromising situations. In this merged state, he could identify with Sophy Hopkey in distress because she was part of him, and he expressed sorrow for her grief, but she could not be seen as a person in her own right. He was sexually attracted to her, but this attraction was felt as intensely dangerous. When reprieved from it he felt like a brand plucked from the fire. He saw his conflict about his sexuality in terms of his decision to be celibate, but the events described raise the question as to whether celibacy was used as a protection from a fear that a consummated sexual relationship would result in the loss or destruction of himself. The idea of it appeared desirable but also lethal.

His strong reaction to Sophy Hopkey's acting against his approval, without his knowledge or control, and asserting her separateness from him resulted in the almost unbearable feelings he described. There was a feeling of being abandoned and torn apart from his merged state with Sophy, and temporarily from God. God 'let[ting] loose his inordinate affection' on him, so that the poison drank up his spirit, suggests that he felt overwhelmed and poisoned by the anger and hate at being abandoned. As long as he experienced the relationship as being merged with an idealised Sophie, he felt no anger, envy or hatred, but having been forcibly separated, he was left overwhelmed by all these feelings: 'the pains of hell'. Eventually having looked up 'with groanings that cannot be uttered' he managed to feel that God was restored to him. Once separate from Sophy Hopkey, his anger showed itself in his denigration of her and the absence of any concern. It also resulted in the refusal to allow her to take communion, which led to problems with her family and threats of prosecution and to Wesley's subsequent flight from Georgia.

Grace Murray

There were similarities between Wesley's relationship with Sophy Hopkey and that with Grace Murray in 1748–9. He intended to marry Grace Murray but delayed and prevaricated. After a long and complicated series of events, she too married another man. However, there were also significant differences. Although it involved a similar idealisation and involvement in a triangular situation, Wesley was older (45), and his views on marriage had changed. He clearly indicated his intention to marry Grace Murray by going so far as to take part in a ceremony of formal espousal, an espousal 'de Praesenti' (Heitzenrater, 2003, pp. 167–8).

In a letter to Charles (25 September 1749) John included the account, already quoted, of his objections to marriage from his youth up and his reasons for his change of heart. While he had previously taken to heart St. Paul's words in 1Corinthians 7:32–3 – that an unmarried man could more fully devote himself to God – he now quoted Hebrews 13:4: 'The bed is undefiled, and no necessary hindrance to the highest perfection'. He described how this and Bishop Beveridge's *Codex Consiliorum* resulted in a change of mind. The letter continued with his reasons for wanting to marry Grace Murray. He knew her well: she was a widow, in her thirties, and very involved in pastoral care within the Methodist movement. She was a housekeeper in the Orphan House in Newcastle upon Tyne. He saw his marriage to her as a defence '(under God) against unholy desires and inordinate affections – which I never did entirely conquer for six months together before my intercourse with her'. He wrote (in Greek) that he now felt it was 'much better to marry than to burn'. He also thought he would be protected against the 'inordinate affection of women'; they would have less 'hope of success', and his conversations with them would be 'more sparing'. This account was entirely about his own needs and about Grace's qualities as they were useful to him. It is strikingly grandiose. Having written about the amazing 'fruits of her labours', he wrote,

> I particularly insist on this. If ever I have a wife, she ought to be the most useful woman in the kingdom – not barely one who probably *may* be so (I could not be content to run such a hazard) but one that is undeniably so. Now, show me the woman in England, Wales or Ireland, who has already done as much good as GM. I will say more. Show me one in all the English annals whom God hath employed in so high a degree! I might say, in all the history of the

Church, from the death of our Lord to this day. This is no hyperbole, but plain demonstrable fact. And if it be, who is so proper to be my wife?

(BEL, 26, pp. 380–7)

She had become an extension of him, and like Sophy Hopkey, not a person in her own right. In the same letter, he dismissed all objections that might be raised to the match: that she was low born; that she had been his servant; that she had already travelled with him, giving rise to gossip; and that she was already engaged to another (John Bennet). Eventually, encouraged by Charles Wesley, who thought that a marriage between Grace Murray and his brother would destroy the Methodist movement, she married Bennet. Wesley's hesitations and delays ensured that, like Sophy, she married somebody else. Here other factors were influential, such as Charles's determined opposition and Grace Murray's own ambivalence, but had John been determined, he could have overridden both of these, as he did in his subsequent marriage to Mary Vazeille.

The relationship with Grace Murray showed evidence of a greater capacity than before to understand the kind of woman who would be helpful to him personally, and in his work. However, his idealisation of her and his grandiose claims for her goodness demonstrate the same dynamic. In spite of his protestations of devoted love and his belief that she would be a perfect wife, his ambivalence asserted itself. He was not as convinced as he thought he was that the 'bed was undefiled' or that marriage protected him from the pit of fire he associated with fornication.

Mary Vazeille

In February 1751, John told his brother Charles that he was resolved to marry. Soon after this, he precipitately married Mary Vazeille, whom he hardly knew. His marriage may have been an attempt to quash rumour-mongering about him, which was rife. Usually, he did not respond to such rumours, but on this occasion, the last straw seems to have been the repetition of a story by the Bishop of Exeter, which was subsequently printed (Heitzenrater, 2003, p. 36).

Unlike Grace Murray, his wife was not steeped in Methodism, nor did she share his priorities. She was the widow of a wealthy London merchant, with two sons and two daughters. To prevent speculation about his being a fortune hunter, Wesley settled her £10,000 property on her and the children (Rack, 2002, p. 265). He had informed Charles at the very last minute so that this time it was impossible for him to interfere. Charles was 'thunderstruck' and on 17 February 1751 wrote in his journal, 'Groaned all day, and several following ones, under my own and the people's burden. I could eat no pleasant food, nor preach, nor rest, either by night or by day' (MJCW, p. 602). He had met Mary Vazeille previously and referred to her as 'a woman of sorrowful spirit' (MJCW, p. 578).

The early letters between Wesley and his wife were affectionate, but from the beginning he was very insistent in urging her to become involved in good works. They married in February 1751, and on 11 March he wrote with a list of demands, which among other things urged her to sell her jewels, help the poor, and visit prisoners (BEL, 26, p. 541). He continued to travel and was absent a great deal. She tried accompanying him initially, but found it too arduous. As the marriage progressed, she became increasingly suspicious of his activities, accusing him of involvement with other women, and even of adultery. She opened his letters (he had previously given permission for her to do this), using the contents to embarrass him and to demonstrate the truth of her accusations. Rack (2002, pp. 266–7) writes of her 'pathological jealousy, suspicion and uncontrollable rage' and quotes Hampson's biography, which tells of finding Mrs. Wesley 'foaming with rage, with her husband on the floor, and some hair in her hand, torn out by the roots' (Hampson, 1791, II, p. 127). The problems became increasingly serious, until eventually she left him. There were reconciliations and further separations, until a final separation was confirmed in his last letter to her in October 1778. When she died and was buried in 1781, he was not aware of it till several days later.

A diagnosis of 'pathological jealousy', hinted at by Rack, depends on a variety of factors and implies a *delusional* belief that a partner is being unfaithful. It often involves some of the behaviour reported of Mrs. Wesley, such as the opening of letters, the searching for evidence and the outbursts of rage, sometimes even murderous rage. However, before applying this label it is important to have some knowledge of the behaviour of the partner and to add that the fact that a person is pathologically jealous does not exclude infidelity on the partner's part. It is therefore important to examine Wesley's relationships with other women in the Methodist movement.

Correspondence with women

Wesley was in contact with many Methodist women. With some he maintained a correspondence over a long period of time. Schmidt (II, 1953–66, p. 142) dated these letters from 1757, but there is evidence that they began before he married. A letter to James Hutton (14 May 1739) mentions a Miss S. Burdock (Sally), and Baker notes that at least eighteen letters were exchanged between Wesley and Burdock between June and October of that year (BEL, 25, p. 649, n.6). As Baker points out, most of the women were single, separated or widowed, and the letters usually stopped when they married, 'whether through motives of prudence or courtesy' (BEL, 25, 86). The longest correspondence lasted thirty-two years, but usually they lasted from fifteen years to twenty years (Schmidt, II, 1953–66, p. 142).

Much of the content of the letters concerned the work the women did in the society and their spiritual progress. Wesley was tireless in his interest: he had a vast capacity for remembering details of their situations, and his efforts to encourage them and exhort them to greater works of goodness never flagged. 'Perfection' was a constant theme, as he urged them towards inner and outer holiness. He clearly saw the letters as an important part of his pastoral care. To examine the form of the letters, the style, the language, and the patterns they follow is not to ignore or diminish this conscious attempt to teach and offer care, nor is it to fail to acknowledge its usefulness.

Most of the women were in their late teens or twenties, though several of his long-term correspondents were growing older, as he was. He was not immune to feminine beauty or 'comeliness' but was particularly attracted by what he called 'sweet seriousness', where 'seriousness' at that time meant a concern with religious matters. To Ann Bolton (12 August 1770), his letter ended, 'The spirit of your last letter engages me much. I dearly love seriousness and sweetness mixed together' (Telford, V, p. 197). He liked simple 'puritan' dress. And to Mary Bishop, who ran one of the Methodist schools (21 May 1781), he expressed anxiety that, in some of the children, some of the 'simplicity' had been lost, that '[m]ore of the world seems to be crept in'. He wanted 'good breeding' to be preserved without affectation (Telford, VII, pp. 62–3). He exhorted her to 'Make such Christians as Miranda.[3] . . . Let it be said of the young women you educate, Grace was in all her steps, heaven in her eye, / In all her gestures sanctity and love' (Telford, VII, p. 63). It was this combination of grace, gentility, seriousness, simplicity, purity and lack of affectation that he found irresistible.

As in the other relationships, there was a strong element of idealisation, particularly at the beginning of a correspondence. Even at the age of eighty-four, he wrote to Hetty Rogers (12 October 1787) of a young woman he had recently met in the Channel Islands:

> Jane Bisson I saw every day. She is nineteen years old, about the size of Miss Ritchie, and has a peculiar mixture of seriousness, sprightliness, and sweetness, both in her looks and behaviour. Wherever we were, she was the servant of all. I think she exceeds Madame Guyon in deep communion with God.
>
> (Telford, VIII, p. 18)

Wesley's image of his correspondents was often that they were vulnerable, in need of protection, and dependent on God's care and forgiveness, but also on him; his language established and maintained the relationship in these terms. For instance, he wrote to a 'Miss March' (11 November 1760), 'I believe I understand your state better than you do yourself. Do not perplex yourself at all about what you call it. . . . Certainly you do need more faith; for you are a sickly, tender plant' (BEL, 27, p. 211). And to Ann Bolton (21 December 1770), he wrote, 'But you need to be nursed like a little child. Therefore, write soon and freely to. . .' (Telford, V, p. 216).

The promotion of this image of weakness and vulnerability, together with his encouragement of 'openness' and the assurance he gave of confidentiality, all tended to foster dependency on him. His second letter to Mary Stokes (4 April 1771) says,

> Only know to whom you speak and then you cannot be too free. Open the window in your breast. I pray never be afraid of writing too large letters:

you must not measure yours by mine; for I have a little more business than you. . . . Your weakness and tenderness of constitution, without great care, may prove a snare to you.

(Telford, V, pp. 235–6)

The dependence on himself was conflated with dependence on Christ; he urged 'needy' correspondents to depend on Christ for their help and succour. He wrote to Elizabeth Briggs (31 May 1771),

[A]s yet you are but a little child, just a babe in the pure love of Christ. As a little child, hang upon Him, and simply expect a supply of all your wants. In this respect reasoning profits you nothing; it is just the opposite to believing, whereby you hearken to the inward voice, which says, 'Open thy mouth wide and I will fill it'.

(Telford, V, pp. 254–5)

The imagery often had an erotic quality, as it did in this letter. Other examples include the letter to Ann Bolton (25 October 1772), 'I long to have you more and more deeply penetrated by humble, gentle, patient love' (Telford, V, p. 342), and his relationship with Sally Burdock, when he first met her: 'I was desired by a young woman to go into her chariot, whom I found quite awakened, and longing for Christ, after having been for some time the finest, gayest thing in Bristol'. She later wrote, 'I believe I love you as well as I do papa', and her family later forbade her to consort with Methodists (BEL, 25, p. 649, n.4). It was also evident in his letters to Ann Loxdale, whom he met in March 1781. In his first letter, he said that she reminded him of 'Miss Ritchie' and that they both 'breathe(d) the same spirit', and then, 'Your heart is toward mine as mine is toward thee: there need be no reserve between us. I hope you will always "think aloud" whenever you speak or write to me' (Telford, VII, p. 53). In a third letter (14 July, 1781) he wrote:

You remind me of what occurred when my dear Hetty Roe first mentioned you to me. I almost wondered I should feel so much regard for one I had never seen! But I can taste your spirit, and rejoice to find that you are so near.

(Telford, VII, pp. 73–4)

His comparisons between the women occurred frequently in his letters, suggesting that there was a commonality in the role they fulfilled, similar to the interchangeability of the Cotswold women. In the early stages of the correspondence, there was usually a sense of excitement: Wesley wrote frequently, urging them to tell him their worries and stressing the confidential nature of the exchange. He emphasised their 'sameness', nearness and unity and their special significance to him; he showed evidence of agitation if they showed signs of 'cooling' towards him, or towards God. Both at the beginning and if their letters became less frequent, he would include a long list of questions, often about their health, mood, sleep, thoughts and dreams, urging introspection and encouraging confidences:

'You see how inquisitive I am, because everything relating to *you* nearly concerns *me*. . . . You are *now* my joy and comfort' (Telford, VI, pp. 231–2).

A letter to Miss March (6 July 1770) showed how he lost his sense of separateness:

> When I speak or write to you, I have you before my eyes, but, generally speaking, I do not think of myself at all. I do not think whether I am wise or foolish, knowing or ignorant; but I see you aiming at glory and immortality.
>
> (Telford, V, p. 193)

However, by April 1780, in a letter to Sarah Crosby, there is a sense that he thought he might be on dangerous territory:

> I speak of myself very little to any one, were it only for fear of hurting *them*. I have found exceeding few that could bear it; so that I am constrained to repress my natural openness. I scarce find any temptation from any *thing* in the world; my danger is from *persons*. Oh for a heart to praise my God, / A heart from sin set free!
>
> (Telford, VII, p. 19)

Psychological defences

How then did Wesley deal with his distressing feelings and the conflicts in his relationships? He was preoccupied with self-examination and with striving for perfection, but he had a capacity to blot out instances when he had been hurtful to others. This is seen in his journal account of his feelings as he prepared for possible court proceedings against him in Georgia; he justified his actions and denied that his own behaviour had been destructive. His deep fears about his own aggression are heard in the mouths of his accusers. He wrote, '[An] account given of me to all company was that I "was a sly hypocrite, a seducer, a betrayer of my trust, an egregious lyer and dissembler, an endeavourer to alienate the affections of married women from their husbands"'. It included a long list of terrifying accusations, and he thought he was seen as so monstrous that the people would rather die than let him carry on (BEJ, 18, pp. 540–1). He had just emerged from a triangular situation with Sophy, and her husband. Sophy had been an exciting but terrifying sexual object for him; part of herself, her child, had died, and he had been accused of having a role in that death. The accusations must have resonated with the feelings of love, hate and murderousness of his own Oedipal struggles. These deep feelings and impulses could not be faced, they were labelled 'corruption and abomination', his damaging of others could not be contemplated, and the accusations were dismissed as unthinkable or absurd.

However, he was not untouched by such fears of his own destructiveness. His journal account of his feelings six days after embarking on his voyage home described a state of distress, with depressed mood, agitation and anxiety. He could not account for his uneasiness over a few days, as the sea was calm. He prayed fervently for help, and gained a temporary peace. But he rationalised that any uneasiness in the absence of bodily pain must be owing to the sufferer's inner conviction that he was not a true believer. Five days later, he felt weighed down and full of sorrow, though unable to give a reason for it, and he felt unable to instruct the people on the boat as he usually did. In the evening, he did manage to teach one of the cabin boys and felt less distressed. A week later, he was chastising himself for lack of faith; for forgetfulness of God, except at times when he feared death; and for pride in previously believing that he could gain holiness through his own efforts. Having gone to Georgia to save his soul and convert the heathen, he now felt farther than ever from being a Christian, instead feeling 'much nearer that mystery of Satan'. He then described being saved from being completely lost by reading St. Cyprian's words, 'O my soul, come not thou into their secret! Stand thou in the good old paths'. This inspired him to preach again, and having resolved to preach, he felt restored. Subsequently, his anxiety and depression disappeared (BEJ, 18, pp. 207–10).

In this way, he was rescued from a state of spiritual depression, which he called being 'in orco' (in the infernal regions; BEJ, 18, p. 210, n.4). He argued against those (the mystics), who would advocate his continuing to struggle in the 'infernal regions' as a way of achieving spiritual growth, and against those who would suggest that his recovery was not a blessing but a curse. He described them as blasphemers. And yet four days later, as they approached Land's End, he was praying for his deliverance from his fear of death, and again he was lamenting his unconverted state: 'I went to America to convert the Indians, but Oh! who shall convert me?' On 29 January, when Lizard Point was in view, he wrote 'that I am "fallen short of the glory of God"; that my whole heart is "altogether corrupt and abominable", ... "a child of wrath", an heir of hell'. His only hope was to throw himself on the mercy of Christ for his redemption (BEJ, 18, pp. 210–15). He labelled his inner badness 'corruption and abomination' and hoped for forgiveness, but could not accept that this could happen; he could only blot out his agitation by activity and preaching. Although his dark side could be labelled in this way, the actual hurt he had caused others by his behaviour could not be faced. Alongside his uneasiness, depression, and prayers for redemption, went his self-justification that Sophy Hopkey was deceitful and ungrateful. To address her miscarriage and his own behaviour in Georgia would have been to confront the fears relating to his sexuality and his destructive or even murderous anger and hatred.

In order for it to be manageable, his 'corruption and abomination' had to be converted into a more 'acceptable' sin. He managed this by attributing his fear and agitation to his being 'so far an unbeliever', rather than to the actual nature of the 'corruption and abomination'. However, being 'so far an unbeliever' was not merely a more acceptable explanation: it also described a truth about himself that was at the root of his inability to face up to his deeper 'unacceptable' feelings; he was indeed unable to believe that his 'badness' could be forgiven. At such times of crisis, during which he had an uncomfortable awareness of an internal turmoil and a fear of being overwhelmed by unmanageable feelings and urges, he felt agitated and uneasy or weighed down and depressed. In Kristevan terms, the abject was not 'elaborated' but was labelled 'corruption and abomination'; for Wesley it could not be fully thought about or put into words, and he was left with an 'inexorable carnal remainder' (Kristeva, 1980, p. 120).

He dealt with his unbelief by reverting to the 'good old paths'. These for him, as for Susanna Wesley, were working, teaching, strict religious observance and self-examination, all aimed at increasing faith and holiness. Like most people, he was less uncomfortable with atomistic sins, voluntary transgressions, which there was a possibility of conquering through his own efforts, than with the idea of inner destructiveness. The former also offered some distraction from the latter. Aspects of the 'good old paths' were essential for Wesley in shoring up his image of himself as acceptable. These were actions that would have confirmed his sense of his own goodness: offering advice, finding cures for physical illness, raising money for the poor and preaching the hope of salvation. He was not only active but powerfully active. It was necessary for him to feel indispensable, to know the minutiae of events and to keep control of individuals, of groups and of the movement itself. As a result, he was criticised by some for his ambition and accused of being dependent on power (Rack, 2002, pp. 536–7).

He used the Bible as a weapon and to preserve his self-esteem. As early as the Oxford period, when he was criticised for eccentricity, intolerance and excessive strictness, he preached his sermon on 'The Circumcision of the Heart'. He portrayed one who was 'circumcised of the heart' as appearing foolish before the world but 'satisfied to await his praise on the coming of Christ', thus proving to his own satisfaction that his way was the right one (Källstad, 1974, p. 97). Källstad also describes Wesley's way of reducing 'cognitive dissonance' by identifying himself with a biblical model, or finding biblical texts, which confirmed his belief in providence (Källstad, 1974, pp. 104–6, 188–90). This also gave him a sense of meaning and of being in the right. An example was his choosing biblical readings about Naboth and Michaiah, two figures who were unjustly persecuted, at the time when he was feeling criticised over his relationship with Sophy Hopkey (BEJ, 18, p. 544).

Wesley believed that a desire to serve others drove all his actions. For instance, in December 1734, it had been suggested that he return to Epworth as a curate to continue his sick father's work. In a long letter, assuring himself and his father that the sole aim in his decision making was to glorify God, he justified his intention to stay in Oxford, where he believed he could best become as 'holy' as possible, so that he could 'most promote holiness in others'; he was sure there was 'no place under heaven so fit for [his] improvement as Oxford' (BEL, 25, pp. 397–409). This provoked an exasperated response from his brother Samuel: '[W]hy do I write? For a plain reason. It is my duty, if I can, to please and profit my father and mother and secondly to inform and profit you'. He felt that all John's reasonings were false 'except that of your being assured'; he argued each point and made a series of accusations, including John's neglect of his priestly calling. He wrote: 'I see your love to yourself but your love to your neighbour I do not see' (BEL, 25, pp. 411).

Once decided upon an action, there was little that would deter him, even (or perhaps especially) in the face of quite frightening evidence of risk. This was obvious in his dealings with the Morgan brothers, William and Richard, two students from Ireland, whom he supervised at Oxford. The older brother, William, was a devout member of the Holy Club and strict in his observance of its ascetic practices. He became psychotic and had to return to Ireland; religion and the Wesley brothers figured prominently in his psychotic symptoms. Eventually he killed himself. It is not clear whether the religious practices were instrumental in his deterioration, but Wesley was blamed by many for his death, and the Rector of Lincoln College was concerned about his effect on students. Wesley entered into correspondence with William's father, Richard Morgan Snr., who, in spite of his anxieties, having read Wesley's reassurances, decided to entrust his younger son, Richard, to his care. Wesley was unwilling to consider that he had had any role in William's illness. In spite of requests from the father that he should be more lenient with Richard, and Richard's protestations to his father about his oppressive treatment, Wesley used the same intrusive methods in his attempts to 'save the soul' of the younger son (BEL, 25, pp. 357–62, 364–71).

Wesley's pervading sense of inner deadness, or coldness, his fear of falling into nothingness and a sense of something missing have already been referred to. Any unacceptable feelings, such as destructive anger or hatred, had to be kept out of his consciousness; but this could not be achieved without an associated blocking out of loving and joyful feelings. Because this deadness was such an unpleasant feeling, he was driven to get rid of it in various ways. One way to gain a feeling of being alive was by preaching and offering salvation to others. This allowed him to witness the experience of others, and he saw it as evidence that they (and he) could be forgiven and acceptable to God. Another was through his interactions with women with whom there was no possibility of a sexual relationship; these also made him feel alive. The erotic excitement temporarily blotted out the deadness. However, where there was a risk of marriage, with the prospect of sexual intercourse, his ambivalence manifested itself. There was a powerful wish for sexual contact but an equally powerful fear of it. His reactions ('a brand plucked from the burning') suggest that this fear had associations with being burned, no doubt aggravated by threats of the fires of hell, which were part of his religious beliefs, and his experience in the rectory fire, which meant death and the loss of himself. There may also have been very early experiences associated with this fear, as we will see.

His failed marriage to Mary Vazeille has been attributed by some to his wife's 'delusional jealousy' and her disturbed and violent behaviour. There is an alternative explanation for her jealous, 'mad' behaviour. It is possible that she sensed accurately the erotic content of Wesley's letters to women; and that his explanations, which indeed were true *for him*, conflicted with her more accurate interpretations. Just as Sophy Hopkey had been confused by the contradictions between his words and his behaviour, this discrepancy would also have led to his wife's confusion. Wesley saw only her unacceptable behaviour and his own long-suffering patience. In 1774, he offered her forgiveness and reconciliation:

> I love you still, and am as clean of other women as the day I was born. At length know *me*, know *yourself*. Your enemy I cannot be; let me be your friend. Suspect me no more; asperse me no more; provoke me no more. Do not any more contend for mastery, for power, money, or praise. Be content to be a private, insignificant person, known and loved by God and me.
> (Telford, VI, p. 102)

Over this same period, he continued to write to his many women correspondents and clearly saw his wife's unease as unreasonable. Mary was a widow with children and had therefore experienced sex within marriage. Wesley's anxiety about sex raises the question as to whether the marriage was ever consummated; if not, this would clearly have added to her suspicions. These contradictions could well have caused her to doubt her own instincts, to feel confused or mad and to be consumed by impotent fury. If she began to behave in a 'crazy' fashion, this was different from the psychotic illness known as 'morbid jealousy'. Whatever her psychopathology, Wesley succeeded (to his own satisfaction) in locating all the disturbance in their relationship in her.

How does the psychoanalytic theory help to understand Wesley's struggles?

In addition to the effects of 'evangelical nurture' on all the Wesley children and on Susanna herself, and of being in a large family, each child would have been affected differently by their order of birth. This, as well as the constitutional characteristics of each child, would have evoked a particular response from the parents.

By the time John was born, eight children had died. At a time of high infant, child and maternal mortality, there would have been a widespread fear of losing a child and fear for the safety of the mother during childbirth. With Susanna having lost so many children, the fear of death could never have been far away, both during her confinements and during the infancy of each child, but there are some factors which could have affected John Wesley particularly.

John was born thirteen years after his brother Samuel and was the first male child to survive after him. There was a particularly bleak five-year period before John was born in 1703, in which the Wesleys lost a baby (sex unknown) and two sets of twins. The first set of twins were male (John and Benjamin) and the second, a boy and a girl (John Benjamin and Anne). It was following the reconciliation after the parents' temporary separation, and ten months after the death of these twins, that John Wesley was conceived. As sometimes still happens, it was common practice in the seventeenth and eighteenth centuries to name a child after a previous one who had died; it is likely that this reflected an attempt to ameliorate the loss by replacing the dead child.

In the literature, the term *replacement child* has usually been used to describe a child who was conceived within six months of the death of a previous one. However, the crucial element is not the actual time which elapses, but whether the mother has succeeded in grieving adequately for the lost baby before becoming pregnant again. It is difficult for mourning to continue during a further pregnancy (Rowe et al., 1978, pp. 166–70). Before having John, Susanna had repeatedly conceived very quickly after losing a child; the effect of losing five babies in the years before his birth is hard to imagine. It seems unlikely that she could have grieved successfully for each child separately. The sex of the babies she had lost would have been important in her hopes for John and her expectations of him. Although she had lost two daughters, three had survived, but she had lost five, or perhaps six, sons. The closeness of these losses and the naming of consecutive boys 'John' suggest that there was some hope that each could replace the others and that John would have had to struggle with some of the hazards associated with being a 'replacement child'.

If another pregnancy supervenes while the mother is mourning a lost child, her unresolved grief can adversely affect her relationship with the new baby (Thistlethwaite, 2006, pp. 125–6). While the 'replacement child' is perceived as particularly desired, loved and precious, the 'ghost' of the previous child or children can distort the individual and exclusive relationship between the child and its mother. This is likely to compromise the necessary close mirroring and attunement between the mother and child and the mother's capacity to see the child as a unique individual with a need to develop in his own particular way. If the mother is not closely attuned to *this* particular baby, and there is confusion caused by the dead baby's presence in her mind, there is likely to be a failure of containment. When the infant's projections are distorted by the mother's preoccupying phantasies (as they would be in unresolved grief for a dead baby), there is difficulty in containing the child's primitive fears. Instead of being made tolerable, in Britton's words, 'the uncomprehended is made incomprehensible'; there is a sense of 'nameless dread', a 'fear of being overwhelmed by uncontained, untransformed, psychic elements or of living in the aftermath of annihilation' (Britton, 1998, pp. 54–6). This resonates with Wesley's fear of falling into nothing and his need to 'wall off' a chaotic, disturbing part of himself, the contents of which remained 'unsymbolised'. This was evident in his anxiety, agitation, unease and depression on his return voyage from Georgia. If this were the situation for Susanna and John as a baby, then later in his childhood, her belief that he was destined by divine providence for a 'special' role, reinforced by his rescue from the fire, could only have added to her difficulty in relating to him as a unique person.

In Chapter 4 a further possible result of a failure of containment was discussed. It can be experienced as an attack on the child's link with the mother as a good object. In order, to preserve the mother as a good object in the child's mind, the child has to deny the failure of containment and attribute it to a third force, equated with the father. In such a situation, in the child's phantasy, any linking together of the parents would feel catastrophic, as it would 'reconstitute the mother as a non-receptive, malignantly misunderstanding maternal object' (Britton, 1998, pp. 53–4). It is possible that Wesley's difficulty in seeing his parents as a sexual couple was related to such fears.

When the lost child is idealised by the parents, as commonly occurs, there is pressure on the 'replacement child' to live up to unrealistic expectations and the child has difficulty establishing his or her own identity (Poznauski, 1972, pp. 1190–3). John was said by his father to be precociously reasonable and thoughtful, suggesting that he learned to use his intellect and control his feelings very early. There were high expectations of all the children, and they all learned to tolerate frustration at an early stage; but it is possible that the expectations, demands and frustrations were too harsh for John. Instead of a gradual separation from the mother involving a slow disillusionment at a rate that he could manage, he appears to have been precociously independent. Both failure of containment and a too rapid disillusionment would have made it difficult for him to establish a 'good-enough' maternal internal object.

Wesley's repeated relationships with women whom he saw as perfect and with whom he could feel merged suggest that they were attempts to re-create or rectify the earlier mother/child relationship. If he had had difficulty internalising the function of a 'good-enough mother', which would have enabled him to care for, or 'mother' himself, he would have been driven to find external substitutes. Such a lack of internal structure can result in a persistent sense of futility, emptiness and depression; it can be associated with an apparent confidence, arrogance or 'charisma', but there is a rigid and brittle crust which is vulnerable to narcissistic injury. This picture is not inconsistent with the one that Wesley presented.

These suggested difficulties for Wesley in the early mother/child relationship can also be seen in Kristevan terms, and this gives some insight into his ambivalence about his sexuality. At the beginning of the process of separation, there is a loss of the child's omnipotence and a sense of emptiness and fragility. The idealising identification with the 'father of individual prehistory' is a support in facilitating the child's move into the world of language. There is an intense attraction back to the merged bliss of the first relationship but an equally intense fear of being sucked back into maternal chaos and meaninglessness. The boundary between mother and child at the point of separation is the 'abject' and is associated with ideas of flesh, filth, defilement and death. According to Kristeva, the fear of the terrifying woman becomes a screen for the terror at the absence of the mother, felt as death. And yet, this terror of the woman and the 'abject', which has come to symbolise absence or death, is for Kristeva a further mask which covers what she calls 'the zero of subjectivity'. 'It is the necessity to represent nothingness as *something else* in order to maintain the cover over the *central void* that founds the abjection of mother' (Crownfield, 1992, p. 25). Wesley's sense of his mother's absence from him was acute, and more than he could easily bear, so that a smooth negotiation of his separation from her, which should have been facilitated by an adequate, loving, accepting paternal function, would not have been easy for him. In these terms, Wesley found himself at the mercy, on the one hand, of his fears of falling into nothing, covered but represented by the chaotic, devouring mother and evoked by the prospect of sex; and, on the other hand, of the Oedipal father, of words and laws. The powerful attraction of sexual union terrified him and was associated with fears of destruction. It is not clear whether he ever risked a sexual relationship, but he was certainly reassured by 'pure' women in puritan dress, who were 'serious' in religion and simultaneously inaccessible sexually. The 'good old paths' represented a retreat to the safety of an identification with, and obedience to, the Oedipal father.

He would have been helped if had he been able to hold on to and internalise what Kristeva sees as the Christian symbolism of *agape*. *Agape* as 'unconditional love', she suggests, offers a 'spiritual enactment' of the archaic love of the pre-Oedipal period. This is the overflowing of divine love in response to feelings of loss and emptiness, induced by the mother's loving the 'not-I'. This was what Wesley was desperate for and thought for a moment he had found in 1738 in Aldersgate Street, but he had to keep his 'unacceptable' feelings separated off and so was also denied access to his own loving aspects, his own joy and God's forgiveness. He was unable to relinquish his own omnipotence and his fear of God as a punishing parent.

Joyce McDougall writes movingly about conflicts and deficits in early relationships with parents, which give rise to confusion and mental pain, and which the individual attempts to deal with by 'erotic' solutions of one kind or another. She sees them as attempts, in difficult circumstances, to preserve the individual's sexual and personal identity. She relates how a mother's own feelings about body image, bodily functions and erogenous zones are unconsciously communicated to her child. A mother can either enhance or inhibit a baby's 'motility, emotional liveliness, intelligence, sensuality and bodily erogeneity' (McDougall, 1995, pp. 180–6). A failure to enhance these attributes can result in a lack of responsiveness. It is possible that Susanna Wesley, in her handling of John, passed on to her son at a very early stage, something of her attitude to the 'corrupt body', and/or she conveyed to him her fears of excessive or uncontrolled emotions. Neither his sense of himself as a potent sexual being nor his emotional liveliness would have been enhanced. His fear of sexual contact, which meant falling into chaos and death, together with his lack of liveliness and potency, would have been likely to lead to another solution, which would preserve his sexual identity and self-esteem.

McDougall writes of perverse, eroticised solutions to early conflicts. So far as is known, Wesley did not engage in perverse sexual acts of this kind; he did, however, engage repeatedly in relationships which had an erotic and compulsive quality to them. It is possible therefore that they were prompted by similar dynamics to those described by McDougall. She writes of possible effects of an absence of a reassuring parental object: 'When sexual desire arouses terror, this lack of essential introject leaves a vacuum, so to speak, for the creation of a *sexually addictive solution* to the psychic conflict and mental pain'. Such compulsive activity is usually experienced as good, because it blots out unpleasant feelings such as anxiety and guilt or sometimes unacceptable or dangerously pleasant ones (McDougall, 1995, p. 184). Wesley experienced his idealised relationships with women as 'good', while being oblivious to his breaking of boundaries. McDougall describes how the erotic solutions can be used to avoid the following: conflicts about adult sexual or love relationships, severe anxiety or depression (with feelings of inner death or a fear of disintegration), loss of identity or facing a void. Because this kind of solution can give only temporary relief, it has to be repeated so that the illusion of omnipotent control is maintained (McDougall, 1995, pp. 187–90). The erotic excitement in Wesley's relationships with young women who were inaccessible gave him a sense of aliveness. By 'flirting' with sex he could repeatedly reassure himself that he was potent and effective, but the actual characteristics of the situation kept him safe. Of course, consciously, he saw his interventions in these women's lives as motivated entirely by Christian love and pastoral care, as do most of his commentators.

McDougall writes about children who feel destroyed by their early success. They are so precocious and independent that they miss out on the caring that is appropriate for a child of their age. As a result, they are left with a sense of not existing, of feeling that they merely fulfil a role for their parents. They do not feel recognised and have to *beg* for attention. They fulfil the role expected of them but at great sexual and social cost (McDougall, 1995, pp. 205–8). This is reminiscent of the serious, precocious little John, who later had to ask his mother to hold him in her mind before God once a week.

McDougall also suggests that when the child does not have an established image of the parents as a sexual couple (as Wesley seems not to have had) then:

> the mental representation of the mother's sex (which she transmits to her child) becomes that of a limitless void. The child runs the risk of projecting into this void all the off-shoots of infantile megalomania, without encountering any obstacle. The fantasy of the mother's inner space then appears constantly enticing yet at the same time terrifying.
> (McDougall, 1989, p. 45)

If such were the case for Wesley, the terror of being lost in the meaningless chaos of the maternal matrix would have been evoked or intensified by the possibility of sexual intercourse in later life.

We have seen that in the paranoid/schizoid position, splitting and projection are described by Klein as the way in which unmanageable feelings of inner destructiveness are dealt with. In healthy development, a move to the 'depressive position' involves an integration of the loving and hating aspects of the object and the self, with the withdrawing of projections. A failure to achieve this has several consequences: a persistence of the use of projection, a failure to tolerate ambiguity in the self and others, an acting out of duty according to rules rather than out of concern for the other, a tendency to polarise good and evil, and the use of omnipotent defences. There is difficulty in relating to people, as separate individuals, rather than as fulfilling a need. The individual is moralistic, rather than moral.

Evidence has been given that Wesley showed many of the features of 'paranoid/schizoid' functioning in his relationships. His feelings were separated off from his grandiose, 'special', omnipotent self, or projected on to others. This was necessary to maintain his self-esteem. Of particular note in this context was his capacity to substitute one woman for another, both in the Cotswold group and among his women correspondents. They fulfilled the same function.

A further manifestation of a failure of individuals to reach the depressive position is their difficulty in using symbols helpfully as a source of growth. For Ricoeur, their use requires an initial acceptance of what the symbol offers, followed by thought and interpretation of the meaning. He contrasts this process with the presupposing of a meaning already there. The 'enigma' must be preserved (Ricoeur, 1978, p. 47). Kristeva has suggested that the suffering wounded Christ might be used to symbolise the traumatic separation of the child from the archaic relationship with the mother, thus helping the individual to negotiate the process. In Wesley's case, the evidence suggests that in his unconscious identification with Christ and other biblical figures they were not used as transforming objects, as offering a space within which to recognise himself, but as ways of confirming or justifying his actions. By seeing himself as Naboth when he felt persecuted, he did not have to explore *why* he might be being criticised. He identified with, or *became*, the object; the biblical figure did not act as a separate symbol to be thought about, interpreted or seen beyond.

'Falling into nothing'

John Wesley's need to keep his parents apart in his mind and his fear of 'falling into nothing', raise the possibility that, as described by McDougall, he would have perceived his mother's sex as a 'limitless void' and that his fear of being drawn into it would have been exaggerated by the threat of sexual intercourse. His responses to others, to events and to Christian beliefs suggest that his deeper, negative feelings had to be kept out of consciousness. In Kleinian terms, because he had not succeeded in dealing with his early persecutory anxieties, the boundary between conscious and unconscious had become more rigid and less porous. In Kristevan terms, the 'abject' had to be so firmly separated off that it was not accessible for symbolisation and therefore could not be brought into dialogue with the 'symbolic'. He was left with his sense of inner coldness, deadness and powerlessness; with uncertainty and fear related to his sexuality. His destructiveness felt so bad that he could not bear to face it fully but instead experienced a nameless dread, a fear of falling into nothing. As he said in his old age (2 June 1785), he dared not rest, while he believed there was 'another world' (Telford, VII, p. 272).

Notes

1 Here several words were cut out of the letter.
2 See Chapter 3, p. 37.
3 Miranda was the subject of Chapter vii of Law's *Serious Call*. She was described by Telford as '[a] Sober reasonable Christian'.

References

Abelove, H., 1990. *The Evangelist of Desire: John Wesley and the Methodists*. Stanford: Stanford University Press.
Britton, R., 1998. *Belief and Imagination: Explorations in Psychoanalysis*. London/New York: Routledge.
Clarke, A., 1823. *Memoirs of the Wesley Family*. London: Printed by J. and T. Clarke.
Crownfield, D., 1992. Intertext I. In *Body/Text in Julia Kristeva*. Albany: State University of New York Press.
Freud, S., and Breuer, F., 1893–5. *Studies on Hysteria*. Pelican Freud Library. London: Penguin Books, 1991.
Hampson, J., 1791. *Memoirs of the late Rev. John Wesley*, vol. III. Sunderland: Printed for the author.
Heitzenrater, R., 2003. *The Elusive Mr Wesley*. Nashville: Abingdon Press.
Källstad, T., 1974. *John Wesley and the Bible: A Psychological Study*. Uppsala: Uppsala University, Doctoral Dissertation.
Knox, A., 1828. Remarks on the Life and Character of John Wesley. In R. Southey, *The Life of Wesley and the Rise and Progress of Methodism*, ed. C. Southey. New York: Harper and Brothers, 1847.
Kristeva, J., 1980. *Powers of Horror*. Translated by L. Roudiez. New York: Columbia University Press, 1982.
Langford, P., 1992. *A Polite and Commercial People: England 1727–1783*. Oxford: Clarendon Press.
McDougall, J., 1989. *Theatres of the Body*. London: Free Association Books.
McDougall, J., 1995. *The Many Faces of Eros*. London: Free Association Books.
Moore, R., 1974. Justification Without Joy. *History of Childhood Quarterly*, 2, pp. 31–52.
Poznauski, E., 1972. The Replacement Child. *Behavioural Paediatrics*, 81(6), pp. 1190–3.
Rack, H., 2002. *Reasonable Enthusiast: John Wesley and the Rise of Methodism*. London: Epworth Press.
Ricoeur, P., 1978. The Hermeneutics of Symbols and Philosophical Reflection. In eds. C. Reagan and D. Stewart, *The Philosophy of Paul Ricoeur*. Boston: Beacon Press.
Rowe, J., Clyman, R., Green, C., Mikkelsen, C., Haight, J., and Ataide, L., 1978. Follow-Up of Families Who Experience a Perinatal Death. *Paediatrics*, 62(2), pp. 166–70.

Schmidt, M., 1953–66. *John Wesley: A Theological Biography*, three volumes. Translated by Norman Goldhawk et al. London: Epworth Press, 1962–73.

Thistlethwaite, H., 2006. The Replacement Child as Writer. In ed. P. Coles, *Sibling Relationships*. London/New York: Karnac.

Waller, R., 2003. *John Wesley: A Personal Portrait*. London: SPCK.

Wesley, J., 1749. *An Account of an Amour of John Wesley*. London: British Library. Add. MSS 7119.

Wesley, J., 1755. *Queries Proposed to the Right Reverend and Right Honourable Count Zinzendorf*. London: n.p.

Figure 8.1 Charles Wesley

Chapter 8

Charles Wesley (1707–88)

There are fewer reliable sources of first-hand material about Charles Wesley than there are about John. He kept a journal from 1729, and Jackson (1849) published extracts from 1736 to 1756, with a selection of his letters. There are many gaps in this edition. They are because of Jackson's lack of knowledge of shorthand (used by the Wesleys for material they wanted kept confidential) and probable deliberate omissions aimed at protecting John Wesley and the Methodist preachers from Charles's opinions about their plans and behaviour (Lloyd, 2007, pp. vii–viii). Until recently, the information from his sermons and letters was also very patchy, but now more reliable material is available: Baker (1995) wrote a valuable brief portrait of Charles Wesley from manuscript letters; Newport (2001) published a complete collection of the sermons of Charles Wesley;[1] Lloyd (2007) has drawn directly on manuscript material in his important book on Charles Wesley's influence on the development of Methodism, the manuscript journal (MJCW) which includes shorthand material has been published (2008); and in 2013 the first volume of Charles Wesley's letters was produced (CWL), with a second volume awaited. I am grateful for permission to use material from these sources. For some letters after 1756, however, the only source remains Jackson.

Early experience: childhood and youth

John was a small boy of four when Charles was born in 1707. Their brother, Samuel, was much older (born 1691), and as we have seen, it is likely that John's birth had fulfilled the parental longing for another male child. Although another son was lost, between John and Charles, this loss was followed by the birth of a baby girl before Charles's birth. Another set of twins was born two years after Charles, of whom only one, Kezia, survived (SW, p. 8).

It is thought that Charles was born two months prematurely. According to Best, Susanna kept him wrapped up in soft wool for the first eight weeks, during which time he did not cry or open his eyes (Best, 2006, p. 14). Whether or not this was the case, it is likely that, as a premature baby, he received a great deal of close and careful attention from his mother. Tyson suggests that this began a 'pattern of frailty and illness throughout his life' (Tyson, 1989, p. 3), and while there is no reason why prematurity alone should lead to ongoing physical vulnerability, it may have led his parents to see him as fragile, which would have affected their handling of him in childhood and beyond.

Like John, Charles would have been affected by his birth order and by the losses his parents had suffered. It is hard to imagine Susanna's state of mind as she coped with her repeated pregnancies, the nursing of her babies, and the loss of so many children. However, unlike the bleak period with its multiple infant deaths prior to John's birth, and although Susanna had lost one other child, she had subsequently successfully delivered and was caring for a healthy baby girl when Charles was born. It seems less likely that she would have been preoccupied with previously lost children or to be struggling with unresolved grief than she had been in 1703. In which case, she would have been more emotionally available to relate to her new baby as a unique individual, and more capable of acting as a container for his unmanageable feelings. Charles would have been less vulnerable to the problems associated with being a 'replacement child' than John had been.

The brothers had four older sisters, as possible extra 'maternal' supports; and for Charles, as the younger of the two brothers, John would have been an important figure. Silverstone has written about the ways in which 'in the search for containment and care, siblings can nurture and care for each other in a lively and vital way'. They can provide 'love and sustenance' and 'withstand ruthless use'. They can be a source of nurturing and a reassurance that inner hatred is not lethal, and a testing ground for boundaries and for learning to manage incestuous wishes (Silverstone, 2006, pp. 243–4). Little is known about how the brothers related to each other in childhood, but evidence from their later life suggests that John fulfilled at least some of these roles.

John was sent to Charterhouse School at the age of eleven, while Charles, aged eight, went to Westminster School. Although Charles left home at a younger age, Westminster was the school at which his brother Samuel taught. In a letter of 28 April 1785, Charles looked back: 'At eight years old, in 1716, I was sent by my father to Westminster School, and placed under the care of my eldest brother Samuel, a strict churchman, who brought me up in his own principles' (Baker, 1995, p. 7). His 'own principles' involved Samuel's High Anglicanism, a passionate interest in the classics and love of poetry (Clarke, 1823, pp. 364–6). Seventeen years older than Charles, Samuel had taken Holy Orders and was a reliable and dutiful son, who supported his parents and his brothers and sisters, financially and emotionally, as far as he was able; Clarke quotes a grateful letter from his father, acknowledging all his care and generosity (Clarke, 1823, p. 462). His presence at Westminster must have greatly improved Charles's school experience. He was clearly an important 'paternal' support. This was shown at a later date, when Samuel became very angry when John Wesley persuaded a reluctant Charles to go with him to Georgia (Lloyd, 2007, p. 29). Also, when Charles found himself in trouble there, he confided in

Samuel, questioning his own faith, wondering if he should have allowed himself to be ordained and wishing he could come home. Samuel wrote back that he should 'never spare unburdening [himself]' to him and that, while, in general, it was wrong to start something and not finish it, he was sure that Charles's 'coming back to England [would] not be looking back from the plough', as he would still be able to exercise his ministry. This was unlike the usual demands that Charles would have experienced at home, which always involved taking the most difficult path. The support continued in spite of Samuel's dislike of some of John and Charles's unorthodox methods, such as field preaching; and Charles continued to confide in him until Samuel's death, aged forty-nine (Clarke, 1823, pp. 391–5). Such 'paternal' support, particularly at the time of separation from home, for a child whose own father was unpredictable and often absent, was a significant advantage, of which John was deprived.

The necessity of preparing themselves for a life totally dedicated to God's purpose was impressed on all Susanna's children: she wrote to Samuel, at the age of fourteen, reminding him that he had been dedicated to the church from birth and hoping he would fulfil this calling by 'bringing many souls to heaven' (SW, p. 48). However, there is no evidence that Charles was subjected to the additional pressure of being specially chosen among his siblings, as John was.

The many differences in the influences on the two brothers in early childhood, subtle or more obvious, can never be known in detail. However, from the available material three emerge. First, it is possible that, as a premature baby, Charles had extra attention and that if he were considered fragile, demands on him were less severe. Secondly, he had extra paternal support from Samuel from childhood into adult life. Thirdly, and unlike John, he did not have to face the hazards of being a 'replacement child' or of being seen as having a special destiny. If, as this suggests, Susanna was more able to function as a good container for his chaotic feelings, allowing his primitive fears to become more tolerable, he was unlikely to have experienced her as unreceptive or 'attacking'. As a result, he would not have needed to employ the defensive manoeuvre aimed at preserving her as a good object, by projecting all the hostility into the father (Britton, 1998, pp. 53–4). There would have been less need to deny any link between his parents. If Charles could hold an image of a good, sexual parental couple in his mind, as it seems he could, he would not have had to confront many of John's difficulties. There would also have been other benefits for him, regarding his creativity.

Oxford

Charles followed John to Oxford, to the same College, Christ Church. In the year that Charles matriculated, 1726, John was elected a Fellow of Lincoln College. At this time Charles clearly admired John: he relied on him to solve problems and to resolve difficult situations. Indeed, Charles's first known poem was written in

January 1728 in a letter lamenting John's absence, when John worked as a curate in Lincolnshire for two years:

> Nor yet from my dim eyes THY form retires!
> (The cold empty starving grate before me makes me add the following disconsolate lines)
> Nor cheering image of thine absent fires.
>
> (CWL, p. 21)

When Charles first went up to Christ Church, he enjoyed the social life, and in his first year he was easily distracted from his studies. When John talked to him about religion, his reply was 'What! would you have me be a saint all at once?' and then he would 'hear no more' (Baker, 1995, pp. 10–14). In 1728, there was a change, possibly related to a failed love affair. He became more serious and began to write about his previous 'lethargy' and his 'former state of insensibility'. He attributed the change to John's and his mother's influence (CWL, p. 27). A letter to John (5 May 1729) was full of anxious introspection regarding his spiritual state; he described how he was strictly organising his life around religious activities and striving not to waste a minute: 'I'm assured, if I have no business of my own, the devil will soon find some' (CWL, p. 30). In the same letter, in response to John's raising the subject, he described needing a remedy for his 'coldness'. However, he appeared to be using this word in a different sense from John. Charles wrote that having been 'utterly inattentive at public prayers' for thirteen years, he could not expect to find a warmth he had never known 'at his first seeking'. He then continued with a description of receiving the Sacrament without being properly prepared and of being surprised that he felt 'greater warmth than usual'. John sometimes used 'coldness' in this sense, but it usually reflected a more persistent state of the absence of feeling (CWL, pp. 29–32).

The brothers shared the intense fear and horror of inner badness, of 'the world, the flesh and the devil', which had been a life-and-death struggle for their mother. Charles continued his struggle to gain salvation, through serious study, the avoidance of women, carrying out good works and receiving the Sacrament frequently. When in 1728 he joined with a group of like-minded friends to form the 'Holy Club', there must have been a noticeable change to a more serious demeanour, which was commented on when he went to stay with Samuel. Charles wrote to John, 'They wonder here I'm so strangely dull (as indeed mirth & I have shook hands and parted), & at the same time pay the compliment of saying I grow extremely like you' (CWL, p. 29). This last comment seems not to have been ironic, as there were many other expressions at that time of his wish to be with John, to agree with him or to be like him. Charles became as rigorous as John in leading the ascetic life but, like him, failed to find any sense of peace or acceptance.

The extent of John's early influence over Charles was clearly shown in 1735 by Charles's reluctant agreement when John persuaded him to become ordained, a prospect he said he dreaded, and his decision to go with him to Georgia (Charles talked of these decisions and of John's powerful ability to persuade him to do things against his will in a letter to Dr Chandler written much later, in 1785; Wesley, 1785). In spite of this, the brothers remained close. Charles wrote in his journal (28 March 1739) of an episode when he was afraid that John would be killed by his enemies if he travelled to Bristol. He was persuaded to stay an extra night but left the following day. Charles wrote, 'The next day he set out, commended by us to the grace of God. He left a blessing behind. I desired to die with him' (MJCW, p. 169).

The close bond of mutual appreciation and loyalty between them continued, particularly from the time of their conversions until 1749. They worked closely together and complemented one another, making them a very powerful evangelising force (Lloyd, 2007, pp. 42, 62). Both were Arminian and opposed the Calvinism of George Whitefield. They both engaged in field preaching, travelled widely and published hymn books together. However, Charles had a hot temper, and there were numerous episodes when they became extremely angry with each other.

The relationship become more strained after 1748. It was aggravated by Charles's giving up the itinerant ministry in 1756, which John saw as his withdrawing his help, and it was sustained by ongoing disagreements about the disciplining of lay preachers and the prospects of separation from the church (Lloyd, 2007, pp. 89, 116). Three events in particular upset Charles profoundly: John's plan to marry Grace Murray in 1749, his marriage to Mrs. Vazeille in 1751 and his decision to ordain preachers in 1784, which would lead to separation from the Church of England. The last dispute, which resulted in friction and conflict over a long period, provoked Charles to anger in verse and by letter: on July 27 1786, he wrote, 'I believe you have been too hasty in ordaining. I believe God left you to yourself in that matter, as He left Hezekiah – to show you the secret pride in your heart' (Baker, 1995, p. 140). Writing to Henry Durbin, who had informed him of the three ordinations in September 1784, he impugned John's integrity: 'I trust I shall be able, like you, to leave behind me the name of an honest man. Which with all his sophistry he can never do . . . I call you . . . to witness that I have had no hand in this infamous ordination' (Baker, 1995, p. 135).

Charles's anger is reflected in his verses:

W[esley] himself and friends betrays,
By his own good sense forsook,
While suddenly his hands he lays
On the hot head of C[oke]:
Yet *we* at least shou'd spare the weak,
His weak Co-evals *We*,
Nor blame a hoary Schismatic,
A Saint of Eighty-Three.

and in the well-known lines:

> So easily are Bishops made
> By man's, or woman's whim?
> W[esley] his hands on C[oke] hath laid,
> But who laid hands on Him?
>
> (Wesley, 1784a, MS Ordinations 1 and 5, in Baker, 1962, pp. 367–8)

Charles's apprehension about his brother's power and authority continued. Writing about lay preachers in a letter to Lady Huntingdon of 4 August 1752, Charles proposed that they should not give up their trade in order to preach. He was concerned that, if they became financially dependent on John Wesley, the extent of his authority over them would not be kept 'in due bounds', that their financial independence would act as

> guard against that rashness and credulity of his, which has kept me in continual awe & bondage for many years, therefore I shall insist on their working as the one point, the single condition, of my acting in consort with him, because without this I can trust neither them nor him.
>
> (CWL, p. 324)

In spite of his anger and the irreconcilable differences between them, Charles wrote a hymn in 1779, praying for John's long life, sung by the Society in Bristol (now in the John Rylands University Library, Manchester). In the letter to Dr Chandler (28 April 1785), he wrote, 'Thus our Partnership here is dissolved but not our friendship. I have taken him for better or worse, till death do us part; or rather, re-unite us in love inseparable' (Wesley, 1785, letter MS ordinations, in Tyson, 1989, p. 60). There was a great deal of bitterness, but they remained inextricably involved with each other.

There was a pattern, which was played out repeatedly: it was likely to have been one familiar from childhood. Charles would become overtly angry and would make sure John was aware of his feelings, while John would assume the moral high ground and become more domineering or would tend to withdraw. During these arguments, Charles would become very despondent. When he heard that John was planning to marry, without having consulted him, he wrote (13 December 1749),

> He brought down my strength, and I am next to useless for when I preach, which is seldom, my word is without power or life; my spirit is that of the whole people, all are faint and weary; all seem on the brink of desperation.
>
> (CWL, p. 273)

However, no matter how profound the disagreement, it was always followed by a reconciliation. The serious disagreement over John's ordination of three ministers, to minister to the newly independent Americans in 1784, was followed by a poem which was a prayer for John Wesley and the Methodist people: it referred to the strong bond between them from their infancy, when they were 'true yokefellows'. They were one in 'nature', and 'judgement' and their hopes, fears and hearts were known to each other, 'attuned in perfect unison' (Wesley, 1784b, MS Brothers, 9 in Baker, 1962, p. 371).

For much of their lives, there was a sense of a deep attachment between them which helped them to weather many crises. But in later years, there was a change in Charles. He was more able to resist pressure from John and staunchly held to his own opinions. He was no longer an itinerant and led a more settled family life. He continued to oppose John in many decisions about the future of the Methodists. In spite of Charles's ambivalent feelings and their sometimes prolonged periods of dispute, John appears to have served as a loved, admired and resilient model and support for him, at least until the 1750s. In Silverstone's terms, he was a sibling who could withstand ruthless use. Charles could risk attacking him and knew he would survive; this would have been an important reassurance for him that his hatred was not lethal (Silverstone, 2006, p. 244). It is less likely that Charles served the same purpose for John, who had more difficulty in expressing his deep feelings; his anger leaked out in ways of which he was barely aware.

Pre-conversion experience

In February, 1736 during the voyage to Georgia, Charles wrote a letter to two women friends from the 'Cotswold Set'. He was despondent because all his strenuous efforts towards salvation had failed to bring any assurance or peace, and he had only a fluctuating hope that service in the New World would bring some relief. What is striking, however, is the rapidity with which his mental state changed over a period of nine days, while writing. It shifted from despair (he regretted that he had survived the crossing and said that he was carrying his hell with him) to enthusiastic religious exaltation, from self-denigration and envy of John's devotion to God to 'an interval of ease' and a hope that God could save him (CWL, pp. 50–2). Like John, he was impressed during the voyage by the Moravians' lack of fear during storms, and their calmness in the face of death, but he seems to have been disinclined at that stage to look at their different way to salvation, with its stress on salvation through the blood of Christ. Like John he clung to his intention to struggle on towards 'perfection' through his own desperate efforts (Best, 2006, pp. 60–1).

His troubles in Georgia have been well documented. There were malicious rumours of sexual misconduct, which Oglethorpe, his employer and Governor of the colony, initially believed. Charles was charged with 'mutiny and sedition' (MJCW, p. 10). He was finally exonerated, and he and Oglethorpe were reconciled, but he never became popular with his parishioners. Oglethorpe's comments suggest that his unpopularity was due to his High Church formality, his inexperience, his naivety in relating to people, and his failure to deal with rumour and gossip (MJCW, p. 14). When he was leaving, Oglethorpe told him, 'You are of a sociable temper, and would find in a married state the difficulties of working out your salvation exceedingly lessened, and your helps as much increased' (MJCW, p. 46). All the evidence suggests that Charles was not guilty of the accusations made against him, but he was ostracised by the community and deprived by Oglethorpe for a time of the ordinary physical necessities of life. As often happened when he was unhappy, he became physically ill with the 'flux' and a fever, and it became clear that the only safe course was for him to return to England.

'Conversion' experience

On his return from Georgia, his mental state was even more despairing. He had not only had his hopes dashed – that he would be saved though Christian service – but he was also in a severely debilitated physical state. He wrote to John from Boston on his way home, exclaiming that the sense of self-preservation must be very strong if it made such a 'wretch' as he willing to go on living: 'I know no greater pleasure in life than in considering it cannot last for ever' (CW, p. 60). He had failed to live up to his own expectations and felt that the extent of his failure had been disguised; he saw himself as a whited sepulchre (Best, 2006, p. 74).

For some months after his return, in September 1736, he hoped he could return to Georgia. In January 1738, in another letter to John, he said, 'The fiery furnace, I trust, shall purify me, and if emptied of myself, I would defy the world and the devil to hurt me' (CWL, p. 65). But he remained ill and was suffering debilitating treatments from his doctors, who told him that a return to Georgia would result in certain death (CWL, p. 68).

It was in this state of mind that, like John, Charles came under the influence of Peter Böhler. On 24 February 1738, the journal records that he was suffering from a toothache, enough to 'separate soul from body'. He had just been treated for pleurisy; his doctor had expected to find him dead at the second visit, and he had been violently medicated and bled three times. Böhler visited him during this illness and prayed for his recovery 'with a strange confidence'. He asked him if he hoped to be saved, and why. Charles replied, 'Because I have used my best endeavours to serve God'. Böhler shook his head and said nothing. 'I thought him uncharitable', wrote Charles, 'saying in my heart, "What are not my endeavours a sufficient ground of hope? Would he rob me of my endeavours? I have nothing else to trust to"' (MJCW, p. 97). In April 1738, there was some improvement, but he became ill again, and the bleeding was repeated. Again, Böhler was authoritative and influential:

> In the morning Dr. Cockburn came to see me; and a better physician, Peter Böhler, whom God had detained in England for my good. He stood by my bedside, and prayed over me, that now at least I might see the divine intention, in this and my late illness. I immediately thought it might be that I should again consider Böhler's doctrine of faith; examine myself whether

I was in *the faith*; and if I was not, never cease seeking and longing after it, till I attained it.

(MJCW, p. 100)

For the first three weeks of May 1738, he was convinced that he did not have faith in the Gospel: 'In the afternoon I seemed deeply sensible of my misery, in being without Christ'. He spent all his time praying, reading scripture and discussing religion. On 17 May, having read 'Luther on the Galatians', he found Luther 'nobly full of faith' and was astounded that he should ever have thought the doctrine of 'justification by faith alone' a new doctrine. It was 'not an idle, dead faith, but a faith which works by love, and is necessarily productive of all good works and all holiness'. He then 'laboured and waited and prayed, to feel "who loved *me*, and gave himself for *me*"' and finally gained an assurance, from reading Luther, that God would 'finish the work'. Then he 'slept in peace' (MJCW, pp. 103–4).

There was intense pressure on him to undergo a 'converting' experience: he was staying in the house of a Mr. Bray, 'a poor ignorant mechanic, who [knew] nothing but Christ'. He was very ill with breathlessness and pain and required medical attention. He was surrounded by people who had experienced conversion, one of whom told him he would not rise from his bed until he believed, and more than once he 'received the sacrament; but not Christ' (MJCW, pp. 101–4). There were Bible readings, which indicated to him that he could expect to experience 'healing' faith. On 21 May, from his bed, he heard a voice, which he took to be that of Mr. Bray's sister, saying, 'In the name of Jesus of Nazareth, arise, and believe, and thou shalt be healed of all thine infirmities!' It was confirmed that this was indeed her voice, that she had had a dream of opening a door when somebody knocked and of finding Jesus there. She had wakened in fear, felt uneasy throughout the day and then had a religious experience in evening prayers. Charles's account was that she felt 'enlarged in love and prayer for all mankind, and commanded to go and assure me from Christ of my recovery, soul and body'. She was encouraged by her brother, and after Charles heard her words, he searched the scripture for confirmation that they were from God. He found several confirming texts and then gained a sense of peace: his 'temper' was 'mistrust of my own great, but before unknown, weakness'. He wrote,

I saw that by faith I stood; by the continual support of faith, which kept me from falling, though of myself I am ever sinking into sin. I went to bed still sensible of my own weakness (I humbly hope to be more and more so), yet confident of Christ's protection.

(MJCW, pp. 106–8)

On going to sleep, he dreamt of facing two devils, one under his feet and the other facing him, but they 'faded, and sunk, and vanished away' when he told them he belonged to Christ (MJCW, p. 108).

He describes subsequent struggles against Satan. He believed Satan was discouraging him from writing hymns or proclaiming his faith, accusing him of pride, but he managed to finish what later became known as the 'conversion hymn', 'Where shall my wond'ring soul begin?' At the sacrament four days later (25 May 1738), he had a further experience:

> in the prayer of consecration I saw, by the eye of faith, or rather had a glimpse of Christ's broken, mangled body, as taking down from the cross. Still I could not observe the prayer, but only repeat with tears, 'O Love, Love!' At the same time, I felt great peace and joy.
>
> (MJCW, p. 111)

Following these experiences, his health improved. He was energised to write more hymns and preach sermons, and he had a strong urge to share his experience as widely as possible. This was the beginning of his ministry, but like John, he could not rest securely in a place of peace and joy but continued to sink into periods of despondency.

Character and relationships

It has been suggested that Charles Wesley had an 'almost a manic-depressive personality', having inherited his father's passion, poetic creativity, and tendency to mood swings, while John resembled his mother in being more calm, rational and intellectual. Rack (2002, p. 252) describes Charles as of a 'less robust constitution' than John, possibly accounting for 'his later vacillations of behaviour'.

The evidence suggests that there is an element of truth in the 'head' versus 'heart' contrast, and John appeared to think so; on 28 February 1766, he wrote a letter to Charles, urging that they should cooperate better together: 'If I am (in some sense) the head and you the heart, may it not be said, 'the whole head is sick and the whole heart faint?' (Telford, IV, p. 322). However, the situation is more complex than these dichotomies and the apparent parental resemblances suggest, as is Rack's implication that the more overtly emotional brother was in some sense less psychologically sound.

Nothing could be more different from John Wesley's 'going along in an even line' than Charles's mood changes. These striking, rapid swings were obvious in the letter already quoted to the Cotswold women on the way to Georgia. He himself commented that his mood switched according to the content of the letter. Only ten days after his conversion experience, he described an episode of depression and deadness (MJCW, pp. 114–15). It is quoted here because it clearly describes an alteration which was crucial to his future experience and which enabled him to deal with further episodes of depression. He could by then hold on to the idea that the episodes were transient, that they would pass and that God remained a loving figure, in spite of his present doubts. On 1 June 1738, he wrote that he 'could not pray, being utterly dead to the sacrament'. The following day, he was 'still unable to pray; still dead in communicating; full of cowardly desire of death'. For two more days, the deadness, heaviness and aversion to prayer continued, and he went to church, where 'the prayers and sacraments were exceeding grievous to [him]'. He wrote that he could not help asking himself,

> '[W]here is the difference between what I am now, and what I was before believing?' I immediately answered, that if darkness was not like the former darkness, because I was satisfied. There was no guilt in it, because I was assured it would be dispersed; and because, though I could not find *I loved God or feel that he loved me, yet I did and would believe he loved me notwithstanding.*
>
> (my italics; MJCW, p.114)

The same evening, he reluctantly joined a group of worshippers and wrote that through prayer, he helped one of them to believe. There was great joy and thankfulness, singing and praising God. Charles's faith was 'confirmed' and '[t]he weight was quite taken off'. This assured him that the best cure for being 'cast down' and 'most unable to help ourselves', was to 'labour . . . for our neighbour' (MJCW, 114–15).

When the 'weight was quite taken off', he became enthusiastic, energised, his health improved, and he began preaching 'faith in Christ'. This improvement in mood continued: he discussed his experience wherever he went and urged others to share it. To those of the same mind, this was a great time of rejoicing, but the reaction of Mrs. Delamotte (a friend who was not of his opinion) suggests that his excitement and insistence could be overwhelming. She accused him of 'seducing' her children (to his beliefs) in her absence, and when he reiterated his experience of 'instantaneous faith', 'she started up, said she could not bear it and ran out of the house' (MJCW, p. 125).

There were many instances of his mood being depressed, of his feeling inadequate to his task, and of his wanting to escape from his responsibility. In a letter to George Whitefield (10 August 1739), just over a year after his conversion, he wrote,

> I am continually tempted to leave off preaching and hide myself, like J. Hutchins. I should then be freer from temptation and at leisure to attend to my own improvement. God continues to work *by* me but not *in* me, that I can perceive. Do not reckon on me, my brother, in the work that God is doing; for I cannot expect He should long employ one who is ever longing and murmuring to be discharged.
>
> (MJCW, p. 183)

As with John, there were many instances of his mood lifting, from preaching, reading, talking to friends or helping somebody in need, and usually when his attention had been brought back to the Gospel message. In his journal (6 August 1738), he wrote, 'I preached at Islington and gave the cup. In the afternoon, I read prayers in a church in London, and preached again. I was faint, and full of pain when I began; but my work quite cured me' (MJCW, p. 142). A month later there was an episode during which he felt that God had left him in 'desertion'. One minute, he was 'weak and faint in mind', with no strength and wanting to be released from his ministry while, the next moment, having found a sign from God in the scriptures, he was preaching 'with power'. He described children, soldiers and others shouting and roaring:

> the enemy raged exceedingly . . . I never felt such power before . . . I saw God had great work to do among us by Satan's opposition. I lifted up my voice like a trumpet, and in a few minutes drove him out of the field.
> (MJCW, p. 199)

It was during this period (1738–9) that he wrote some of his finest hymns, including 'And can it be' (*Hymns and Sacred Poems*, 1739, 'Free Grace', pp. 117–9):

> Long my imprison'd Spirit lay
> Fast bound in Sin and Nature's Night:
> Thine Eye diffus'd a quick'ning Ray;
> I woke; the Dungeon flam'd with Light;
> My Chains fell off, my Heart was free,
> I rose, went forth, and followed Thee.

The mood swings from despondency to elation clearly continued after his conversion experience, and like John his mood was lifted by activity, but there was a difference in the way he felt, which he was able to describe. He felt less guilty and could continue to believe that he was loved by God through periods of depression and even when he felt temporarily deserted by him.

The evidence suggests that he suffered from marked mood swings, with excitement which was sometimes marked enough to irritate other people; but there is not enough evidence to indicate that he was suffering from a manic-depressive (bipolar) illness. Although his outspokenness sometimes upset people, so far as is known, his mood changes never interfered with his ability to function or form relationships. In fact, Charles's access to his feelings resulted in his being able to be compassionate towards people in distress and to relate in a loving way to his wife and family.

Man of the heart

Pastoral care

Although Charles Wesley is sometimes depicted as preferring to mix with the aristocracy and middle- and upper-class Methodists, rather than with the poor (Heitzenrater, 1992, p. 185), his journal does not support this. It includes many instances which demonstrate his work as an effective pastor; he regularly ministered to the sick, the dying, the mentally ill and to prisoners. A letter to his wife (22 September 1755) describes his care of a dying man, whom he visited one afternoon. He was called to him again in the night and stayed for several hours until his doctor arrived. The following day he visited 'our brother Cowper' in the 'mad-house' (CWL, p. 399). He did indeed mix with the aristocracy, particularly in his later life, in order to ensure that his musically gifted sons received necessary teaching and opportunities to perform, but much of his ministry was with the poor.

One example of Charles's pastoral work, during early December 1753, gives considerable insight into his character (Tyson, 1989, pp. 325–32).[2] He describes a period of seven days, during which he travelled from Bath to London and back to his home in Bristol again. He went to visit his brother John, who was very ill in London, but while there, he heard that his wife had developed smallpox, and he had to return home. At the time, Charles was caring for a John Hutchinson, who was clearly in a very disturbed, if not psychotic, state. He was afraid to leave Hutchinson alone because of his condition and so took him with him on both journeys. He describes this period as a time of torment, '*as in hell*'. He suffered verbal abuse and physical violence: during a stay in an inn, he found himself dragged into Hutchinson's room with him. He was locked in, until the servants broke down the door. The journal for the following day reports that during the night Hutchinson had been 'sorely tempted' to cut his own throat. There were periods of calm, when he would beg forgiveness, but then further outbursts of rage and '*relapses into his strange madness*'.

Charles's account shows him as a man of extraordinary resilience, who was able to think about another's needs at a time when he was very anxious about his brother and then his wife. He saw the experience as Satan using Hutchinson as a messenger to 'buffet him', but he recognised the other's need in spite of the abuse and aggression, and he courageously tolerated the behaviour without retaliating. Charles persevered, largely alone, ensuring that Hutchinson was safely looked after, for what must have felt like an eternity. There is no suggestion that he saw this as a 'saintly' action or that he was 'preening' himself because of his worthiness; it is clear that he would rather not have been doing it but merely saw it as necessary. His own comfort and peace had to take second place.

There are many other examples which show the same capacity for empathy. He often wrote to the bereaved, and while he held the same beliefs about mourning as John Wesley, that there should be a limit to grieving, he would not introduce this thought until he had first acknowledged and sympathised with the mourner's pain (Baker, 1995, p. 123). His capacity for empathy, for putting himself in another's shoes, is also demonstrated in the way he speaks in the voice of a woman in labour in several poems. These poems for 'women in travail' must have been unusual poems for a man to write in the eighteenth century:

Whisper to my list'ning soul,
Wilt Thou not my strength renew,

Nature's fears and pangs controul,
And bring Thy handmaid thro'?

(*Hymns for the use of Families*, Hymn liii,
'Lord, I magnify thy Power')

Relationships with women

There is evidence in the journal that he maintained contact with his sisters, was supportive to them in their troubles, and was concerned about their religious struggles. On 20 January, 1727, he wrote affectionately about his 'poor' sister Hetty, who was in London for only a week before he had to leave: 'little of that time did I lose, being with her almost continually: I could well almost envy myself the deal of pleasure I had crowded within that small space . . . we both wished it had been longer' (CWL, pp. 21–2).

As a young man, he had a brief relationship with an actress, Molly, which, according to a letter to John (5 January 1729), resulted in his becoming more discriminating about women:

> I shall be far less addicted to gallantry, and doing what s[ister-in-law] Nutty [Ursula Wesley] with less justice said you did – liking women merely for being women . . . but enough of her – I'll blot my brain and paper no longer with her.
>
> (CWL, p. 25)

He was also part of the 'Cotswold Set' and clearly enjoyed their company, so much so that he wrote to John in May 1729 saying he dare not go to Stanton Harcourt without him, 'for as I take it strong pleasure w[oul]d be dangerous to one in my unconfirmed condition' (CWL, p. 31). The letter already mentioned, written on the voyage to Georgia, does not have quite the extravagance of John's letters to these women, but he was intimate enough with them to share his fears and his confused and changing feelings. His reaction to the danger of the 'strong pleasures' of the 'Cotswold Set', suggests that, as for John, they represented something of the 'serpent in Eden'.

When Charles married, twenty years later (April 1749), it was only after a great deal of doubt and soul-searching. He was sure of his feelings for Sally Gwynne but required confirmation from John and many other Methodists that this was the right thing to do, for himself, for Sally and for the Methodist society. Part of his anxiety was about money, as she was better off than he. He was very hesitant and diffident and not sure that he was good enough for her. He wrote (5 February 1749) urging her not to '*expect too much*! I am a man of like passions – compassed about with infirmities, weak in faith, & wanting in all things' (CWL, p. 225). However, his later letters to Sally and the evidence from the journal suggest that, once married, the relationship gave him a close confidante (he described her as 'his best friend') and the security of feeling loved. In spite of the trials due to his itinerant ministry, his ill health and their loss of five children out of eight, there is nothing to suggest that they ever ceased to be emotionally close and mutually supportive. While he was not slow to give advice to Sally regarding the upbringing of the children, he nevertheless respected her opinion as to what was best for them: they acted together as a parental couple. He gave up his itinerancy in 1756, spent more time at home in Bristol and in London and was happiest when they were together. In a letter of 11 April 1760, when he was hoping that she could come to stay in London, where he was working, he wrote,

> You will not mistake my tenderness for indifference. The greatest earthly blessing I could obtain, were a sight of you and the children; but I should buy it too dear, if you came unwillingly. Therefore do as you find best in your own heart. Come with Charley, or without him, or not at all. Your will I shall receive as the will of Providence.
>
> (Jackson, II, p. 234)

These expressions of longing for her company, of wanting to be at home with his family, became stronger as he grew older and less inclined to continue his itinerancy.

There are many letters which show his intense interest and involvement in the care of the children. He wanted to know about their progress in detail; wrote poems about their struggles, including teething problems; and was deeply concerned about their health and education. Like John he recommended his mother's methods, urging Sally to adhere to 'Locke's rules' which were the 'whole secret of education', but he clearly found it difficult to be as consistent and severe as the rules suggested. He thought his son Charley was so easy to manage that he need not be 'chastis[ed] too severely' (Baker, 1995, p. 109). One of his *Hymns for the use of Families* (Hymn lxiv, 'How fast the chains of nature bind') shows that he believed there were dangers in being both too lenient and too severe. He describes the merciless severity of those who treat their children as 'beasts' or 'slaves', which results in a 'yoke severe' that they can never escape. His hymn provides a clear picture of how 'evangelical nurture' results in a level of anger and hatred which is difficult to manage; it is hard to 'throw off the yoke'. Surprisingly, however, in the light of this, some of the hymns he wrote for children were quite terrifying in their reference to hell and damnation and their urging good behaviour. They suggest that his mother's fears for a child's soul, prior to a conversion experience, remained with him. Yet his daughter Sally wrote of her father:

> So *kind and amiable* a *character* in domestic life can scarcely be imagined. The *tenderness* he showed in *every weakness*, and the sympathy in *every pain*, would fill sheets to describe. But I am not writing his eulogy; only I must add, with so warm a temper, he was never heard to speak an angry word to a servant, or known to strike a child in anger; and he knew no guile.
>
> (Watson, 1831, p. 410)

In addition to having to suffer his episodes of depression, the fact that he was so emotional meant that, as his daughter Sally recognised, he also had to struggle at times to control his anger – 'the old man'. Sometimes this would erupt, as when he left the 1755 Methodist Conference early in protest that it had not been definite enough in prohibiting Methodist preachers from administering communion (Best, 2006, p. 239). Similarly, when he became angry about John's intention to marry Grace Murray, he acted impulsively and intervened in a way which may have been destructive to some extent of John's future happiness; certainly, it affected his own future relationship with John.

There are several reports of his losing his temper and frightening people by his loss of control. Best quotes John Cennick, a leading lay worker, who was a Calvinist and became involved with Charles in an argument about 'election': 'Charles fell into a violent passion and affrighted all the table, and rising from the table, he said he would go directly and preach against me, and he accordingly did' (Best, 2006, p. 146). On other occasions, his anger would appear in forceful verbal or written confrontations, as in his arguments with John over the question of ordination. Like John, while he was not physically violent, he had a 'biting' wit, with a ready use of irony, sarcasm and ridicule. This tone is captured in a letter to his wife (9 May 1755). He was writing ironically about John's wife, whom he disliked and found impossible to deal with:

> I met my good angel, & sister[-in-law] [Mary Wesley]. I have done her honour before the people, & behaved (tho[ugh] I say it) very much like a gentleman: only that I took a French leave, that is, left Leeds without telling either her or her husband. He will follow me quickly with a querulous letter, but I am hardened to causeless reproofs.
>
> (CWL, p. 371)

After Charles's death, in an account published with his sermons (Wesley, 1816, pp. xxxii–xxxiv) and quoted by Tyson (1989, p. 9), his wife wrote that his chief love had been to be with his family, whom he had treated with tenderness and kindness. However, such gentleness she thought was not part of his 'temperament' but based on his 'divine principles'. She stressed his humility and his capacity to rejoice in other's superior talents, rather than to be envious. Like John, he could forgive and be reconciled with his enemies, but unlike John, he never regained his trust in those who had once let him down. While this account, coming from his wife, may well be biased, as may his daughter's account, they were the people closest to him, and it is of interest that both were aware that, although kind and gentle, he had to struggle with altogether different internal impulses.

Reason and discrimination

Charles Wesley was indeed an emotional man, and this is the aspect of his personality which is usually contrasted with John's more rational and intellectual character.

But this is an oversimplification. The evidence shows that Charles was also capable of being analytical, sceptical, diplomatic and of acting with common sense.

In 1778 Samuel Johnson is reported to have talked to James Boswell about John Wesley's susceptibility to believe in the supernatural and said that he thought that Charles was a more 'stationary', less gullible man (Newton, 2007, p. 58). When he preached, he was particularly careful not to accept bizarre behaviour in his listeners as evidence of divine intervention: on 10 January 1739, he wrote in his journal, 'We had some discourse about agitations; no signs of grace, in my humble opinion' (MJCW, p. 158); on 22 April 1739, 'Talked with the Count [Zinzendorf] about motions, visions, dreams and was confirmed in my dislike to them' (MJCW, p. 171); and on 24 May 1739, 'I believe not every spirit, nor any till I have tried it by the fruits and the written word' (MJCW, p. 174). While he believed that many could be 'struck down, both soul and body, into the depth of distress', he dealt with those he considered to be blaspheming by imitating the spirit of God, very firmly indeed. They were moved to a corner of the room or taken outside, where they could not be seen and were then ignored:

> Another girl, as she began to cry out, I ordered to be carried out. Her convulsion was so violent as to take away the use of her limbs, till they laid her and left her without the door. She immediately found her legs and walked off.
> (MJCW, p. 350)

For Charles, fits and convulsions were devices of Satan, which interfered with his work (MJCW, pp. 350–2).

He could be diplomatic. The journal (18 November 1740) describes his response, when asked to reprove Howel Harris, the Welsh evangelist, in public for preaching predestination:

> I smiled at Satan's imprudence, but turned aside the question with mildness, and thanks to the proposer . . . I quashed all farther importunity by declaring, 'I am unwilling to speak of my brother Howel Harris, because, when I begin, I know not how to leave off, and should say so much good of him as some of you could not bear'.
> (MJCW, p. 289)

Although he often persisted with his preaching and travelling in dangerous situations, there were times when common sense prevailed. At a time when both he and John had suffered violence and been pelted with dirt and stones (8 February 1744), he concluded that they should take more care about where to preach and 'wait upon God':

> [A] false courage, which is a fear of shame, may otherwise betray us into unnecessary dangers. . . . To seek redress by law, unless we are very sure of obtaining it, is only to discover our own weakness, and irritate our opposers.
> (MJCW, pp. 386–7)

Although he was often impulsive and easily emotionally involved with people, he did not flinch from imposing on the lay preachers the necessary standards of education, morality and preaching. Similarly, if it were thought necessary to expel a member from the society, he was able to do it but not without misgivings. On 16 July 1740 he wrote, 'I was forced to cut off a rotten member. But I felt such love and pity at the time, as humbled me into dust. It was as if one criminal was made to execute another' (MJCW, p. 273).

Dependence and conformity

While he was impulsive and driven by emotion, he was far from being a revolutionary. There was a lack of confidence in himself and his own opinions. Particularly as a young man, he had a tendency to rely on others: he worried about the 'proprieties', and he had a preference for the 'status quo'. The lack of confidence in himself and his opinions was obvious in his anxieties prior to his marriage. His tendency to rely on others has been discussed by Edwards, who saw the two main contenders for his allegiance as John and their elder brother Samuel. Samuel, as a High Churchman, was distressed by the brothers' field preaching, which he described to his mother as a 'spreading delusion'. Having been heavily influenced by Samuel as a boy, Charles deferred to John at Oxford and in the early days of their ministry, but Samuel's influence prevailed in Charles's later insistence that no action should be taken which might lead to separation from the Church (Edwards, 1961, pp. 33–7). Certainly, he was passionate about the need to stay in the Established Church throughout his adult life, and this may have reflected the influence of Samuel and his father; but later in his life, he was able to resist pressure always to go along with John's wishes, he was clear about his own beliefs, and he defended them vigorously.

Emotional pain

The overall picture of Charles is a complex one. He was a man of intense feeling and, as with John, there were many contradictory elements. Some of the ways in which he dealt with his feelings were useful in contributing to his ability to relate to people empathically and kindly, as described by his wife and daughter. They led to his gaining the reputation of being a 'man made for friendship' (Gill, 1964, p. 38) and added to his abilities as a preacher and pastor. Other defensive responses, or symptoms, made life more uncomfortable for him.

In addition to being able to experience and acknowledge feelings of sadness, anger and exhilaration, he was able to share his feelings with his wife. His letters suggest that he trusted her enough to let her know about feelings he was embarrassed about or ashamed of, whether they were trivial or serious. For instance, in writing to her about his preaching (15 May 1749), he confessed, 'To any but you I durst not tell how strangely I was carried out, for fear of pride' (CWL, p. 260).

His poems and hymns helped him deal with his feelings, for instance in coping with loss. Intellectually at least, his beliefs about death coincided with those of John and of Susanna Wesley: that God's will must not be questioned and that there should be rejoicing that the loved one was welcomed into paradise. However, having lost their first child John (Jacky), aged sixteen months, he wrote several hymns about the dying and death of children. They served two functions for him. First, they included an outpouring of searing grief:

> Those waving hands no more shall move,
> Those laughing eyes shall smile no more:
> He cannot now engage our love,
> With sweet insinuating power,
> Our weak unguarded hearts ensnare,
> And rival his Creator there.
>
> (*Funeral Hymns*, 1759, Hymn 20, On the Death of a child, Dead! Dead! The Child I lov'd so well!)

Second, the verses were a space in which he could externalise and wrestle with his conflicting responses to his loss. In some he manages with great difficulty to resign himself to what he sees as God's omniscient will and in *Hymns for the use of Families* (Hymn lxi, 'Helpless Babe'), he goes so far as praying for the death of a child, if God, in his prescient wisdom, can foresee a life of 'misery and vice'. The hymn ends: 'Save a helpless child from sin, / Snatch him now to endless rest'.

On the other hand, in Hymn xcix, in which the subject is 'we', he intercedes for himself and his wife and asks forgiveness for praying that a sick child might live but then in the third verse manages to write that he submits their will to God's. He struggles through the next five verses, oscillating between praying for the 'faith of *Abraham*' and praying for the child not to die. Finally, in this hymn (unusually), he cannot manage to resign himself to the child's death, and throws himself on Christ's mercy ('his bowels'); it ends:

> Father, aright we cannot pray -
> But Jesus reads the troubled breast -
> O let His bowels speak the rest!
>
> (*Hymns for the use of Families*, 1767, Hymn xcix, 'Father, thy froward children spare')

Here his grief overpowered what he believed would have been the right response, but he was able to trust that Christ could 'read the troubled breast' and forgive the grieving parents; it is difficult to imagine John Wesley ending a hymn in such a way.

Charles was able to face his own destructiveness more directly than his brother could. He used the same conventional vocabulary to describe the sinful state (the corrupt body, worldliness, self-love, inbred sin, blind or dead in sin, heart of stone, the old Adam), but there is no sense that these were abstract labels. That he related them to instances in his life in which he felt he had been destructive, is shown in his journal from December 1744 to February 1745 (MJCW, pp. 431–5). He wrote that he had 'innocently brought such a burden' on his friends, particularly one of them. He expected no 'further communication of good' from the friend and intended 'never more to see *that person* (if without sin I may forbear) till we *stand* together at the judgement seat'. In January 1745, accusations were made against him in the presence of Lady Huntingdon, but he gave no details about them. In February 1745, he sent a declaration to the Bishop of London. There had been charges of his 'committing or offering to commit lewdness' with one E.J. He denied any such action, and the bishop was satisfied. He wrote a hymn at that time, in which he *felt* his 'shame' and 'dishonour' and recognised that while free from 'outward vice', 'Inwardly, like other men, / Wholly born in sin I am'. The hymn continued with a plea for God's righteous judgement and his love (Jackson I, pp. 390–1). Also in February 1745, there is another letter to a 'friend':

> The loss of all things and life itself is nothing to the loss of a friend. If my burden weighs you down I must communicate no more. But whatever becomes of me the foundation stands sure. Farewell my sorrowful friend, for I know I have infected you.
>
> (MJCW, p. 435)

It is not at all clear what has happened between these friends, or who was involved, but there is no doubt Charles's 'sinfulness' to him is real, serious and to be owned. It had to be confronted, but he was aware it was too appalling to be faced all at once:

> Shew me, as my Soul can bear,
> The Depth of Inbred Sin;
> All the Unbelief declare,
> The Pride that lurks within;
>
> (*Hymns and Sacred Poems*, 1742, part II, 'Christ, my Hidden Life, appear')

But Charles also saw the need for self-love. In August 1786, he wrote to his son Charles, 'Self-love is not in itself sinful. There is a right and just self-love, which sets a man upon securing his only true (that is, his eternal) happiness' (Jackson, II, letter xcvi, p. 275). The combination of self-love and knowledge of a capacity for destructiveness, meant that Charles developed a degree of tolerance for ambivalence in himself and others. His hate and anger were, for the most part, owned rather than projected into others.

Charles became aware that activity, particularly preaching, made him feel better. In a letter, probably written around 1764–6, he wrote, 'My work, I know very well keeps me alive, more than it wears me out' (Jackson II, letter lxix, p. 246).

Though less than John's, the amount of travelling and preaching he did was prodigious by ordinary standards. He persisted in travelling in dreadful weather conditions; on 18 November 1744, he described walking to Sunderland and back from Newcastle (some twenty-four miles) in 'hail and snow' so violent that at times that he could hardly 'walk nor stand' (MJCW, p. 428). Similarly, it is thought that he wrote between 6,500 and 9,000 hymns, many while he was travelling on horseback. This degree of persistence has a compulsive quality to it. It is possible that hymn writing was one aspect of his need to work, in order to feel better, partly, as described earlier, by externalising his conflicts and expressing emotion but also as a reparative activity, driven by unconscious guilt.

Like John, Charles preached mainly in the 'plain style', but at times his sermons included features of the rhetorical tradition, with more ornate language, play on words, the inclusion of Greek quotations, and references to the homilies and articles of the Church of England (Newport, 2001, pp. 44–5). However, the most outstanding feature of his preaching was the passionate outpouring of emotion it involved. After his conversion experience, he increasingly preached without notes and often on a random text from the Bible. He knew he was a good preacher. As in his letters to his wife, in his journal (7 August 1739) he wrote of his success in preaching and of the pride and guilt that accompanied it: 'Too well pleased with my success, which brought upon me the buffetings of Satan' (MJCW, p. 183).

He would become so carried away with emotion, that his sermons were often very long, and at times he felt so transported by his feelings that he felt that his words were 'not his own'. On 13 August 1744, in Cardiff, he wrote, 'Enlarged in the Castle on our Lord's lamentation over Jerusalem, and many wept, because they knew the time of *their* visitation. In the Society I was borne as on eagle's wings. All were partakers of my faith and joy' (MJCW, pp. 417–8).

Charles was not only a passionate preacher; he was also very much aware of his power over people. His journal of 18 March 1740 tells how he was able to calm hostile rioters:

> Preached at the usual place from Isaiah 11[:6], 'The wolf also shall dwell with the lamb', etc. Set my eyes on the man that had been violent with me on Sunday, and testified my love. He thanked me, and seemed melted.
> (MJCW, pp. 224–5)

Although at first he was even more reluctant than John to preach in the open air, his preaching formed an important and effective part of his ministry. He did not match John's extraordinary levels of activity, but he nevertheless preached energetically and frequently throughout most of his life.

We have seen that before his 'conversion' he suffered significant bouts of depression, with guilt, and wished that he could die. He would become physically ill under stress, as he did in Georgia. When he did not deal with disturbing feelings consciously, they would manifest themselves physically. One of his friends, Dr Whitehead, who was also one of his medical advisors, wrote an account of his death, and he described him as having had 'a weak body, and a poor state of health, during the greater part of his life' (Tyson, 1989, p. 480). There were frequent episodes of illness, and his journal describes his having suffered from 'fevers', or the 'flux', or 'pleurisy', and a variety of symptoms such as headaches, weakness and pains on many occasions. It is possible to relate some of the episodes of illness to times when he was under emotional pressure, such as his time in Georgia and the period of spiritual turmoil prior to his conversion, but there is not always a clear association. The episodes themselves were often severe enough to provoke his doctors to drastic treatments, which could only have exacerbated his weakness. His journal of 6 August 1740 describes the beginning of a fever, which lasted almost two weeks; throughout this time his doctor attended 'constantly' and 'bled' him. There was little hope that he would survive, but he began to recover when Jesus 'touched [his] hand and rebuked the fever'. It took him a further two weeks to return slowly to normal, but he 'had little use of [his] legs and none of [his] head'; there were rumours that he had died. He saw such 'visitations' of illness as God's way of chastising him, and wrote that, after this episode, he was 'more desirous and able to pray, more afraid of sin, more earnestly longing for deliverance, and the fullness of Christian salvation' (MJCW, pp. 276–7). At these times of illness and weakness, although he believed the 'chastisement' was for his own good, God nevertheless had resumed his fearful aspects, and Charles had to struggle to hang on to his sense of a loving, forgiving God.

He was not immune from using the more primitive mechanisms which would have been prevalent at the time and which John and Susanna Wesley also used to deal with adversity. God's providence and ultimate beneficence were invoked to explain painful events; illness and suffering were seen as chastening. Persecution was seen in terms of a struggle against Satan, and badness was seen as residing in those who disagreed or who were 'messengers of Satan'. Like John, at times he used identification with a biblical character as evidence that he was on the side of right and randomly opened of the Bible to find texts to confirm religious experience or the rightness of decisions.

As he grew older, he appears to have developed an accepting, even affectionate relationship with his frail and unpredictable body. In a letter to his wife he describes a journey on horseback:

> I crept on singing or making hymns, till I got unawares to Canterbury. . . . Tomorrow I go to Margate, and should willingly bestow a fortnight there on my crazy carcass; but I must officiate at Spittlefields on Sunday next.
> (Jackson, II, letter xvi, p. 214)

Ten years before his death, he wrote, 'I creep along the streets, tottering over the grave. My strength seems to abate daily, perhaps through my long walk' (Jackson, II, letter xciii, p. 270).

Charles Wesley – poet

Kristeva has privileged art and poetry over religion in their capacity to promote a dialogue between the semiotic and the symbolic, and to symbolise unconscious phantasies, which she regards as vital to mental flexibility and growth. Although she has written extensively about the ways in which religious imagery can be used to promote mental stability, she sees most religion as not adequately symbolising the semiotic and as having 'forgotten that it rumbled along over emptiness before lovingly springing toward the solar source of representation' (Kristeva, 1983, p. 42). If this were true, religion would be unable to facilitate change at a deep level. It is interesting to look at Charles Wesley's expression of his religious beliefs in his verse, from the point of view of estimating whether his imagery 'forgets' or engages with the 'emptiness'.

Psychoanalytic theory suggests that an artist is someone who can access phantasies and urges in the unconscious and express them in a symbolised form: Meltzer has written that a creative genius is one who 'permits his own internal objects to give him new ideas – even if he does not understand them or cannot use them: his function is to receive them, and he possesses the art of transmitting them' (Meltzer, 2005, p. 175). Klein and Segal saw creative activity mostly as an attempt to deal with guilt and anxiety associated with early destructive phantasies towards the love objects and aimed at restoring them, while others saw it a seeking for forms which evoked missing aspects of the early mother/child relationship. Art in this second case represents a restoration of the self rather than of the object (Wright, 2009, p. 60). Fairbairn saw the success or failure of art as linked to its capacity to 'represent restitution' both for the artist and the observer or reader. That is, it must offer in a disguised form, an 'atonement' with the superego for destructive wishes and impulses. If there is too much disguise, the artwork is too remote from the destructive impulses it attempts to symbolise to perform its healing function (there is 'over-symbolisation'). On the other hand, if there is too little disguise ('under-symbolisation'), the sense of destruction is too powerful to tolerate (Clarke, 2006, pp. 94–160); this distinction between over- and under-symbolisation is important in looking at John Wesley's response to some of his brother's hymns.

It has been said that in the absence of religious 'rites', Kristeva turns to the 'w-rite-r' who 'becomes the high-priest who undertakes the impossible task of writing the unnameable' (Taylor, 1987, pp. 178–9). Many critics have acknowledged Charles's importance as a writer of sacred poetry. Donald Davie wrote that 'Charles Wesley sounds notes that are outside the range, or outside the intentions, of any other sacred poet in English', though he had reservations about the poetic quality of some the hymns (Davie, 1993, p. 69). He and others have pointed to many aspects in both the form and content of the hymns, which I would suggest, can be seen as promoting a permeability between the semiotic and symbolic and so tending to allow a 'writing of the unnameable'. For instance, Davie described Charles Wesley as a 'poet of vehement feeling', but he also interestingly noted that often the powerful effect of the hymns is achieved by their insistence on 'strong and muscular thought', so that it is not the feelings but the intellectual capacities which are stretched to the limit. In some of the concepts expressed, it is the 'energies of human Reason' which are pushed as far as they can go towards understanding what is beyond words – 'the unperceivable and illogical'. He stressed that this intellectual emphasis and strength 'does not dessicate the emotions but strengthens them' (Davie, 1993, pp. 57–8, 76–9). Davie's description of Wesley's writing as 'pushing reason as far as it can go' to express what is inconceivable and beyond words is reminiscent of the use of language of mediaeval mystic theologians towards God, what Turner described as 'this characteristic apophatic self-subverting utterance'. At this point, words have reached their limit, and such an 'utterance' is disturbing, leading to silence, uncertainty and a state of not knowing. Wesley's verse abounds in examples of paradox, oxymoron and irony, all of which demand vigorous response and arduous thought. This pushing of language to the limit also brings a sense of aliveness and the possibility of change.

In examining Charles Wesley's eucharistic hymns, Frost shows how his theology grows out of his poetic inspiration, from his 'muse', which he, of course, believed was the Holy Spirit. It is expressed through poetic imagery (word music comprising the sounds of words, word pictures, paradox, metaphor, and simile), which brings alive its mystery and allows complex understandings to emerge. He draws attention to Wesley's ability to concentrate and condense images into single phrases or words, using ambiguous meanings or juxtaposing contrasting or paradoxical concepts to expand spiritual insights, for instance the bringing together of the transcendent and the quotidian, and the abstract and the material. There is an intertwining of thought and an openness to the unknown; in other words the 'symbolic' and the 'semiotic', the 'cataphatic' and the 'apophatic', which would resonate at a deep level with the singers' experience. He contrasts Charles's theologising with John's more logical approach (Frost, 1995).

Similarly, Kimbrough comments that Wesley brings his poetic imagination to bear on Holy Scripture and theology and sets them in a 'symphonic language of numerous keys'. Wesley does attempt to clarify theological ideas in his hymns, but also, through his imagination and the use of symbol, metaphor, similes and other linguistic devices, he can powerfully convey 'not only the meaning but the mood of the text'. Kimbrough points out that Wesley is 'changed, redirected, healed or utterly devastated by what he reads in Scripture', and, through his poetic art, he creates not only a 'metamorphosis of the text' but also the possibility of change in the poet and the hymn singer (Kimbrough Jr., 1992, pp. 113–21).

Wesley's hymns are full of allusions to the Bible and overflow with biblical metaphors, but they also draw on Greek and Latin texts and on English poets such as Milton and Herbert. They therefore stir the memory and resonate on many levels. As Davie pointed out, Wesley makes frequent 'inconspicuous reference to ... a hallowed canon, classical or scriptural'. Giving what he described as a 'crude example', he demonstrates how the use of scriptural reference opens up the singer to the semiotic:

> Expand Thy Wings, Prolific Dove,
> Brood o'er our Nature's Night,

> On our disorder'd Spirits move,
> And let there now be Light.
>> (*Hymns and Sacred Poems*, 1740, 'Come, Holy Ghost,
>> our Hearts inspire', Davie, 1967, pp. 70–81)

The Holy Ghost is portrayed in terms of the Creative Spirit in Genesis, 'brooding' (*Paradise Lost* I.21) so that the urbane, understated word *disordered* corresponds with Milton's 'vast abyss' (Davie, 1967, pp. 74–6). This highlights the indescribable extent of the chaos in the depths of the psyche. Davie also draws attention to Wesley's capacity to express ideas with 'poignant simplicity', with a sudden change from complicated, elaborate language to simple words so that the plain statement appears vigorous and direct and arrests the reader. The instance he gives is of Wesley ending a verse of a hymn about Christ's forgiving love: 'this Man receiveth sinners still'. Wesley's enlivening of dead words and metaphors forces the reader to 're-define meanings' through his use of 'contrast, antithesis, [and] juxtaposition' (Davie, 1967, pp. 72–3). It is reminiscent of Kristeva's 'resensitising of language'. In discussing Celine's writing, she describes his 'tamper[ing] with vocabulary and syntax' in a way that induces an emotional response and engages with the semiotic (Kristeva, 1980, p. 137).

Wesley was a poet of strong emotion, and the semiotic is evoked in his poetry, not only by 'tampering with vocabulary and syntax' but also by the use of language evocative of the body and of blissful or painful feeling. A reading of Wesley's hymns suggests that far from his symbolism 'forgetting that it rumbles over emptiness', there is material which can be interpreted as symbolising archaic dynamics and phantasies. It demonstrates that Wesley's religion, as expressed in his hymns, by no means glosses over its bodily and affective roots.

Very early experiences such as those described by Kristeva as the dynamics of love in the 'archaic triad' are in later life evoked by sounds and rhythms and by bodily images: oral images of tasting, feeding, satiety and devouring; images of blissful union, killing, woundedness, brokenness, messiness and of bodily fluids; and images of touching and bodily contact. There is an abundance of such images in Wesley's hymns. The hymns relating to the believer's identification with Christ in his suffering are full of them, and some of the Eucharistic hymns have extreme imagery. Wesley was not fearful of primitive bodily images; the following hymn includes images of the communicant drinking in something good, purple blood, and of identifying with Christ as he is welcomed and strengthened by the loving God:

> Now, e'en now, we all plunge in
> And drink the purple Wave,
> This the Antidote of Sin,
> 'Tis This our Souls shall save:
>> (*Hymns on the Lord's Supper*, 1745, Hymn xxvii,
>> 'Rock of Israel, cleft for me')

There is a verse full of murderousness:

> O what a killing Thought is This,
> A Sword to pierce the faithful Heart!
> Our Sins have slain the Prince of Peace;
> Our Sins, which caus'd his mortal Smart,
> With Him we vow to crucify;
> Our Sins which murder'd GOD shall die!
>
> (*Hymns on the Lord's Supper*, 1745, Hymn cxxxiii,
> 'O Thou, who hast our Sorrows took')

The vivid imagery of blood and wounds in some hymns recalls Merleau-Ponty's description of the body as a 'gaping wound'. For instance,

> Father see the Victim slain,
> Jesus Christ, the Just, the Good
> Offer'd up for guilty Man,
> Pouring out his precious Blood,
> Him, and then the Sinner see,
> Look thro' Jesu's Wounds on Me.
>
> (*Hymns on the Lord's Supper*, 1745, Hymn cxx,
> 'Father see the Victim slain')

It stresses the bodiliness, or 'carnality' of human existence, and the 'holey-ness or gappiness' of the human body (Taylor, 1987, p. 69). The experiences of the 'archaic triad' are evoked by the emphasis on an identification with Christ's suffering and, through God's *agape*, a sharing in his Resurrection and the receiving of a name. These images evoke the suffering of the separated child, who through the identification with the 'imaginary father' is supported in its introduction to the realm of the symbolic.

Wesley frequently uses of the word *heart* in his hymns. Watson relates this to Christ's use of it: 'Thou shalt love the Lord thy God with all thy heart, and with all thy soul, and with all thy mind, and with all thy strength' (Mark 12:30). He points out that 'Heart', comes first in Christ's list and that in many of Wesley's hymns it is shorthand for the whole self. There are many examples in Wesley's hymns in which he despairs over the state of his heart: 'Loathsome and foul and self-abhorr'd, / I sink beneath my sin', what Yeats calls the 'Foul rag and bone shop of the heart', which suggests images of waste, mess, unwanted and rejected objects: 'the untidy accumulation of loves, hatred, the anger and remorse of life'. According to Watson, Wesley goes beyond the expected self-examination of Puritanism and, through his use of Christian symbols and images and his language of tasting and feeling, he is able to show the way he 'experiences' what is foul about himself. Wesley does not avoid what is hardly bearable: 'Fain would I know as known by Thee / And feel the Indigence I see' (*Hymns and Sacred Poems*, 1739:

'Father of Lights, from whom proceeds', titled 'A Prayer under Convictions'). Of course, he also seeks to 'feel' and taste God's forgiveness: 'Should know, should feel, my Sin forgiven, / Blest with this Antepast of heaven!' (Watson, 2014, pp. 396–400).

We have seen that, in some forms of Christianity, according to Kristeva, the 'abject', as sin, is 'displaced' and 'absorbed into speech'; and because 'I repent of my sins' becomes the 'very site of spiritualisation', the abject is not adequately 'elaborated'. Because it is not adequately symbolised, the subject is left with the unsymbolised 'abject', a 'fearsome ineradicable evil', an 'inexorable carnal remainder'. I would suggest that through his use of carnal imagery of brokenness, woundedness, sickness and suffering and through his ability to put into words, for himself and for the singers of his hymns, the way in which he experiences (tastes and feels) his dark, 'foul' side, his 'filthy', 'inbred' sin, Charles symbolises and 'elaborates', rather than 'overreaches' Kristeva's 'abject'. In this way, the hymns symbolise what Tillich was describing, when he wrote of God's participation in the ambiguity of the human situation. Through the death of Christ, 'Divine removal of our guilt and punishment is not accomplished by overlooking their depth but by entering into them in love so deeply as to transform us' (Kelsey, 1997, pp. 93–4).

T. B. Shepherd notes that Charles's poetry shows 'the longings, the prayers, the backslidings, the repentance, the sense of sin, the raptures, the ecstasies, and the peace and joy of the believer' but also that 'he brought into English verse the note of *rapture* perhaps more than any other poet'. Less averse to 'mysticism' than John, Charles frequently used metaphors which express ideas of vast spaciousness to convey the idea of salvation for all – boundless, fathomless, overflowing oceans of water, and fire, rising higher and higher, 'giving light to the feast with joy ineffable, bliss-transporting, triumphs and dazzling raptures' (Shepherd, 1940, pp. 106–16). The third verse of the hymn 'Come Holy Ghost, all-quick'ning fire' is an example:

> Eager for Thee I ask and pant,
> So strong the Principle Divine
> Carries me out with sweet Constraint
> Till all my hallow'd Soul be Thine
> Plung'd in the Godhead's deepest Sea
> And lost in Thy Immensity.
>
> (*Hymns and Sacred Poems*, 1739, Part II, 'Hymn to the Holy Ghost', p. 184)

In this hymn Wesley uses Shakespeare's 'love's sweet constraint' (from *All's Well that Ends Well*), as a benevolent force, and the image of a swimmer being swept away by the tide, before being 'plunged' in the 'deepest sea' and 'lost' in 'the fathomless sea of God's infinite love'. As Watson suggests, the singer is encouraged to feel and experience God's love as strong and irresistible and, as like water, touching him everywhere: 'drowning the singer in its immensity' (Watson, 1997, p. 15). This merging with a loving presence is reminiscent of the idealised merging with Kristeva's 'imaginary father', very different from the oppressive 'evangelical' parent.

In the last chapter, mention was made of John Wesley's dislike of the sexual imagery used in a religious context by the Moravians. In his journal (6 September 1742), he referred to reports from some of his congregation, who told of their sensations of Christ's blood being poured over them, 'down their throat' or 'like warm water upon their breast and heart', and of its bringing peace and joy. He wrote that he could not deny that some of these experiences might be from God, but mainly he attributed them to the 'mere empty dreams of an heated imagination' (BEJ, 19, p. 296). He had also preached a sermon that year against the Moravian overemphasis on blood and wounds (Podmore, 1998, p. 76). There is evidence that he had longings to let go of his controlling ego and experience a primitive merging, in that he published and sang those hymns of Charles's which expressed these longings but that he struggled with anything too visceral. While he translated German hymns and adapted poems 'of fervour and inward piety', which included the language of love and images of boundless heights and abysses, he disliked sentimentality and wanted to avoid what he described as 'every fondling expression' (Watson, 1997, pp. 206–14). In Fairbairn's terms, so far as John was concerned, the unconscious phantasies were under-symbolised, and he was confronted too directly with his primitive feelings. For similar reasons, when John edited Charles's hymns he omitted anything he considered 'namby-pambical' such as *dear*, or *lover*, when addressing the Deity. As Davie (1993, pp. 60–1) suggested, John appeared to be fearful of the 'physicality' of 'baby-talk' and of 'mawkishness'. For instance, he suggested leaving out verses which portrayed the infant Jesus as a messy, helpless baby. So it is likely, according to Davie, that he would have had difficulty with the idea of 'the God Incarnate sucking at a human nipple':

> Our GOD ever blest
> With Oxen doth rest,
> Is nurst by his Creature and hangs at the Breast'
>
> (*Hymns for the Nativity of our Lord*, 1745, Hymn xvi, 'O Mercy Divine')

A few of Charles Wesley's hymns are maudlin, sentimental or gruesome, but in most of them, he is able to make extensive use of 'carnal' language and imagery of merging and union while retaining a sense of balance. Manning writes of one of his most 'mystical' hymns that 'nothing short of inspiration keeps the daring emotion sane and reverent and orthodox' (Manning, 1942, p. 29). The hymn, which includes the lines 'A Child of Man, / In Length a Span, / Who fills both Earth and Heaven' and 'Those Infant-Hands shall burst our Bands and work out our salvation' (*Hymns for the Nativity of our Lord*, 1745, Hymn vi, 'Join all ye joyful Nations') is one of the hymns John Wesley thought 'namby-pambical'. He felt some verses should be omitted (Baker, 1962, p. 59).

Davie believed that in such hymns, Charles is saved from 'mawkishness' by his use of paradox. He also suggested that by using what others have described as 'vulgar' language and being literal-minded; for instance about messy, suckling babies, he could draw out the real implications of the Incarnation. He felt that to avoid such realities would, in fact, have been more coy or mawkish (Davie, 1993, p. 62). While the use of paradox, as well as other rhetorical devices, avoids mawkishness, the structure of the poem itself offers a framework to contain the bodily images and the images of merging. In Kristevan terms, by these means the better hymns achieve a balance between the semiotic and the symbolic.

Psychoanalytic aspects

John Wesley had a difficult struggle to stay in touch with a good, forgiving image of God by 'practising the presence', and had frequent need to resort to obsessional defences. Charles, who had had more access to potentially good objects in his early life, and who may well have experienced his mother as more emotionally available to him, appears to have had less of a struggle to remain in touch with his good objects, though for him, too, it was sometimes difficult. It is clear from his Journal that after the conversion, he had a capacity to tolerate ambivalence in himself and others. He was more in touch with his feelings than John was, and could feel both joy and sadness. From the examination of his relationships, it is clear that he had a greater capacity for concern and empathy for those close to him than John did.

There is not enough information about how Charles related to his siblings and friends prior to his conversion to make a useful comparison with his later relationships, nor is there enough information to deduce whether his capacity for feeling changed. If he related to other people in the same way both before and after the conversion, this would suggest that he had always been less dominated by his bad internal objects than John was. If there was a change on conversion, this, too, would tend to indicate that he had not been so much in their grip as to prevent change. There are several pointers which suggest that some change did occur: it has been demonstrated that subsequently his episodes of depression had a different quality; although there were times when he doubted his love for God, and times when God resumed his frightening aspect, there was a continuing assurance that God loved him and that he could be forgiven; and he was less burdened with guilt. After all, the devils at his head and feet in his post-conversion dream, did fade and sink and vanish away.

Charles Wesley is best known for the hymns he wrote after 1738, when his productivity increased exponentially, and it is tempting to conclude that his conversion increased his creativity. However, there is evidence that as a young man at Oxford, he translated Virgil and knew the works by heart, and Baker speculated that he 'versified purple passages from the major classical poets', as he did from the scriptures later. None of this material survives but that he did 'versify' is clear from John Wesley's account. He described Charles's bursting into his Oxford room, 'full of the muse', in a 'fine frenzy', disturbing all John's tidy arrangements, reciting some poetry and then leaving (Baker, 1962, p. xii). He was writing poetry before his conversion, and Beckerlegge concludes that, had he not had that experience, 'no doubt [he] would have written masses of facile verse, numbering him among the best of the minor poets in English literature', but he became a 'sacred poet *par excellence*' (Beckerlegge, 1992, p. 32).

Nobody can say what he would have become, but there does appear to have been a striking change, and his writing 'Where shall my wond'ring Soul begin?' in the days after the conversion suggests a recognition of a new state of affairs in his inner world. Beckerlegge attributes this to 'deep religious emotion', but it can also be described in terms of an increase in creativity, resulting from an integration of internal objects, with an increase in inner stability and ego strength. As discussed, several authors have written of the need for a degree of integration of internal objects and of aspects of the self in order for an individual to be creative, both in the sense of being open and flexible in responding to new experiences and ideas and as applying to artistic creativity. An internal combined object in which paternal and maternal elements, (not necessarily aligned with the external parental figures), and loving and hating aspects of relationships are integrated, is developed and becomes a resource or Muse, on which an artist can rely.

The foregrounding of a God of *unconditional* and *forgiving* love, which John and Charles Wesley found in reading Luther, would have evoked the maternal, agapeic aspect of God, which contrasted with the prohibiting critical God of the Law. From the increase in his creativity, it seems likely that Charles did achieve some integration of these aspects of the Deity and of conflicting aspects of himself. As a result, in a deeper way than before, Christ could now represent for him a judge *and* an advocate – a common theme in his hymns, where he was again following Milton (*Paradise Lost*, X, 36, 58–62, pp. 77–9). Meltzer writes of the integration of the maternal and paternal elements into the 'combined object', as described by Klein. She saw the combined object 'as a "powerful" object in its emotional evocativeness, but she also saw in it a quality not visible in the external parents – namely its mystery and creativity, its essential privacy and perhaps sacredness' (Meltzer, 2005, pp. xv–xvi).

The fact of Charles's increased creativity does support the supposition that his conversion facilitated a process of integration. As a result of the integration of his good and bad objects, there would have been an increase in ego strength so that he felt safer to access unconscious phantasies. Nobody ever achieves a full integration of their internal objects, and there is evidence that Charles continued to struggle with unsymbolised and unintegrated parts of himself: he continued to become sick when he was under physical or mental pressure; he often had to resort to working harder to fend off his persisting bouts of depression, when God felt like a harsh, demanding parent; and he never had complete control of his temper. Although his hymn writing was likely to have been one positive benefit of his integrating experience, and although it would also have offered a continuing opportunity for further integration for himself and others, there was a residual compulsiveness about it, which reflected an ongoing struggle.

Charles was able to use Christian symbolism to achieve some integration. He was able to enjoy mutually satisfying relations with others, and his creativity was encouraged and freed. In Kristevan terms, the imagery and form of his hymns demonstrate his capacity to symbolise unconscious phantasy and to hold a tension between conflicting feelings and between the symbolic and the semiotic. This is not to suggest that such creativity is necessary for this kind of integration to occur in an individual, but it is fortunate that, in Charles's case, his hymns provide some evidence of the process. The process occurring in others would be through a similar response to Christian symbolism, possibly facilitated by hymns such as those of Charles Wesley, which would be manifested in other subjective or objective changes.

Notes

1 Newport points out (2001, p. 71) that most were written by Charles Wesley but that some were produced by editing and copying John's material. Early in his career, as was not an uncommon practice at the time, when preaching, he would sometimes read John's sermons.
2 Tyson has transcribed hitherto unpublished material, including shorthand sections (in italics), from a fragment of manuscript found separate from the main journal manuscript and combined it with published material. This fragment is mentioned by Kimbrough and Newport but not included in their published manuscript journal.

References

Baker, F., 1962. *Representative Verse of Charles Wesley*. London: Epworth Press.
Baker, F., 1995. *Charles Wesley as Revealed by His Letters*. London: Epworth Press.
Beckerlegge, O., 1992. Charles Wesley's Poetical Corpus. In ed. S. T. Kimbrough, Jr., *Charles Wesley: Poet and Theologian*. Nashville: Kingswood Books.
Best, G., 2006. *Charles Wesley: A Biography*. Peterborough: Epworth Press.
Britton, R., 1998. *Belief and Imagination*. London/New York: Routledge.
Clarke, A., 1823. *Memoirs of the Wesley Family*. London: Printed by J. and T. Clarke.
Clarke, G., 2006. *Personal Relations Theory: Fairbairn, McMurray and Suttie*. Hove: Routledge.
Davie, D., 1967. *Purity of Diction in English Verse*. London: Routledge & Kegan Paul.
Davie, D., 1993. *The Eighteenth-Century Hymn in England*. Cambridge: Cambridge University Press.
Edwards, M., 1961. *Sons to Samuel*. London: Epworth Press.
Frost, F., 1995. The Eucharistic Hymns of Charles Wesley: The Self-Emptying of Glory of God. *Proceedings of the Charles Wesley Society*, 2, pp. 87–92.
Gill, F., 1964. *Charles Wesley the First Methodist*. London: Epworth Press.
Heitzenrater, R., 1992. Charles Wesley and the Methodist Tradition. In ed. S. T. Kimbrough, Jr., *Charles Wesley: Poet and Theologian*. Nashville: Kingswood Books.
Jackson, T., ed., 1849. *The Journal of the Rev. Charles Wesley, M.A., Sometime Student of Christ-Church Oxford*, vols. I and II. London: Wesleyan Methodist Book Room.
Kelsey, D., 1997. Paul Tillich. In ed. D. Ford, *The Modern Theologians*. Oxford: Blackwell.

Kimbrough Jr., S. T., 1992. Charles Wesley and Biblical Interpretation. In ed. S. T. Kimbrough Jr., *Charles Wesley: Poet and Theologian*. Nashville: Kingswood Books.

Kristeva, J., 1980. *Powers of Horror*. Translated by L. Roudiez. New York: Columbia University Press, 1982.

Kristeva, J., 1983. *Tales of Love*. Translated by L. Roudiez. New York: Columbia University Press, 1987.

Lloyd, G., 2007. *Charles Wesley and the Struggle for Methodist Identity*. Oxford: Oxford University Press.

Manning, B., 1942. *The Hymns of Wesley and Watts*. London: Epworth Press.

Meltzer, D., 2005. Creativity and the Countertransference. In ed. M. Williams, *The Vale of Soul-Making*. London/New York: Karnac.

Newport, K., ed., 2001. *The Sermons of Charles Wesley*. Oxford: Oxford University Press.

Newton, J., 2007. John and Charles Wesley: Brothers in Arms. In eds. K. Newport and T. Campbell, *Charles Wesley: Life, Literature and Legacy*. Peterborough: Epworth Press.

Podmore, C., 1998. *The Moravian Church in England, 1728–1760*. Oxford: Clarendon Press.

Rack, H., 2002. *Reasonable Enthusiast*, 3rd ed. London: Epworth Press.

Shepherd, T.B., 1940. *Methodism and the Literature of the Eighteenth Century*. London: Epworth Press.

Silverstone, J., 2006. Siblings. In ed. Prophecy Coles, *Sibling Relationships*. London: Karnac.

Taylor, M., 1987. *Altarity*. Chicago/London: University of Chicago Press.

Tyson, J., ed., 1989. *Charles Wesley: A Reader*. Oxford: Oxford University Press.

Watson, J., 1997. *The English Hymn: A Critical and Historical Study*. Oxford: Clarendon Press.

Watson, J., 2014. Sacred Poetry: Watts and Wesley. In ed. S. Prickett, *The Edinburgh Companion to the Bible and the Arts*. Edinburgh: Edinburgh University Press.

Watson, R., 1831. *The Life of the Rev. John Wesley A.M.* London: Wesleyan Conference Office.

Wesley, C., 1784a. MS Ordinations, No. [I] and [5]. In ed. F. Baker, *Representative Verse of Charles Wesley*. London: Epworth Press, 1962.

Wesley, C., 1784b. MS Brothers, No. 9. In ed. F. Baker, *Representative Verse of Charles Wesley*. London: Epworth Press, 1962.

Wesley, C., 1785. MS letter. In ed. J. Tyson, *Charles Wesley: A Reader*. Oxford: Oxford University Press.

Wesley, S., 1816. A Remembrance of Charles Wesley by Sarah Wesley. In C. Wesley, *Sermons of the Late Charles Wesley*. London: Baldwin, Craddock and Joy.

Wright, K., 2009. *Mirroring and Attunement*. Hove: Routledge.

Chapter 9

Theological differences

A theological clash?

It is sometimes maintained that what John Wesley said in prose was said more effectively and elegantly by Charles Wesley in poetry. This implies that they were in total agreement theologically. Their names appear together on the title pages of *Hymns and Sacred Poems*, 1739, 1740, 1742, and *Hymns on the Lord's Supper*, 1745, suggesting a close similarity of belief. The preface of the last-named book was extracted by John from Daniel Brevint's *On the Christian Sacrament and Sacrifice*, 1673, and Rattenbury (1948, pp. 12–13) uses this as evidence that they were in complete agreement about the doctrines involved. He attributes most, if not all, of the hymns to Charles and writes that 'Charles Wesley gives Brevint wings, and adds very significantly the confirmation of Methodist experience to Brevint's doctrine'. He can find no 'theological clash whatever' between Brevint's prose and Wesley's verse. But Rattenbury's eloquent rhetoric conceals differences in belief and emphasis, as well as in their emotional responses to Christian symbolism and practice.

Meissner called for research aimed at understanding the level of interaction between the developmental needs of the individual and the influence of a particular modality in a religious tradition.[1] Is an individual attracted, gratified, repelled or dismayed by particular aspects of religious symbolism and practice according to his psychological structure and developmental needs? In this chapter, I examine the different responses of John and Charles Wesley to five modalities: their conversion experiences, 'mysticism', Christian perfection, the meaning of suffering and the Trinity.

Conversion experiences

The effect of the 'evangelical nurture' to which John and Charles Wesley were subjected has repeatedly been referred to, and it has become clear that they both struggled with fears of inner destructiveness prior to their conversion experiences. At Oxford, each used ascetic practices to try to gain inner and outer purity. Charles's starving and vomiting, referred to in Susanna Wesley's letter of 25 October 1732, suggest that he was considerably disturbed during that time. Haartman (2004, pp. 72–3) describes oral sadism (greed, envy, voraciousness and destruction) as the 'diabolical hallmarks of carnality' and the 'repressed underside of evangelical nurture'. Starving and vomiting act out opposite impulses and could have been experienced as an act of atonement, a denial of the child's wilfulness. Just as John saw fasting as a way of averting the wrath of God (BES, I, p. 601, Sermon 27), so too did Charles, who also resorted to these means, probably as a way of dealing with similar underlying feelings. We have already seen that he had difficulty in managing his anger.

They both found themselves in a state of turmoil prior to their conversion experiences, having failed to find a sense of acceptance by God through their own efforts. They were aware of their failures and 'sinfulness', but, as we have seen, Charles was more able than John to relate the concept of sinfulness to his own capacity to hurt others. In Haartman's terms, they were in a state of desolation, in a position which re-created their childhood experience: a hell of separation from the parent/God through their own sin, wilful children from whom the parent/God is withholding love, as at the Fall. Each of them was in the grip of his critical superego and ripe for Böhler's intervention. The split parental image, resulting from excessive demands and a lack of containment, was projected into their image of God, a punitive, wrathful image which often obscured any loving aspects (Haartman, 2004, pp. 27–9).

Like John, Charles believed that change was not possible unless the believer became aware of his sinfulness. They had both preached 'the Law', in order to induce the 'necessary' state of 'induced mourning' in their listeners. As Charles wrote in his journal of 4 June 1740: 'The promises to the unawaked are pearls before swine. First the hammer must break the rocks, then we *may* preach Christ crucified' (MJCW, p. 264). Before 1738, each of them was in a mental state which resembled that induced by their preaching, and it was at that point that Böhler offered a God of love, an opportunity to cease striving and to identify with an ideal, loving, forgiving object. In the presence of such an object, the believer may feel safe enough to examine the extent of her own badness and to repent. In this place of safety there is an opportunity for the conscious acknowledgment of primitive rage; it can be faced in a context in which repentance is met with acceptance and forgiveness. As discussed previously, according to Klein, in infancy the 'badness' of the bad internal object is compounded by projection into it of the child's own 'badness'. The withdrawal of these projections becomes possible as unconscious anger becomes conscious and is owned. This allows more contact with the loving aspects of the superego figures, those aspects which inspire and encourage. In this way, the foregrounding of a loving God can be seen as offering an opportunity for an integration of the split images of God and for an integration of good and bad internal objects.

The degree of difficulty that an individual has in achieving this integration depends on the degree to which the inner world is dominated by bad objects. The greater the sway of these objects, the more difficulty there is in holding on to a forgiving image of God and developing a self-soothing internal structure. However, if this kind of integration does occur in the 'conversion' experience and in subsequent struggles with disappointments, it can be seen as facilitating a shift towards Klein's 'depressive' functioning. In Kristevan terms, the offering of a God of love as a symbol of the 'imaginary father' also evokes the dynamics of the archaic triangle. As Crownfield (1992, pp. 59–60) describes it, there is the creation of a triadic space in which the subject is affirmed and validated by the 'mythic Third Party', a space which is 'open to love, to another, to others and relationships, and the possibility of love of neighbour and even of enemy'.

John's experience has often been described as a prime example of instantaneous transformation. However, he was unable to experience the joy he had anticipated, and many doubts remained. What is usually remembered is that he described his heart as 'strangely warmed' and felt an assurance that 'He had taken away my sins, even *mine, and* saved *me* from the law of sin and death' (BEJ 18, pp. 249–50). John's struggle with 'deadness' and 'coldness' is relevant here. The words he heard from Luther's Preface to the Romans were important:

> Faith is a divine work in us, which changes us and makes us newly born of God, and kills the old Adam, makes us completely different men in heart, disposition, mind and every power, and brings the Holy Spirit with it. O faith is a lively, creative, active, powerful thing, so that it is impossible that it should not continually do good works. It does not even ask if good works are to be done, but before anyone asks it has done them and is always acting.
> (Schmidt, 1953–66, I, p. 263)

'Power' is referred to twice here, and there is an offer of liveliness, of spontaneity and of a new start. It is an offer of becoming alive, of being made powerful and being relieved of the unbearable burden of sin. To John, it must have felt as if the words were meant specially for him; they defined exactly what he needed; they spoke to his dead, powerless, 'uncorrected heart' and offered a reworking of his early experience.

This sense of being addressed and recognised at a deep level would, indeed, have been a 'new' experience. At the same time, he was in a situation where his brother had had a 'conversion' experience three days previously, and he was surrounded by people who were waiting for it to happen to him. This new feeling was identified as the expected change, but he quickly questioned it. He was worried because he felt no joy. He had been moved because his deep needs had been addressed so accurately, but the feeling of assurance did not last. His fears about his unconscious hate and anger were so strong that they had to remain separated off, and he could not sustain, for more than a brief period, a belief that he was acceptable to God. His doubts remained, the central deadness continued, and he had to preach constantly to reassure himself, through his own words and others' experience, that such a wiping away of 'corruptions and abominations' was possible. While he desperately wanted to believe in an entirely loving God/parent, the evidence suggests that he could not let go of his 'ancient' belief that his badness was the cause of parental wrath. A loving God would forgive others, whatever their crime, but not someone as destructive as he believed himself to be. In this respect, his experience was like that of his mother. While teaching justification and sanctification by faith, he could not believe it for himself. At times he grasped it briefly, but it repeatedly slipped away from him, and his emphasis on the need for good works continued throughout his life.

In 1935 Cell postulated that John Wesley had achieved an almost miraculous synthesis of the two great principles separated at the Reformation: the Catholic ethic of holiness and the Protestant ethic of grace (Cell, 1935, pp. 360–1); more recent scholars have argued over where to orientate John's theology and whether it might be seen as a bridge or synthesis between traditions (Maddox, 1990, pp. 29–30). It is not clear if he set out to achieve such an ecumenical synthesis, but the conjunction of these themes is at least in part a consequence of his own inner struggle. His difficulty in believing in the God of *agape* meant that although he desperately hoped that he could be saved instantly by faith, he could not allow the symbolism of salvation by faith to reach his dark side. He could not allow the image of the wounded Christ fully to evoke the true nature of his 'abject'. This was *labelled* 'corrupt and abominable', but then by the use of the various defences described, the extent of the destructiveness was not fully faced. He was left with an 'inexorable, carnal remainder' (Kristeva, 1980, p. 120), which had to be separated off, leaving him feeling cold and dead. After listening to Böhler and his witnesses, reading the Bible, praying in the hope of achieving justification and reading Luther's translation, he identified his emotional reaction as his 'conversion'. But he connected the symbolism only to the label and not to his own depths. He did not feel joy, nor did he experience a lasting assurance of acceptance. Although he became greatly loved by many and worked hard for the welfare of others, his adult relationships with those close to him showed little evidence of a capacity to show concern, except when he felt merged with an ideal object; his lack of empathy with his sisters in their troubles was striking. He also continued to struggle to tolerate ambivalence. These ongoing difficulties suggest that his 'conversion' experience did not result in increased integration of his internal objects. He could not sustain a triadic balance in the face of the dyadic alternatives; his fear of the abject encouraged a dyadic merger with the Law of the Father.

In this sense, John, who helped thousands to use the symbolism of the Atonement in a way which transformed their lives, could not help himself. He had to make do with the 'good old paths'. This is not to minimise the effects of his preaching and example, or to suggest that he did not believe what he preached. He was a 'wounded healer', who offered a sense of purpose, hope and forgiveness to thousands, and his very woundedness was one of the reasons he could reach his listeners in such a powerful way. He himself struggled on with great perseverance, as his mother had done, and, as Rack suggests, he grew to accept his lack of direct *experience* of acceptance with more tranquillity as he got older, accepting that this was how God had chosen to deal with him (Rack, 2002, p. 549).

Charles, on the other hand, although he too was not free from doubt or periods of depression after his 'conversion', did describe a clear change in the quality of the feelings of 'darkness' before and after the experience. We have seen that on 3 June 1738 he wrote that he believed that his guilt would be 'dispersed' and that whatever his temporary doubts, 'yet I did and would believe he loved me notwithstanding' (MJCW, pp. 114). He could believe in a God of love and forgiveness, and tolerate the presence of a 'third party' so that he gained a space offering 'triadic subjectivity'. This was reflected in his capacity to relate to others as whole people, to show concern and to be more creative; all evidence of 'depressive' functioning. He became more able to resist pressure to conform to John's wishes, but he still had alarming outbursts of temper. The change suggests that Charles's conversion facilitated integration, implying that the previous balance of good and bad internal objects in his inner world was more advantageous for him than it was for John.

Mysticism

In the 'mystical theology' of the fifteenth century and previously, the whole of religious practice was considered 'mystical', particularly the Eucharist. John Wesley used the term *mystical* in a more modern sense, to mean that which required a retirement from the world in order to develop 'inner holiness'. It concerned the 'experiencing self' in relation to God's presence or in union with God.

Both brothers were strongly influenced by William Law, and their reading included the writings of the mystics (Berger, 1992, pp. 207–8). Nevertheless, in the preface to *Hymns and Sacred Poems* John outlined his objections to the 'mystic divines'. His objections were aimed at those who emphasised 'the inner light' over the scriptures, the sacraments and service to others (particularly the Moravians, whom he called the 'still brethren'). The preface included his opinion that a cultivation of holiness of heart was a form of 'works righteousness' and that those he called 'holy solitaries' ('a Phrase no more consistent with the gospel than Holy Adulterers'), whom he thought 'self-absorbed', could never demonstrate that 'Faith working by love is the *length, breadth, depth and height of Christian perfection*' (1739, p. vii). Charles would have agreed with him. For him 'true stillness' involved activity:

> Hence I magnified the love of Christian ordinances, exhorting those who wait for salvation to be as clay in the hand of the potter, *by* stirring themselves up to lay hold on the Lord. God gave me much freedom to explain that most active, vigorous, restless thing: true stillness.
>
> (MJCW, p. 324)

Although both described *mystics* as the enemy of true religion, Charles's complaints were mainly aimed at the 'still brethren' and those Methodists who were tempted to join them. While he did not *advocate* a withdrawal from other people or from religious practices, he was less uncomfortable than John with these other aspects of 'mysticism'. Both were concerned about the tendency to discourage people from attending communion and were worried about the 'spectre of Antinomianism' (Green, 1945, pp. 180–4). But John had more ambivalence and deeper reservations about it. These are demonstrated in his extreme personal responses, as in the language of 'Holy Adulterers' and in his reaction to his old mentor, William Law.

John Wesley associated Law, whom he had met in 1732, with the mystics. Law had introduced him to *Theologica Germanica*, the principal collection of mediaeval mystic writing (Heitzenrater, 1995, p. 52). Some years later (15 May 1738), in a letter to Law, John set out his reservations. It was written just before his 'conversion' experience. In it he accused Law of failing to teach him about salvation by faith as the free gift of God and of failing to tell him that he 'had not faith'. He suggested that this failure was because Law himself lacked faith. This elicited a surprised and ironic response from Law, who insisted that in many conversations with John, he had never avoided the subject: 'you never was with me for half an hour without my being large upon that very doctrine which you make me totally silent and ignorant of' (BEL, 25, pp. 540–3).

The degree of anger in his letter suggests that John may have had some inkling that it was the deeper parts of himself that he needed to approach if he were to be healed. The same violence of his reaction appears again in another very long, detailed, open letter (39 printed pages) which he wrote almost twenty years later on 6 January 1756. It ends by his urging Law to 'renounce, despise, abhor all the high-flown bombast, all the unintelligible jargon of the Mystics, and come back to the plain religion of the Bible, "We love Him, because He first loved us"' (Telford, III, p. 370).

In Georgia John had read the biographies of Lopez and de Renty and, although fascinated by them, had reacted against them. The mystics offered an opportunity to explore deeper aspects of himself, but he had his sights set on Böhler's quicker solution, the idea of which was less disturbing for him. However, he remained ambivalent about mysticism. He saw it as the enemy of reason and distrusted it because of its appeal to the emotions, yet he translated German hymns which contained passionate images of love and union and published his brother Charles's hymns, albeit with some editing of the 'fondling' language. While attacking mysticism, he advocated piety and 'devotion of the heart', and his preaching often provoked powerful emotional reactions with conviction of 'assurance'. He did not dismiss these emotional reactions, but assessed them over the longer term by their 'fruits'. The fascination and attraction for him of the idea of merging with an all-loving (non-wrathful) God was evident in the hymns he translated or sanctioned and in his provoking 'blissful' states in others, which he could only observe. At the same time, his fear was evident in his attacks on Law, who was perceived as the embodiment of these notions. Such ambivalence suggests an important underlying conflict. It mirrors the ambivalence previously described in a sexual context: not only his fear, as well as his fascination, with the maternal *chora*, attractive as a source of merging and bliss, but also an abhorrence of the maternal abject, with a threat of loss of control, of structure, of meaning and, ultimately, for him, of a loss of self.

Unlike John (but like his mother), Charles believed that on occasions, God chose to withdraw from a believer, in order to make more vivid to him the extent and seriousness of sin. When he was 'in desertion', he could be reassured, for instance by Isaiah 54:7, 'For a small moment have I *forsaken thee*, but with great mercies will I gather thee' (MJCW, p. 199). For Charles these 'dark night of the soul' experiences came from God and were vital for self-knowledge. However, John attributed them to man's withdrawal from God (a re-creation of the early experience of the sinful child and withholding parent). In a letter (24 April 1777) to Ann Bolton, who felt she had been deserted by God, John reassured her that this was impossible and that her present state was more likely due to a disorder of her liver. For him, 'desertion' was an improper 'Papist' term (Telford, VI, p. 261). Charles could hold on to a sense of God's goodness towards him, even while feeling temporarily abandoned, but for John the idea of God's withdrawal was too painful. It is possible that John rejected the idea of God's withdrawal intellectually, as incompatible with a loving God, but it is also possible that it reflected his difficulty in holding on to his internalised good objects. Failure to establish an internal 'good-enough' mother, as seems likely to have been the case for John, interfered with the development of his capacity to be alone. As a result, an exaggerated fear of abandonment would have persisted, leading to a fear that God's withdrawal meant a permanent abandonment.

Charles's hymns show that he was more comfortable with 'mystical' aspects of his faith; they are passionate, with metaphors of 'boundlessness' and union. They concentrate on the experience of the presence of God, of closeness or union with Christ, of being filled up with Christ or lost in Christ, often expressed in terms of bliss or ecstasy. Tyson (1989, p. 7) notes that John was not convinced that Charles ever 'got the "poison" of mysticism out of his system'. He wrote that 'some of the later hymns savour a little of Mysticism, I have rather corrected or expunged them; but I have no thought at all of printing them' (Telford, VIII, p. 122).

Christian perfection

John Wesley's ideas about perfection were modified after his 1738 experience (though he claimed in his *Plain Account of Christian Perfection* (1767) that they had not changed since 1725). Rack describes how his experiences, in Aldersgate Street and subsequently, led him to change what was originally a 'simple notion of justification, new birth, assurance and sanctification, all achieved in a moment' to a belief in a more gradual process, through several stages and 'culminating in the gift of perfection'. He had become aware that many of those who claimed instantaneous perfection following 'conversion', including himself, continued to be tempted and to succumb. Justification then came to be seen as a 'door' to a process through which perfection could gradually be achieved, just before death.

The concept of 'perfection' itself became complicated. For John, as elucidated by Rack, perfection did not involve being perfect in the customary sense of the word; it meant loving God with one's whole heart, mind, soul and strength. 'Perfection' still allowed for the presence of 'infirmities and temptations'. There were two types of sin: one was conscious and therefore could be resisted, once 'domination over sin' had been acquired. This was 'a voluntary transgression of a known law which it is our power to obey'; the second type was a falling short of the perfect law of God. John believed that this second type of unconscious sin did not act as a barrier between the 'two-way flow of love' between Christ and the believer. Perfection which eliminated it could be achieved only *after* death. The first kind, 'voluntary transgression', was what he concentrated on in his writings about perfection (Rack, 2002, p. 399). For Charles, the concept of 'perfection' posed fewer problems. He saw it as attained more gradually but as the rooting out of all sin, including inbred or unconscious sin, and a restitution of the 'image of God'. It was achievable only on the threshold of death. John wrote to him on 9 July 1764, '"Where are the perfect ones?" I verily believe there are none upon earth, none dwelling in the body . . . at least I never met an instance of it; and I doubt I never shall' (Telford, V, p. 20).

The degree of psychological integration experienced by the two brothers is reflected in their view on this subject of Christian perfection. Charles, who achieved more acceptance of his inner destructiveness, saw that dealing with this destructiveness would be a constant and gradual struggle throughout life. This struggle was with every kind of sin, including 'deep-rooted' sin; John, whose destructiveness had to be kept out of consciousness, desperately hoped for and insisted on the possibility of instantaneous perfection but saw the chances of gaining it as possible only if it concerned 'voluntary sins'. His doctrine of perfection outlined his internal predicament: it was as if he were aware at some level that there was an unreachable area inside himself, which he was powerless to alter. His doctrine included a second type of sin (unconscious, inbred or original sin), which he believed could not come between man and God and could be wiped out only after death.

There is evidence that John came to look more kindly on himself as he grew older. As described by Tyson (2001, p. 33), in the early years after the 'conversion' experience, he distinguished between 'almost' and 'real' Christians. The former were morally scrupulous, valued the sacraments and saw their main priority as the service of God, but they had not had an experience of 'saving faith'. 'Real' Christians, on the other hand, felt an assurance that they were justified, born again, and sanctified. The latter were saved through their faith, while the former remained 'heirs of hell'.

However, in 1754 he wrote of those who were doing their best to serve God, in spite of their not having 'saving faith'. He described them as 'servants', rather than 'sons' of God. By then, he believed that through Christ, 'servants' were accepted by God though they might be unaware of it. He extended this acceptance by God to 'almost' Christians, and he amended his original journal entry of

February, 1738, in which he had written, 'I who went to America to convert others, was never myself converted to God'. In 1774, he inserted a less severe entry, 'I am not sure about this' (Tyson, 2001, pp. 35–6). His doubts and lack of lasting assurance about his own status as 'son' or 'servant' persisted, but he came to the view that, although a 'servant' lacked a sense of assurance and peace, he was at least accepted without knowing it. A 'son', on the other hand, was justified, experiencing a sense of freedom from guilt and a relationship of love and confidence with God (Tyson, 2001, p. 37).

Suffering

For both John and Charles, the healing of sickness by the 'Great Physician' was used as a metaphor for the redemption from sin by Jesus Christ. This must have been a familiar idea to them from other poets and hymn writers; it was also a metaphor used by their mother. She wrote to Charles on 19 October 1738, saying, 'Jesus is the only physician of souls, his blood the only salve that can heal a wounded conscience' (SW, p. 174). The idea of blood as a salve or balm, describes the priestly function of a Christ who is touched by our 'infirmities' and can make us whole in soul and body, as in Charles's hymn:

> He shares our pain, and grief, and fear,
> Wounded with every wounded soul,
> He bleeds the balm that makes us whole.
> *(Short Hymns on Select Passages of the Holy Scriptures,*
> 1762, II.349, Hymn 683, on Hebrews iv.15)

For John, salvation was not merely an escape from hell or the achievement of heaven, which he considered a 'vulgar' idea, but a restoration to health and wholeness. The forgiveness of sin and holiness were 'interwoven' with God's healing of the damage caused by sin. It was a healing of body and soul, inside and out (Maddox, 2007, p. 7). Both brothers would have seen the God of *agape*, as shown in Christ, as a source of strength and comfort in trouble. We have seen that Charles wrote poems for women in labour. In these he hoped they would gain comfort from an image of the suffering Christ with which they could identify. Kristeva held the view that a believer's identification with Christ's agony and abandonment was a use of Christian symbolism to 'sublimate' the loneliness and melancholy separation of the child from the mother. For the Wesleys, an identification with Christ's suffering, an imitation of Christ's self-emptying and his life as servant to others, was the way a Christian seeking redemption had to live. By following the Via Dolorosa, the believer became like Christ. Thomas à Kempis's *The Imitation of Christ* was one of two books John advised his lay assistants to leave behind as they travelled among his followers as resources to safeguard their physical and spiritual health (the other was his own book *Primitive Physick*) (Maddox, 2007, p. 8).

Participation in the suffering Christ was central to Charles's theology and the conventional, contemporary belief in the substitutary atonement appeared in his hymns. Tyson has argued that in much of his thought, he also saw the effects of suffering conventionally: that only Christ, through the Holy Spirit, was able to heal and renew but that suffering induced humility and patience, which contributed towards 'inner renewal' and eventually to the heavenly inheritance. However, there were also some instances when Charles went beyond the traditional and emphasised the purifying and saving effects of suffering itself. He made a clear connection between the purifying and 'purging' action of suffering, which led to perfection:

> The more my sufferings here increase,
> The greater is my future bliss;
> And Thou my griefs doth tell:
> They in Thy book are noted down;
> A jewel added to my crown
> Is every pain I feel.
> ('Poetical Works', 5, 70–1, quoted in Tyson, 2007, pp. 218–24)

His view that suffering was sent by God as a test, to be endured patiently, and that it could lead to perfection would have enabled him to tolerate his physical distress and weakness more easily. It is not surprising that images of sickness and suffering were important in his theology and in his hymns.

While John would have agreed that suffering induced patience and forbearance, and that Christian discipleship involved self-denial and participation in Christ's suffering, he did not accept that suffering itself could lead to perfection and the gaining of the heavenly reward. When such ideas appeared in Charles's hymns they gave rise to John's irritated editing. In one of his *Short Hymns on Select Passages of the Holy Scriptures* (1762) I, 98, no 307, on Deuteronomy ix.7, Charles wrote,

> A rebel to this present hour!
> Yet now for all thy mercy's power
> I ask with contrite sighs
> To end my sin, but not my pain:
> I would lament till death,* and then
> Rejoice in Paradise.
> (At the asterix, John has added 'God forbid!')

John, who was generally healthy, responded to suffering more actively. Health and healing were prominent in his thinking, and the promotion of physical and spiritual health was an important part of his ministry. Extensive advice and prescriptions appeared in *Primitve Physick*. The book went to twenty-three editions and was used and in print until the 1880s. Maddox (2007, pp. 4–6) points out that it was not merely a collection of 'old-wives' tales', as has been suggested, but was based on his wide reading of current medical literature. John clearly saw his role as including that of a physician, dispensing 'physick' and good advice about healthy ways of living.

These differences reflect the attitude of each of them to his own body. Charles had experienced a great deal of pain and sickness and had learned to live with his physical weakness. The hope that suffering would bring a reward would have been comforting and sustaining. John, on the other hand, had to maintain an active, 'healthy' (but brittle) shield, to protect him from any feelings of weakness. He energetically researched ways in which he could achieve this and advocated his methods to others.

Trinity

There is no doubt that, as an Anglican priest, John Wesley's theology was Trinitarian. When he was very ill on the night before he died, he was singing, 'To Father, Son and Holy Ghost, / Who sweetly all agree' (Heitzenrater, 203, 331). His sermon on 'The New Creation' (1785) describes the goal of Christian life in Trinitarian terms:

> And to crown all there will be a deep, an intimate, an uninterrupted union with God; a constant communion with the Father and his son Jesus Christ, through the spirit; a continual enjoyment of the Three-One God, and of the creatures in him!
>
> (BES, II, p. 510)

The writings of both the Wesleys on the Trinity have to be seen against the cultural background of the late seventeenth and early eighteenth centuries: as Vickers suggests, the increasing emphasis on reason at that time led to the view that 'faith' involved assenting to 'intelligible propositions' (*assensus*), rather than a personal trust in God (*fiducia*). As a result, there was pressure on theologians to demonstrate that the doctrine of the Trinity was intelligible. Many attempts were made, and almost all of them were concerned with the *immanent* Trinity; that is, they were attempting to describe the 'divine nature', the relations between the Three Persons, the Three-in-One. They were challenged, in particular, by the Socinians, who criticised the doctrine as unintelligible (Vickers, 2007, pp. 278–82).

Unlike these theorists, John's beliefs on the Trinity, as defined in his letter of 18 July 1749, 'To a Roman Catholic', are expressed in terms of the *economic* Trinity; that is, he outlines the roles of each of the three persons of the Trinity in relation to Creation, the Incarnation, and human Salvation, but does not speculate about the relationships between them in the eternal divine (Heitzenrater, 2003, pp. 192–5). He was suspicious of metaphysical speculation, and in a letter to Mary Bishop (17 April 1776), warned against it, referring her to Charles's hymns, which he suggested showed the effect of the Trinity on 'our hearts and lives' (Telford, VI, p. 213).

Only one published sermon by John Wesley on the Trinity still exists. In his introduction to it, Outler writes that it is his only extended written comment on this doctrine. However, the text (1 John 5:7, 'There are three that bear record in heaven, the Father, the Word, and the Holy Ghost: and these three are one') is recorded as having been used in his oral preaching twenty-three times, suggesting that it was a favourite topic. In the extant sermon, John bases his belief in the 'fact' of the Trinity on scripture and tradition. Most of the sermon is spent encouraging his listeners to be content to accept the 'fact' of the Trinity, just as they accept many 'mysterious' facts which are believed as a matter of course, for instance the sun's resting or moving in the heavens, or the existence of earth, air, souls, and bodies (BES, II, pp. 373–85). This mystery of the Trinity, God as Three-in-One, and the roles of the Father, Son and Holy Spirit in human lives are central to John's thought, but he avoids any explication of the diversity in unity of the immanent Trinity or its meaning or implications for believers. Rack plausibly suggests that this may have been owing to John's embrace of empiricism and his dislike of arguments about ideas for which there was little evidence (Rack, 2002, pp. 381–2).

Charles Wesley published his *Hymns on the Trinity* (1767) when he was sixty years old. By then, his thought about the Holy Spirit (as understood from this and his earlier book *Gloria Patri*, or *Hymns to the Trinity* [1746] and from his sermons) had become increasingly complex and prominent, until a comprehensive doctrine of the economic Trinity emerged (Vickers, 2007, pp. 282–7). However, Charles made no separation between the economic and the immanent Trinity, and his understanding of the immanent Trinity arose not from speculation or from attempts to make it appear intelligible but from his beliefs about the actions of the Three Persons and their relationship to human beings. There is no attempt to produce a systematic theology, but he does not avoid introducing the technicalities of Trinitarian doctrine into his hymns, sometimes managing to condense very complex ideas into a small space:

> Hail Father, Son and Spirit, great
> Before the birth of time,
> Inthron'd in everlasting state
> JEHOVAH ELOHIM!
> A mystical plurality
> We in the Godhead own,
> Adoring One in Persons Three,
> And Three in Nature One.
>
> (*Hymns on the Trinity*, No. lxxxvii, on 'The Plurality and Trinity of Persons')

His thoughts about the immanent Trinity are embodied in his hymns, and this context allows an emotional as well as a rational response, as the hymns were intended to be sung. Knowledge is offered in the context of the believer's relationship with God. Unlike the Anglican divines who tried to understand the immanent Trinity intellectually, in order to convince the rationalists of the day, and unlike his brother, who discouraged 'speculation', Charles entwined the immanent and the economic in his poetry. The concepts appear in a doxological setting of praise and prayer. They are embedded in metaphor and poetic imagery and structured by the form of the poetry so that they are enlivened and experienced rather than merely intellectually known. Charles believed that this knowledge was imparted through the Holy Spirit, the 'Divine Interpreter' and any 'knowledge' of the Trinity could only arise from its indwelling in the human heart:

> Furnished with intellectual light,
> In vain I speak of Thee aright
> While unrevealed Thou art:
> Thou only can suffice for me,
> The whole mysterious Trinity
> Inhabiting my heart.
> ('Hymns and Prayers to the Trinity', Hymn xix, in *Hymns on the Trinity*, 'Thee, great tremendous Deity')

Kimbrough has written about the 'verbal icons' in Charles Wesley's hymns, which he sees as acting like visual icons in the Orthodox tradition, 'as windows through which to glimpse the way of holiness, to interpret faith and practice, to celebrate the saints, to explore the mystery of God and to approach God' (Kimbrough, 2007, p. 170). In this way Charles's words could be seen as bringing to life for the believer, the *allegoria amoris* which is the Trinitarian narrative of the Incarnation.[2] In addition, the agapeic accepting love of the 'imaginary father' in Kristeva's archaic triangle is mirrored in the forgiving, accepting, unmerited, ceaseless, free love of God, which appears in many of the hymns. Through Charles's hymns on the Trinity, knowledge of God is through the Spirit and the Son, based on a personal relationship involving both feeling and reason; it is a 'sapiential' knowledge.[3] Kimbrough quotes Charles himself in asserting that the indwelling of the Spirit is a sharing of the 'life divine', which 'make[s] the depths of Godhead known'. There is 'a mystic power of godliness' beyond human intellect that enables one to grasp spiritual truths (Kimbrough, 2016, pp. 29–30).

In addition to technicalities of doctrine, Charles preserves the mysterious, apophatic element of the immanent Trinity; for him, it is more than has been revealed through the *actions* of the Three Persons (Vickers, 2007, p. 291). There are many hymns which describe the incomprehensibility and mystery of God:

> Beyond our utmost thought,
> And reason's proudest flight,
> We comprehend Him not,
> Nor grasp the Infinite,

> But worship in the mystic three
> One God to all eternity.
>
> ('Hymns and Prayers to the Trinity', Hymn xli, *Hymns on the Trinity*, 'We God the Father praise')

As expressed in the following hymn, Charles's thoughts on the Trinity are very close to what Moltmann calls the 'Open Trinity'. They include 'perichoresis', which for Moltmann is not only an 'intimate indwelling and complete interpenetration of the persons one in another' but also an understanding that 'Trintarian unity goes out beyond the doctrine of persons and their relations': 'it seeks the inclusion of creation'; it 'invites participation' (Moltmann, 1992, p. 86, in Grenz, 2004, pp. 81–2).

> The Spirit is Life, we know and feel
> Who life to us imparts;
> And God doth in Three Persons dwell
> For ever in our hearts:
> Our life is One: a Trinity
> In Unity we love,
> And gladly die from earth, to see
> His Face unveil'd above.
>
> (*Hymns on the Trinity*, No. cxxiii, 'He is our life, the Lord our God')

There have been many references in the psychoanalytic theory previously discussed to the presence of a 'third party' within relationships, and the way in which this provides the space for reflection, thought and creativity. The growth of Charles's understanding of the Trinity as shown in his sermons and his fascination with it as shown in his *Hymns on the Trinity* show that he experienced his relationship to God as triadic. The believer is indwelt by the Holy Spirit (the love between Father and Son), just as the child in the Kristevan archaic triangle is identified with the mother's love for the 'imaginary father' (the love for the 'not-I'). This triadic rather than a dyadic relationship, would offer the possibility of balance, in Kristevan terms, between the semiotic and the symbolic, a balance which has been shown to be evident in Charles's hymns.

He emphasised the plurality as well as the unity of Trinitarian life and subscribed to the traditional belief that human beings are in the image of the Triune God. To be in this image has implications for relationships and for living in the world. The plurality in unity of the Trinity, spanning time and space, and eternity, when mapped on to human relationships, allows not only for separateness, distinctiveness and identity but also for mutual erotic, kenotic and agapeic loving. This 'Open Trinity', and the participation in it of human beings, would be reflected in the world in acts of welcome, forgiveness, kindness and compassion in a community which encompassed diversity in unity (Moltmann, 2000, p. 118).

When John Wesley published the 1780 *Collection of Hymns*, he was selective about which hymns on the Trinity he included. His omissions and alterations led to less emphasis on the Trinity than on salvation. Campbell remarks on this emphasis and on the omission of more complex, 'explicit and sustained material on the Trinity'. He suggests that John could have been 'presupposing the Trinitarian devotion of the Book of Common Prayer' (Campbell, 2007, pp. 273–4), but, judging from the sentiments expressed in his sermon on the Trinity, it is also likely that he would have regarded such material as approaching worrying speculation. His relative lack of engagement with the internal relationships within the Trinity, a relationship which would be triadic in nature, is consistent with the preferences shown in his experiences in relationships in his life: the difficulty in seeing his parents as a sexual couple and his tendency to become involved in intense, merged idealised dyadic relationships.

The influence of psychological needs

In each of the five theological modalities, John and Charles Wesley faced the same opportunities for relating to religious 'objects'. The observations made show how each of them reacted in a way which was influenced by his psychological needs.

For instance, in their 'conversion' experiences, John had more difficulty than Charles in believing that God could be loving and forgiving to *him*. He was more in the grip of his 'bad' internal objects. In Kristevan terms, his responses were affected by his need to avoid the pull of the restitution of the mother/child dyad, the 'abject', which fascinated but terrified him. His primitive desires and fears had to be separated off, and he resisted any provocation by notions that invoked them (such as 'involuntary sin', illness and weakness, carnality and 'fondling', boundlessness, and a lack of structure). These would have raised fears of losing control and of falling into nothing.

John's terror of the 'abject' and his difficulty in accommodating a 'third' in relationships meant that in response to religious doctrine such as the Trinity and the God of *agape*, which symbolise the 'archaic triangle' and clear 'a space for triadic subjectivity' (Crownfield, 1992, p. 59), he struggled to sustain a 'symbolic/semiotic' balance. He tended to retreat or 'collapse' into a dyadic relationship with the Law of the (Oedipal) Father, which involved sticking to rules and striving to be perfect. This meant that, for him, the Christian symbolism involved was less helpful than it was for Charles in achieving integration of his 'dark side', with its attendant possibilities for growth.

The boundary between what was unconscious and what was conscious appears to have been more permeable in Charles. His 'dark side' was less terrifying, and his ability to acknowledge his destructiveness and weakness was greater. This meant that, in writing his poetry, he could access his internal objects and express unconscious material symbolically. More balance and interlacing of Kristeva's 'symbolic' and 'semiotic' were possible. The desire for merging and the 'abject' were symbolised and accommodated rather than being left as an 'inexorable carnal remainder' (Kristeva, 1980, p. 120) as they were for John; there was evidence of integration. Not only was Charles's ability to tolerate a 'third' seen in his response to the doctrine of the Trinity and the God of *agape*; it was also apparent in his use of poetry as a 'third', between subject and object, which created a place for reflection and self-expression. He appears to have been more able than John to use and profit from the same Christian symbols.

Understanding the difference

One way of portraying the difference between the brothers is in terms of their response to the suffering implicit in the mental structures and defences they developed as children of 'evangelical nurture' and their response to life experiences. Harris Williams draws on Keats's distinction between life as a 'vale of tears' and a 'vale of soul making'. She compares this distinction to Bion's description of two different responses to mental pain. The first response is one in which the pain results in symptoms or repetitive action rather than being *felt* or suffered, and it is 'non-developmental' (John shut off his emotional pain and survived through repetitive activity). The second response is to *suffer* the 'tension of conflicting emotions in the face of new knowledge' (Williams, 2005, p. 104). She describes an emotional experience as a 'poetic marriage of contrary emotions': the coming together of love and hate, which can be 'almost unbearable'. If it can be 'suffered', then new meaning and understanding emerges. She writes that in order to bear this tension, there must be 'an act of faith in which the support of selfhood (what Bion calls "memory and desire") is abandoned in favour of total dependence on the internal object'. 'Internal object' here refers to the 'combined object', which becomes a poet's muse (Williams, 2005, p. 192). Charles appears to have been able to suffer the tension of conflicting emotions and depend on his 'muse' in this way, so that he could express deep meaning in his hymns.

John's threatening internal objects were so harsh and critical that his response to mental pain was to keep these objects out of consciousness, stay healthy and work compulsively. Some of Charles's use of semiotic resonances in his hymns were experienced by John as 'under-symbolised' and resulted in too violent a confrontation with the destructive and sexual aspects of himself. He continued in the grip of his 'bad' objects until old age, being identified with them in his strict demands on himself and others. He understood intellectually what would have helped him but had to make strenuous and unrelenting efforts to maintain his memory of a loving father, while the image of a punitive father constantly reasserted itself. Nevertheless, through his intellectual conviction that redemption was available for all, he was able to help thousands of others to experience it and (at least by the end of his life), he had begun to feel that even a 'servant' could be acceptable to God.

The contrasts seen in the responses of the two brothers to the religious doctrines to which they both subscribed tend to confirm that the degree of change possible through religious experience is intimately related to the degree of domination of the internal world by its 'bad' internal objects. The more powerful they are, the more difficult it is for an individual to engage with the religious symbolism involved, as representing his unconscious phantasies, and so achieve growth and change.

Notes

1 See Chapter 1, p. 18.
2 See Chapter 5, p. 69.
3 See Chapter 2, pp. 27–8.

References

Berger, T., 1992. Charles Wesley and Roman Catholicism. In ed. S. Kimbrough Jr., *Charles Wesley: Poet and Theologian*. Nashville: Kingswood Books.
Campbell, T., 2007. Charles Wesley, *Theologos*. In eds. K. Newport and T. Campbell, *Charles Wesley: Life, Literature and Legacy*. Peterborough: Epworth Press.
Cell, G., 1935. *The Rediscovery of John Wesley*. London: Henry Holt.
Crownfield, D., 1992. The Sublimation of Narcissism. In ed. D. Crownfield, *Body/Text in Julia Kristeva*. Albany: State University of New York Press.
Green, J., 1945. *John Wesley and William Law*. London: Epworth Press.
Grenz, S., 2004. *Rediscovering the Triune God: The Trinity in Contemporary Theology*. Minneapolis: Fortress Press.
Haartman, K., 2004. *Watching and Praying: Personality Transformation in Eighteenth Century Methodism*. Amsterdam/New York: Rodopi.
Heitzenrater, R., 1995. *Wesley and the People Called Methodists*. Nashville: Abingdon Press.
Heitzenrater, R., 2003. *The Elusive Mr. Wesley*. Nashville: Abingdon Press.
Kimbrough Jr., S., 2007. Charles Wesley and a Window to the East. In eds. K. Newport and T. Campbell, *Charles Wesley: Life, Literature and Legacy*. Peterborough: Epworth Press.
Kimbrough Jr., S., 2016. *Partakers of the Life Divine*. Eugene: Cascade Books.
Kristeva, J., 1980. *Powers of Horror*. Translated by L. Roudiez. New York: Columbia University Press, 1982.
Maddox, R., 1990. John Wesley and Eastern Orthodoxy: Influences, Convergences and Differences. *The Asbury Journal*, 45(2), pp. 29–53.
Maddox, R.L., 2007. John Wesley on Holistic Health and Healing. *Methodist History*, 46(1), pp. 4–33.
Moltmann, J., 1992. *History and the Triune God: Contributions to Trinitarian Theology*. Translated by J. Bowden. New York: Crossroads.
Moltmann, J., 2000. An Old Magic Word for a New Trinitarian Theology. In ed. M. Douglas Meeks, *Trinity, Community and Power: Mapping Trajectories in Western Theology*. Nashville: Kingswood Books.
Rack, H., 2002. *Reasonable Enthusiast*, 3rd ed. London: Epworth Press.
Rattenbury, J., 1948. *The Eucharistic Hymns of John and Charles Wesley*. London: Epworth Press.
Schmidt, M., 1953–66. *John Wesley: A Theological Biography*, vols. I–III. Translated by N. Goldhawk et al. London: Epworth Press, 1962–73.
Tyson, J., 1989. *Charles Wesley: A Reader*. Oxford: Oxford University Press.

Tyson, J., 2001. John Wesley's Conversion at Aldersgate. In eds. K. Collins and J. Tyson, *Conversion in the Wesleyan Tradition*. Nashville: Abingdon Press.

Tyson, J., 2007. 'I Preached at the Cross, as Usual': Charles Wesley and Redemption. In eds. K. Newport and T. Campbell, *Charles Wesley: Life, Literature and Legacy*. Peterborough: Epworth Press.

Vickers, J., 2007. Charles Wesley and the Revival of the Doctrine of the Trinity: A Methodist Contribution to Modern Theology. In eds. K. Newport and T. Campbell, *Charles Wesley: Life, Literature and Legacy*. Peterborough: Epworth Press.

Williams, M., 2005. *The Vale of Soul-Making: The Post Kleinian Model of the Mind*. London/New York: Karnac.

Conclusion

Some distance has been travelled in this book, from the two apparently unconnected observations which provoked it: that for some patients in psychotherapy, it is often only through a very intense struggle that change can occur; and that some sincere Christians mean well, and can justify their actions, while acting in a very 'unchristian' fashion.

It was noted at the beginning that these two apparently unconnected observations were linked. They both related to difficulty in accessing unconscious content and coming to know the 'deep truth' about the self. The way in which this difficulty manifests itself in a religious context has become clearer through the experiences of the Wesley brothers. The difference in the way they responded to the modalities of their faiths which offered opportunities to symbolise unconscious material was affected by the degree of anxiety associated with their hidden feelings and phantasies, and the 'nameless dreads' connected with them. For some people the 'dark side' (their unconscious shame, rage, helplessness and destructiveness) is felt to be so unbearable, unmanageable and dangerous, with a fear of loss of the self, that it cannot be confronted directly. Defensive strategies, sometimes including religious rationalisations and/or a rigid separating off of these feelings from consciousness, have to be employed; for such people, change through the use of Christian symbolism is difficult, as it was for John Wesley. The desperate need to gain salvation that both he and his mother experienced felt like a 'life-and-death' struggle. Similarly, individuals whom Kristeva would describe as suffering from 'new maladies of the soul' can experience a 'life-and-death' quality to their struggles in therapy.

Kearns suggests that Kristeva, in her exegeses of religious texts, seeks their 'more sensual and even salvific face' (Kearns, 1992, p. 111). We have seen that Kristeva draws out parallels between complex and multiple meanings of Christian narratives and the believer's struggles with unconscious phantasies, drives and affects, often related to very early experience. Both are narratives of love, of loss, of separation, of the body, of the 'abject' and of the search for meaning. Love is central to her thought; her description of the early development of the infant as an *allegoria amoris* is paralleled in the Christian narrative of Kenosis.

Through the use of Kleinian, post-Kleinian and particularly Kristevan theory, this study can be seen as of Carrette's 'order of the other',[1] and as such it enriches and deepens the understanding of how individuals respond to religious symbols in ways which might be transforming (Carrette, 2007, pp. 104–5, 130–1). Several aspects have been emphasised which would have been less evident in a study using the developmental methods more traditionally used in the study of religion. These aspects include the importance of triadic relating, the 'splitness' of the self rather than the 'autonomous ego', the importance of the unconscious factors and the place of symbolisation in the making of meaning out of unconscious content, and the recognition of non-verbal and non-cognitive ways of knowing in therapy and in religion.

The presence of a 'third' and of triadic spaces is important in Kristevan theory and in religion. In connection with this, the comparison of the 'father of individual prehistory' and the God of *agape* has been discussed. However, while Kristeva gives examples of 'triadic relating' within Christian symbolism, as an atheist she privileges art, poetry and psychoanalysis as sources of these alternatives to narcissism. As Kearns points out, Kristeva wants to avoid a return to religion, 'this dangerous *pharmakon*', as a solution. Nevertheless, Kristeva's work enlarges the understanding of the integrating function of Christian symbolism, and so, in Kearns's words, she 'partially rehabilitates' religion. Kearns admits that she herself 'rehabilitates' it further by using Kristeva's ideas to enrich understandings of religion; she acknowledges that in this she is going beyond Kristeva's brief. In her words,

> Without the refining fire of psychoanalysis and *écriture*, religion, theology and even prayer will all too often remain unreconstructed tools of imposition, repression and terror, leaving no room at all for art, for the body, for the sound of other voices, or for that opening of new psychic and imaginative spaces by which we make room for the numinous in our language and lives.
> (Kearns, 1992, pp. 117–20)

The use of Kristeva in the present book, as a 'refining fire' and 'beyond her brief', has tended to reinforce this message: to confirm that when space exists for imagination and mental freedom, in the presence of a 'third', and where unconscious phantasy is 'sublimated' in religious symbol, and the 'symbolic' and the 'semiotic' are brought together, there is opportunity for creativity and growth. It also supports the possibility of finding such spaces in a religious context, offering what Crownfield calls for: an 'imaginary, erotic, open, optional Christianity', one which could provide 'triadic openness against narcissistic alternatives' (Crownfield,1992, p. 63).

Kristeva describes the bond that any religion establishes between the divinity and its believers as 'an identification' (Kristeva, 1983, p. 143). Such a relationship, if it is comparable to the relationship of the child with the 'imaginary father', facilitates a way of 'knowing' rather than an 'acquiring of knowledge' about the divine, and about the self. It is a being 'grasped by' rather than a 'grasping after' truth (Sykes, 1971, pp. 25–9). This identification is described as a 'metaphoric' identification, and metaphor in Kristevan theory is an attempt to approach meaning and to articulate what is unnameable. The 'amatory identification' has a 'heterogeneous, drive-affected dimension', loaded with 'something pre-verbal, or even non-representable that needs to be deciphered while taking into account the more precise articulations of discourse'. She applauds Bernard of Clairvaux's view that mystical desire retains its 'carnal origins', suggesting that 'such stress on the flesh that withstands amatory idealisation and disinterestedness opens love toward that which eludes consciousness, knowledge, and will: toward the region that today we are quite ready to call the unconscious' (Kristeva, 1983, pp. 29, 168). This heterogeneous, 'metaphorical' identification, this bond between the believer and the divine, enables not only cognitively based knowledge but also 'sapiental' knowing. It illuminates Ricoeur's 'regressive, archaic' hermeneutics as well as 'progressive' ones: Kristeva and Ricoeur would agree that the latter are 'nourished' by the former.

Kristeva's subject is a split subject, 'mortal and speaking', semiotic and symbolic, word and flesh. When she writes of religion as inadequate as a symboliser of the 'abject', she is writing of a religion, which has lost Bernard of Clairvaux's heterogeneity and which concentrates on the transcendent: God as an idealised heavenly power. Moltmann's God would have more in common than does this distant God with the object of the Kristevan infant's idealising identification, the 'imaginary father'. For Moltmann, God is love and an event:

> the event of Golgotha, the event of the love of the Son and the grief of the Father, from which the Spirit who opens up the future and creates life in fact derives.
>
> God is unconditional love because he takes on himself grief at the contradiction in men and does not angrily suppress this contradiction.
> (Moltmann, 2001, pp. 255–7)

In Charles Wesley's words,

> He left his Father's Throne above
> (So free, so infinite his Grace!),
> Emptied Himself of All but Love,
> And bled for Adam's helpless Race.
> (*Hymns and Sacred Poems*, 1739, Part II, 'Free Grace', p. 117)

Kristeva emphasises the need for a dialogue between symbolic and semiotic and between the word and the flesh, a dialogue which is embodied in Charles Wesley's hymns.

Kristeva's belief is that, if change is to occur, it is necessary adequately to symbolise the 'abject'. In *Powers of Horror*, she details the 'codification' of the 'abject' as 'sin'. For her sin is 'subjectified abjection'; this notion of 'sin' leads to what she calls 'super-ego spirituality', which involves conforming and obedient behaviour and speech, so that finally it holds the 'keys that open the doors to Morality and Knowledge' but 'equally open[s] up the path to the Inquisition' (Kristeva, 1980, p. 122). As opposed to facing up to the 'coarse and intolerable truth of man', she believes that the 'abject' as 'sin' becomes displaced rather than elaborated. This kind of 'codification' is reminiscent of the way sin is dealt with in some fundamentalist/revivalist movements as described by Percy, but the exploration of Charles Wesley's hymns compels a further questioning of her reservations about the capacity of Christian symbolism to elaborate the 'abject'.

In the hymns, there are corporeal metaphors of brokenness and woundedness, metaphors of suffering and death, and of merging and ecstasy. The poetic writing has many of the features Kristeva would require of *écriture*, which allow the semiotic to erupt into the symbolic. The 'abject' is not merely set aside and 'codified' as 'sin' but is elaborated and held in dialogue with the 'symbolic' elements; the polluted, broken elements interlace with the loving and saving ones:

> I am all unclean, unclean,
> Thy Purity I want;
> My whole Heart is sick of sin,
> And my whole Head is faint:
> Full of putrifying Sores,
> Of Bruises, and of Wounds, my Soul
> Looks to JESUS; Help implores,
> And gasps to be made whole.
>
> (*Hymns and Sacred Poems*, 1742, 'Wretched, helpless, and distressed', pp. 43–4)

Classification of forms of religion

The imaginative spaces within which Charles Wesley created his hymns existed in the context of a religion which for many believers involved a relationship with an anthropomorphic idealised God, the polarising of good and evil, and rigid certainties and demands. According to traditional theory, such a form of religion would be expected to promote dependency, infantilism and dyadic relating, and to be conducive to closure and defensiveness. However, Charles's 'triadic' response, as we have understood it, undermines the view that forms of religion can usefully be classified in this way as 'mature' or 'immature'.

The different responses of the two brothers to their beliefs, and the degree of integration that occurred in each, have been shown to be inextricably linked with their pre-existing mental structure. In response to Meissner's call for more research relating to the form of interaction with a particular religious modality and the developmental needs of the individual, the evidence from the examples here, at least, suggests an important correlation between the two.

There were opportunities for triadic openness which Charles was able to exploit. He was able, through the use of image and metaphor, to 'sublimate' unconscious phantasy and affect. This would have tended not only to increase the integration in his own inner world but also to have offered the same opportunity to the singers of his hymns. He achieved a symbolic/semiotic balance in his hymns, just as his grandfather Annesley had done in his sermons.

John had more of a struggle. So great was his fear of the 'abject', and his difficulty in holding on to a loving, forgiving father, that he often retreated to a dyadic position in relation to the 'Law of the Father'. Semiotic resonances in Charles's hymns were experienced as 'under-symbolised', and resulted for John in too violent a confrontation with the destructive and sexual aspects of himself. He continued in the grip of his 'bad' objects until his old age, being identified with them in his strict demands on himself and others. While he longed for and feared mystic or sexual merging, and felt vicariously gratified when others responded to his preaching with ecstatic experiences, he himself felt safer with the 'good old ways'. This dilemma was similar to that of his mother: she flicked between the dyadic merging of her 'lucid intervals', and her rigid rule keeping.

The God John preached was the God who 'regards his meanest creature'. In his sermon on 'The General Deliverance' he quoted: 'He sees with equal eyes, as Lord of all / A hero perish or a sparrow fall', but claimed that this was 'extremely pretty but it is absolutely false'. Rather, 'God regards his meanest creature much but he regards man much more' (BES, 2, p. 447). He preached a God who 'regarded', understood and cared for people as they struggled with adversity, whether from without or from within; yet his own fears and dreads were so powerful that he could not quite trust that this care was available for him. He remained driven to earn approval and be faultless, and could not let go or relax his efforts for most of his life.

These differences would suggest that of Aquinas's understanding of the reciprocal effect of nature and grace (not only does 'grace presuppose nature' [*gratia praesupponit naturam*] but 'grace perfects nature' [*gratia perficit naturam*] as well) discussed in Chapter 2, only the former is the case. John's capacity to use religious symbols as a means of 'sublimating' archaic material, which depends on a 'good-enough' early experience, appears to have been compromised. Nevertheless, he continued to be seen as almost saintly by many of his followers. His struggle to be Christ-like and his urging of others to be Christ-like was relentless. He helped thousands pastorally, and through his preaching he offered to others what he himself needed. Like Charles, some of his followers would be comforted, feel forgiven, and use the symbolism he described as a path to integration. Others like himself would hang on to their faith as a pattern of rules and an 'Imitation of Christ'. He was a relentless pilgrim, a struggler for whom there seems to have been little comfort or assurance that he was loved and forgiven, either from his faith or through his relationships. From the details of his life it is clear that he cannot be regarded as having been saintly in the sense of being pure or perfect. He can, however, be esteemed as a kind of 'patron saint' of those like him, 'survivors of narcissism', who because of their terror of the Behemoths of their unconscious, fail to gain awareness and acceptance of their darker sides. They, too, struggle on, often relatively comfortless, with their best attempts at the 'Imitation of Christ', held by the Christian narrative and sometimes managing to be extraordinarily effective 'wounded healers'. Such perseverance would be seen by believers as enabled by God's grace and hence as evidence that Aquinas's second proposition is also true.

John was able to treat himself more kindly towards the end of his life. He had begun to feel that even a 'servant' could be acceptable to God. It was as if having preached of a loving God, of forgiveness and salvation over so many years, his old image of God as a demanding and critical parent had softened to some extent. He died beloved by thousands, whose lives, in spite of his own woundedness, had been given meaning, comfort and hope.

Percy's exploration of the fundamentalist/revivalist tradition offers convincing evidence of factors within it which in theory would be likely to reduce the potential for facilitating change and growth, but the evidence from the Wesley brothers suggests that in a setting which had some similarities to this, they responded differently. So that, while there are elements within the various forms of religion which may tend to inhibit growth and change, believers will relate to each modality in their own way, according to their particular needs and psychological defences. While Charles was able to use Christian symbolism to 'sublimate' unconscious phantasy and achieve further integration, John was held within the framework of the Christian narrative, which gave him stability and purpose, and helped him to minister to his followers. In the light of these differences in the same religious context, it seems unhelpful to label some forms of religion as encouraging 'mature' relating, while denigrating others as leading to stultification. This examination has shown that even a so-called 'immature' form of Christianity can be helpful, either in terms of increased integration or as a containing model or both.

Kristeva has said that at this time of 'crisis' of religion, psychoanalysis, literature (particularly poetry) and art offer hope to the 'survivors of narcissism' through their capacity to reach and symbolise the 'abject', rather than to avoid it or perversely to wallow in it. She writes that 'far from being a minor marginal activity in our culture, this kind of literature, or even literature as such, represents the coding of our crises, or our most intimate and most serious apocalypses' (Kristeva, 1980, p. 208). Although, as she says, reading literature is not a 'marginal activity', the kind of literature she cites does not reach those she describes as the 'masses' who hold Christian beliefs (Kristeva, 1985, pp. 41–2); similarly, there are relatively few people globally for whom psychoanalysis is available, should they want or require it.

Against the possible benefits of religion have to be set Kristeva's fears of its providing the keys to the Inquisition, and also the concerns outlined by Jones about the association between religion, wars and terror. Jones's thesis is that religion's power both to effect personal transformation and to inspire terror are related to the idealisation of texts, beliefs, symbols and practices, so that everything within the religion is seen as good, and what is outside and different, is regarded as 'evil' and to be fought against. He suggests a form of religion without idealisation as a possible solution: the *via negativa*, the apophatic way of the early mystics, which he sees as emerging from ordinary religious practices and narratives and returning to them. Eventually the idealised forms would 'begin to lose their former profundity' and would 'not be outgrown but repositioned'; they would no longer be 'sacred ends in themselves' but means to a greater end: 'imageless prayer' (Jones, 2002, pp. 113–17). This is similar to what Blass (2006, pp. 27–9) called a kind of 'westernised Buddhism' and is seen as more 'mature' form of religion by many psychologists. It is a position which many people reach, and comparable to Ricoeur's *second naivete* (Ricoeur, 1967, pp. 350–1); however, most of the millions of worshipping Catholics and Protestants would see it, as Blass points out, as challenging the truth of their religious claims and would be unwilling and unlikely to make such a shift.

Perhaps the best to be hoped for is that the leaders and teachers in the church could be brought to understand and to share some of the Kristevan concepts discussed: the need for more awareness and acceptance of the 'stranger within', leading to welcome and inclusion of the stranger without; that 'sin' should be met with love rather than retribution; the dangers of a rigid, unimaginative, fundamentalist interpretation of texts, with its often associated ethnocentricity, homophobia and misogyny; a deeper exploration of the meaning of the Trinity for living in a community; and the importance of the symbolism of sacraments, poetry, art, and music, in resonating with deeper aspects of ourselves.

Kristeva has said that psychoanalysis 'asserts the end of codes but also the permanence of love as a builder of spoken spaces' (Kristeva, 1983, p. 382). Here I have attempted to explore the spoken spaces built by love in psychotherapy and religion. The Wesley brothers were creatures of their time, and neither their grandfather's Calvinism nor early Methodism would usually be described as 'imaginary, erotic, open, optional' forms of Christianity. For neither of the brothers, nor their parents or grandparents, could Christianity ever have been optional, but this study has shown that Charles Wesley at least (and possibly his grandfather Annesley) was able to engage with its imaginary, open and even erotic aspects.

I have endeavoured to set out the evidence as fully and fairly as possible, but there can never be a definitive version. In the end this is only one narrative: it is merely *a* story (Bellah, 1977, p. 29).

Note

1 See Chapter 1, p. 20.

References

Bellah, R., 1977. Young Man Luther: A Comment. In eds. D. Capps, W. Capps, and M. Bradford, *Encounter With Erikson*. Missoula: Scholars Press.

Blass, R., 2006. Beyond Illusion. In ed. D. Black, *Psychoanalysis and Religion in the 21st Century*. London: Tavistock Publications.

Carrette, J., 2007. *Religion and Critical Psychology: Religious Experience in the Knowledge Economy*. London/New York: Routledge.

Crownfield, D., 1992. The Sublimation of Narcissism in Christian Love and Faith. In ed. D. Crownfield, *Body/Text in Julia Kristeva*. Albany: State University of New York Press.

Jones, J., 2002. *Terror and Transformation: The Ambiguity of Religion in Psychoanalytic Perspective*. Hove and New York: Brunner-Routledge.

Kearns, C., 1992. Art and Religious Discourse in Aquinas and Kristeva. In ed. D. Crownfield, *Body/Text in Julia Kristeva*. Albany: State University of New York Press.

Kristeva, J., 1980. *Powers of Horror*. Translated by L. Roudiez. New York: Columbia University Press, 1982.

Kristeva, J., 1983. *Tales of Love*. Translated by L. Roudiez. New York: Columbia University Press, 1987.

Kristeva, J., 1985. *In the Beginning Was Love: Psychoanalysis and Faith*. Translated by A. Goldhammer. New York: Columbia University Press, 1987.

Moltmann, J., 2001. *The Crucified God*, 2nd ed. Translated by R. Wilson and J. Bowden. London: SCM Press.

Ricoeur, P., 1967. *The Symbolism of Evil*. Translated by E. Buchanan. Boston: Beacon Press, 1969.

Sykes, S., 1971. *Friedrich Schleiermacher*. Bath: Lonsdale and Bartholomew.

Index

Note: Page numbers in *italics* indicate figures.

Abelove, H. 99, 106
abject: Christian symbolism and 52–3, 159, 186, 188; defining 49; elaboration of 64, 72, 122; fear of 168, 187; imaginary father and 50–1; Kristeva on 12, 14, 20, 49–54, 89, 122, 129, 159; as nameless dread 72; religion and 54, 60, 185; separation of mother and child as 12, 126–7, 129, 179; as sin 52; transformational objects and 63–4
Account of an Amour of John Wesley, An (Wesley, J.) 105
Act of Uniformity 77
agape: Christian symbolism of 127; God of 54, 67–8, 70–3, 88, 158, 162, 168, 173, 179–80, 184; idealisation and 51; New Testament meaning of 51
allegory of love (*allegoria amoris*) 69–70, 177, 183
Annesley, Samuel: as Puritan preacher 77–9, 109; Susanna and 80, 84; symbolic and semiotic 79
Annesley, Susanna *see* Wesley, Susanna
Antinomianism 102, 170
Antonaccio, M. 25
apophatic: in hymns 177; loss and 65; mysticism and 17, 64–6, 156, 189
archaic experience 66–7, 70–1, 157–8
archaic objects 38
archaic triangle 51, 67, 70–1, 89, 167, 177–8
aretegenic theology 27, 39
Aristotle 24
arts: Kristeva on 21, 53, 188; restoration of self and 155; survivors of narcissism and 188; symbolic and semiotic in 46, 53, 66, 155

Attention and Interpretation (Bion) 15
attunement 16, 36, 125

Baker, F. 96, 133, 161
Balint, Michael 57
Beatitudes 27
Beattie, T. 14
Beckerlegge, O. 162
behaviour: Christian identity and 27–8; goodness and 26; moral life and 25; psychoanalysis and 26
benign regression 57, 59
Bennet, John 116
Bernard of Clairvaux 53, 64, 185
Best, G. 133, 148
Beveridge, William 115
Beyond Belief (Stein) 19
biological drive theory 12–13
Bion, Wilfred: faith and 65; on interpersonal processes 15–16; on mental pain 180; on mother as container 16, 35, 43–4, 49; mother/child interactions 44; 'O' concept 16; psychoanalytic concepts of 14; on truth 29
Bishop, Mary 118, 175
Bisson, Jane 118
Black, D. 15
Black Sun, The (Kristeva) 12
Blake, W. 44
Blass, R. 19, 189
Böhler, Peter 95, 140, 166, 168, 170
Bollas, Christopher 14, 37, 41, 57, 62
Bolton, Ann 98, 106, 118–19, 171
Boswell, James 149
Brand, Thomas 78
Brevint, Daniel 165

Briggs, Elizabeth 119
Britton, R. 14, 35, 43–4, 98, 125
Brown, A. 30
Burdock, Sally 117, 119
Burton, John 110

Campbell, T. 179
Carrette, J. 20–1, 184
cataphatic 64–6, 156
categorical imperative 32
Cell, G. 168
Cennick, John 148
Chapone, Sally *see* Kirkham, Sally
Charry, Ellen 25, 27–8, 30, 39
child development: abject and 49; capacity to symbolise 41, 43–5; death instinct 33; early experience and 54–5; ego in 36, 48; evangelical nurture and 87–8, 90; evolution of idealisation and 37; imaginary father and 46–50; internalised combined object and 43–4; Klein on 12, 32–5; Kohlberg on 18; Kristeva on 21, 45; loving relationships and 29; metaphorical objects 48; moral sense and 32–5; mother love and 47–8; nameless dread and 44; negative feelings 35; Piaget on 18; semiotic and 46; transformational objects and 29, 32, 56; transitional objects and 41–2; triangular space in 44–5; *see also* mother/child interactions
children: breaking the will of 84–5, 87; death of 124–5; education of 83–6; evangelical nurture and 87; loving relationships 86–7; precociousness and 128; replacement 125–6
chora 46–7, 51, 60–1
Christian excellence 27–8
Christianity: abject and 52–3, 156, 159, 188; apophatic and cataphatic in 66; aretegenic 27, 39; erotic aspects of 119, 184, 189; ethics and 25–7; freedom from sin in 26; kenotic narrative of 69, 183; perfection and 171–2; psychoanalysis and 11; search for goodness 25–6, 28; traditional beliefs in 19; Trinity and 175
Christian symbolism: abject and 52–3, 186; *agape* and 127; change through 183; Cross as 68, 70; early experience in 51, 54–5; experiential nature of 67; interpretation of 71; Jesus Christ as 68–70, 129, 173; Kristeva on 13–14, 41, 50–4, 155, 173, 183–4; as metaphor 51; resurrection as 68; semiotic and 54; transformative 67; triadic experiences 70–1; unconscious and 13–14, 188; *see also* religious symbolism
Church of England 80
'Circumcision of the Heart, The' (Wesley, J.) 122
clarity 62
Clarke, A. 3, 86, 105
Clarke, G. 36
Cloud of Unknowing 64
Codex Consiliorum (Beveridge) 115
cognitive development 18
Collection of Hymns (Wesley, J.) 179
combined object: creative activity and 71; internalised 43–4, 71; triangular space and 44–5
communication: semiotic and 46–7; symbols and 42, 47, 66
conversion: defensive splitting and 88; desolation crisis 88; evangelical nurture and 93, 165–6; jubilant awakening 88; promotion of integration 89; sanctification 88–9; unitive ecstasy 88
cosmic narcissism 37, 62
Cotswold relationships 107–10, 114, 119, 139, 146
countertransference 15
creative activity: guilt and anxiety through 155; Klein on 155; restitution and 155; *see also* arts; poetry
creativity 42–3
Cromwell, Richard 77
Crosby, Sarah 96, 120
Cross 51; *agape* of 13, 51; symbolism of 68, 70
Crownfield, D. 54, 167, 184

Daniel Deronda (Eliot) 29, 37
dark side 72, 183
Davie, Donald 155–7, 161
death instinct 33, 38
de Certeau, Michael 65
defensive splitting 88
Denys the Areopagite 64
depressive position 33–5, 37, 43, 129
de Renty, Jean-Baptiste 105
desolation crisis 88
detachment 62
development: cognitive 18; faith 18; individual 28; maturity of religious

beliefs and 18–20; moral 18; *see also* child development
disavowal 98
Durbin, Henry 137

Edelstein, M. 46
Edwards, M. 150
ego: Britton on 35; child development and 36, 48, 89; defining 39n2; ethics and 25; Fairbairn on 36; Freud on 32; 'frozen' parts of 36, 38; Klein on 33–5; psychoanalysis and 57; religious experience and 59–60
'Ego and the Id, The' (Freud) 32
ego-ideal 32
ego-psychology 18
Eliot, George 28–30, 35, 37–8
Elusive Mr. Wesley, The (Heitzenrater) 93
epigenesis 18
Erikson, Erik 18
ethics: Christianity and 25–7; defining 24; the good and 24–5; growth and change through 27; intention and 24; New Testament 25
Eucharist 52
evangelical nurture: conversion and 87–90, 93; John Wesley and 93; Protestant temperament and 86–7; Wesley family and 87–90, 124, 147, 165–6
'Evangelical' Protestant group 86, 87

Fairbairn, W. 35–6, 38, 155, 160
Faith and Transformation (Forsyth) 54
faith development 18
fasting 94, 166
father: aspects of 47; idealisation and 37; internalised combined object and 43–4; as 'third party' 46; *see also* imaginary father
feminism 13–14
field preaching 3, 135, 137, 150
Fletcher, John 97
forgiveness: God's 87–8, 95, 102, 118, 121, 127, 169, 173, 188; loving relationships and 26–8; struggle and 58–9
Forsyth, J. 54
Fowler, J. 18, 21
Freud, Sigmund: biological drive theory and 12; disavowal and 98; empirical methods and 12, 15; on father 46–7; on moral behaviour 38–9; on mother/child interactions 38; Oedipus complex 32, 43–4, 46–9; primary process thinking 17; on primitive father-figure 35; on religious beliefs 11, 13, 18–19, 71; on superego and ego 32; unconscious and 20
Frost, F. 156
fundamentalist religion: change and growth in 188; emotional states in 60–1; God as transformational object in 59; immature relating and 3; leadership authority in 60; omnipotence of God in 61; power and 59–61; repetitive songs in 60; revivalism in 61–2; worship practices 60–1

'Genteel' Protestant group 87
Gloria Patri (Wesley, C.) 176
God: *agape* and 51, 54, 71, 88, 173, 179, 184; anthropomorphic idealised 186; Christian excellence through 27–8; contemplative response and 63; dispossession and 17; forgiveness and 87–9, 95, 102, 118, 121, 127, 169, 173, 188; fundamentalist religion and 60–1; imitation of Christ 27–8; immature relating and 21; kenosis 68–70; manifestations of 27; as the non-competitive other 26; objects of beauty and 62–3; omnipotence of 61; ordinary objects and 63; power of 60–1; punitive 88–9; recognition of 56; striving for 64; symbolism and 68–9; as transformational object 56–9, 62; as Trinity 70
good-enough mother 36, 38, 41, 43–4, 126
good/goodness: behaviour and 24, 27; Christian 28; ethics and 24; growth to 28–9; human consciousness and 25; loving relationships and 26; maturity of religious beliefs and 24, 26; morality and 24–5; search for 25–6; self-perception and 26; transformational capacity of relationships and 29
grace 51, 54, 58, 69, 71–2, 78–9, 87
Greven, P. 86–7
growth to goodness: infants and 29; Kleinian theory in 29; relationships and 28–30; transformational objects and 29–30, 63–4; truth about the self and 29–30, 41
growth to maturity: change based on love in 30; development of moral sense 33, 35
Gwynne, Sally *see* Wesley, Sally Gwynne

Haartman, K. 88–90, 166
Haecceitas 66
Hall, Westley 104
Hampson, J. 101, 117
Heimann, Paula 15
Heitzenrater, R. P. 93, 101, 108
Herbert, G. 156
Holy Club 94, 99–100, 109, 123, 136
Hopkey, Sophy 110–16, 120–1, 124
'How Poems Arrive' (Stevenson) 45
human psyche 18
Hutchinson, John 145
Hutton, James 117
hymns: Charles Wesley and 2, 138, 142, 144, 147, 151–3, 156–63, 165, 185–7; conversion 142; John Wesley and 155, 160–1, 165; loss and 151; mysticism and 171; semiotic in 157; symbolic and semiotic in 66, 161; Trinity and 176–9
Hymns and Sacred Poems (Wesley and Wesley) 165, 169
Hymns for the use of Families (Wesley, C.) 147, 151
Hymns on the Lord's Supper (Wesley and Wesley) 165
Hymns on the Trinity (Wesley, C.) 176, 178

ideal/idealised object 33–4, 37
ideal/idealised truth 29
idealisation: child development and 34, 37; in religion 19, 189; unconscious and 185; of women by John Wesley 107, 115–16, 118
identification 18, 48, 184
imaginary father: archaic triangle and 51, 67, 70, 167; Kristeva on 46–51, 54, 67–70, 89, 160, 167, 184–5; mysticism and 185; symbolic and 158, 167
imitation of Christ 27–8, 173, 187–8
Imitation of Christ, The (Kempis) 94, 173
immature relating: defensive forms of 20; fundamentalist religion and 2–3, 21
individual development 28
internal objects: Bion on 44; Charles Wesley and 161; child's ego and 36; creative activity and 44, 155; Fairbairn on 36, 38; John Wesley and 126, 161; Klein on 12, 33, 35, 89, 166–7

Jackson, T. 133
James, William 58–9
Jesus Christ: human condition and 69; identification with 52; manifestations of God in 27, 62; as the non-competitive other 26; redemption from sin 173; resurrection of 26, 51, 68–9, 158; suffering of 51, 68–9, 173–4; symbolism of 51–2, 68–70, 129
John of the Cross 64
Johnson, Samuel 149
Jones, J. 19, 37, 188
Jonte-Pace, Diane 19
jouissance 53, 66, 72
jubilant awakening 88
Judaism 52
Julian, J. 80
Jung, C. G.: consciousness and 39; empirical methods and 11; religious myth and 11

Källstad, T. 122
Kant, Immanuel 32
Kearns, C. 183–4
Keats, J. 16, 180
Kempis, Thomas à 94, 173
kenosis 68–70, 72, 183
Kimbrough, S. T., Jr. 156, 177
Kirkham, Betty 108
Kirkham, Sally 107–9
Klein, Melanie 4; biological drive theory and 12; combined object and 162; on creative activity 155; on development of moral sense 32–5, 38; on father 47; on fear of annihilation 33; on ideal/idealised object 33–4, 37; on internal objects 12, 33, 35, 89, 166–7; on mother/child interactions 32–4, 36, 38; positions 33–5, 37, 129; psychoanalytic concepts of 12, 14; subjective approach to psychoanalysis by 15; on symbols 43; transformation and 72; unconscious and 20
Knox, A. 93, 96, 99
Kohlberg, Lawrence 18
Kohut, Heinz 18, 37–8, 57, 62, 102
Kristeva, Julia: abject concept 12, 14, 49–50, 52–3, 126, 129, 159, 186; archaic experience 66–7, 70–1, 157–8, 177–8; on arts and poetry 21, 53, 155; biological drive theory and 13; child development and 21, 45–7; Christian symbolism and 13–14, 41, 50–4, 67, 127, 129, 173, 183–4; dark side 72; feminism and 13–14; imaginary father 46–51, 54, 67–70, 89, 160, 167, 184–5; influence of Klein on 4, 12, 14; kenotic narrative 69–70; on maladies of the soul 12, 49, 183; mother/child interactions 59, 68–9, 126;

mysticism and 50, 53, 64; on patriarchal systems 14; place of not knowing 66; on poetic language 14; on primary and secondary processes 17–18; psychic space and 49–50, 66; psychoanalytic concepts of 2, 11–14; religion and identification 184; on religious beliefs 13–14; symbolic and semiotic 17, 46–8, 51, 56, 60–4, 66, 72, 161, 185; transformation and 72; triadic spaces 5, 71, 184; unconscious and 20, 184

laboratory of selfhood 28
Lacan, Jacques 12, 46
language: cataphatic 64–5; self and 47; semiotic and 46; silence and 66
Law, William 94–5, 169–70
literature: survivors of narcissism and 188; symbolisation and 50, 53; truthfulness and 29–30; *see also* poetry
Lloyd, G. 133
love: change and 30; child development and 29; God and 13, 27–8; morality and 26, 30; psychoanalysis and 13; in relationships 26, 29
Loxdale, Ann 119

Macmurray, John 36
Maddox, R. L. 174
maladies of the soul 12, 49, 183
malignant regression 57
Matthean texts 27
mature narcissism 37
McDougall, Joyce 127–9
Meissner, W. 18, 21, 59, 165, 186
Meltzer, D. 155, 162
Memoirs of the Wesley Family (Clarke) 3
Merleau-Ponty, Maurice 158
metaphor 48, 51
Methodism: Charles Wesley and 3; early forms of 21; E. P. Thompson on 3; immature relating and 3; influence of Puritanism on 78; John Wesley and 2–3, 101–2; revivalism in 61–2; transformation and growth in 90
Midsummer Night's Dream, A (Shakespeare) 45
Milton, J. 44, 156–7, 162
'Moderate' Protestant group 87
Moltmann, J. 69, 178, 185
Monti, A. 62
moral development 18
morality: behaviour and 28; current views of 25; defining 24; the good and 24–5;
growth to maturity and 33; inner change and 25; Klein on 32–5, 38; love and 26, 30; Winnicott on 38
moral life 25
Moravians 95, 97, 102, 106, 110, 160
Morgan, Richard 123
Morgan, William 123
mother: active role of 35–6; as container 16, 35, 43–4, 49, 126; desire for father by 47–9; idealisation and 37; non-receptive 44; symbolisation and 44–5; as transformational object 29, 32, 37; *see also* good-enough mother
mother/child interactions: abject and 49; attunement in 36, 125; *chora* and 46–7, 60–1; creativity and 42–3; death instinct and 38; development of moral sense 32–3; environmental failures and 38; external/internalised relationship 36; good-enough mother and 36, 43–4, 126; growth to goodness and 29; imaginary father and 46–50, 68, 70, 89, 158, 160; mother as container and 16, 35, 126; object hunger and 37–8; separation and 12, 14, 42, 47–8; symbolisation and 49; transformational objects and 29, 32, 37; transitional space and 42
Murdoch, Iris 25, 28
Murray, Grace 115–16, 137, 148
mystical theologians 64–5
mysticism: affect and 50; apophatic and 17, 64–6; carnal origins of 185; cataphatic and 65; hymns and 159, 171; Kristeva on 50, 53, 64, 185; peak experiences and 58; psychoanalysts and 19; religion and 169–71

nameless dread 44–5, 72–3, 125, 130, 183
narcissistic bliss 37
natural religions 19
nature 54
negative feelings 35, 45, 129
'New Creation, The' (Wesley, J.) 175
Newport, K. 133
New Testament ethics 25
'non-competitive other' 26

object: archaic 38; combined 43–4, 71; defining 6n1; emotionally available 5, 29, 38; good/bad 34–8, 89; idealised 34; identification with 18, 48; ordinary 63–4; projection on 33–4, 39n1; religious 18, 179; symbols and 42–3;

transformational 30, 32, 37–8, 56–63, 73; transitional 42
object hunger 37–8, 57, 102
object-relations theory 19
objects of beauty: contemplative response to 63; detachment and 62; knowing God through 62–3; transformational 62–3
'O' concept 16
Oedipus complex 32, 43–4, 46–9, 89
Oglethorpe, James 112
On the Christian Sacrament and Sacrifice (Brevint) 165
order of the other: process of change and 21; religion and 20, 184
ordinary objects 63–4
other: detachment and 62; non-competitive 26; *see also* order of the other
Otto, Rudolph 58
Outler, A. C. 176

paranoid-schizoid position 33–5, 37, 129
parents: ambivalence to 89; idealisation and 37, 88; imposition of will on children by 84; as sexual couple 43–4, 106–7, 126, 128–9
Pauline texts 27–8
peak experiences 58–9, 61
Pendarves, Ann 107
Pendarves, Mary (née Granville) 107, 109–10
Percy, Martyn 59–62, 70, 186, 188
perfection 171–4
perspectivity 63
Piaget, Jean 18
Pitt, William 97
Plain Account of Christian Perfection (Wesley, J.) 171
poetry: archaic experience and 66; hymns and 155–60; objects of beauty and 62; survivors of narcissism and 188; symbolic and semiotic in 46, 53, 66, 155; unconscious material and 44; *see also* arts
Pope, A. 80
positions 33–5, 37, 43
post-modern thought 16–17
power: fundamentalist religion and 59–61; God and 60; perception of Christ as 61; unburdening of sin and 167
Powers of Horror (Kristeva) 186
Practical Treatise on Christian Perfection, A (Law) 94
Primitive Physick (Wesley, J.) 174

progressive hermeneutics 71–2
projection: defining 39n1; symbols and 42
Protestant temperament 86–7
providence 101, 105
psychic space 49–50, 53–4, 66
psychoanalysis: American 20; behaviour and 26; Christianity and 11; countertransference in 15; ecumenism in 14; empirical methods in 12, 15; engagement with 1–2; European 20; growth and change in 28; higher values in 15; interpersonal processes in 15–16; post-modern thought and 17; reconceived ethics and 14; religious beliefs and 18–21; religious language in 16; as science and art 18; search for goodness 25–6; subjective approach to 15; truthfulness and 29
Puritanism: Methodism and 78; Wesley family and 77–9

Rack, H. 93, 103, 106–7, 117, 142, 168, 171–2
Rattenbury, J. 165
Reasonable Enthusiast (Rack) 93
reconceived ethics 14
regression: benign 57, 59; defining 57; malignant 57
regressive hermeneutics 71–2
relationships: ethical growth and 27; with God 27–8; inner change and 26, 28; loving 26, 29; non-competitive other and 26; transformational capacity of 29
religion: anthropomorphic idealised God in 186; change and 2; developmental needs and 18–20, 187; fundamentalist 2–3, 59–61; idealisation and 19, 189; identification and 184; Kristeva on 188–9; modalities in 165, 183, 187; mysticism and 169–71; natural 19; political orders of study of 20; repudiation of traditional 19–20; terror and 188–9; unconscious and 2
religious beliefs: detachment and 62; developmental needs and 165; Freud on 11, 13, 18–19, 71; fundamentalist 59–61; growth and change through 18; Kristeva on 13–14; object hunger and 38; ordinary objects and 63; peak experiences and 58–9, 61; psychoanalysis and 18–21; regression and 57; symbolic and semiotic in 66; transformational objects and 62

religious myth 11
religious objects 18, 179
religious rituals 49–50
religious symbolism: interpretation of 71–2; mysticism and 53; psychic space and 53–4; repressed conflicts and 89; ritual use of 50–1; as transformational object 72–3; unconscious and 50, 89; unthinkable and 67; *see also* Christian symbolism
repentance 94, 103, 166
replacement child 125–6
resonance 56, 68
Resurrection 26, 51, 68–9, 158
revivalism 61–2
Ricoeur, Paul: archaic hermeneutics and 185; on ethics 24; inner change and 25; on interpretation of Christian symbols 67, 69, 71–2, 129; laboratory of selfhood and 28; on morality 24; *second naivete* 51, 189
Ritchie, Elizabeth 96
Rogers, Hetty 118
Romola (Eliot) 29–30
Rupp, Gordon 79
Ryan, Sarah 100

St. Augustine 28, 56, 64, 70
St. Theresa of Avila 58
St. Thomas Aquinas 54, 187
salvation: Annesley on 78; Charles Wesley and 136, 139–40, 154; conversion and 88; evangelical nurture and 87; by faith 95, 100, 103, 168, 170; forgiveness and 188; as healing process 68, 173; hymns and 159, 179; John Wesley and 94, 100, 103, 105, 122–3, 168, 170, 183, 188; life and death struggle for 136, 183; Moravians and 95; reproof and 103
sanctification 88–9
Schleiermacher, F. 63
Schmidt, M. 102, 106, 117
Scotus, Duns 66
second naivete 51, 189
Segal, Hannah 42–3, 47, 68, 155
self: language and 47; semiotic and 51; symbolisation and 51; transformation of 28; truth about 29–30, 41, 183
self-affirmation 71
self-love 152
self-perception 26
self-psychology 5, 18–19

semiotic: *chora* and 46; Christianity and 54; defining 46; symbolic and 46, 48, 51, 53–4, 56, 60–4, 66, 72; unconscious and 59
Seneca 66
Serious Call to a Devout and Holy Life, A (Law) 94
Sermon on the Mount 27
Shakespeare, W. 45, 159
Shepherd, T. B. 159
Short Hymns on Select Passages of the Holy Scriptures (Wesley, C.) 174
signs 67
silence 66
Silverstone, J. 134, 139
sin: abject and 52, 186; Charles Wesley and 151–2, 166, 172; forgiveness and 89, 173; freedom from 26; John Wesley and 122, 166–7; peak experiences and 58–60; superego spirituality and 52; Susanna Wesley and 85–7
Stabat Mater (Kristeva) 46
Stein, S. 19
Stern, D. 35–6
Stevenson, Anne 45
Strangers to Ourselves (Kristeva) 14
suffering 173–5
superego 32, 38, 155, 166
superego spirituality 52, 186
Swift, J. 80
Sykes, S. 63
symbolic: equation 42–3, 68; expressions 42; hymns 66, 161; semiotic and 17, 46, 51, 53–4, 56, 60–4, 66, 72
symbolisation: capacity for 41, 43–5; semiotic and 46, 48, 51, 53–4
symbols: communication and 42, 47, 66; deliteralising 67–8; dynamic 67; early experience and 67; formation of 42–4; objects as 42–3; psychoanalytic concepts of 66; transformative 67; words as 42; *see also* Christian symbolism; religious symbolism
Symington, Neville 19

Theologica Germanica 170
therapist: pain of 65; regression and 57; as transformational object 57
Thompson, E. P. 3
Tillich, P.: on ambiguity of human situation 159; on Christian symbolism 67–70; dark side and 72; *jouissance*

and 66; self-affirmation and 71; Trinity and 70
transformational objects: child development and 29, 32, 56; God as 56–9, 62; growth to goodness and 29–30, 63–4; mother as 29, 32, 37; objects of beauty 62–3; relating to 37; therapist as 57
transitional objects 42
transitional space 42
triadic/triangular spaces 5, 44–5, 71, 73, 73n2, 167, 184
Trinity: community and 189; fundamentalist religion and 61–2; God as 70; as process 69–70; symbolism of 70–1; Wesleys and 175–9
truthfulness: ideal/idealised 29; literature and 29–30; psychoanalysis and 29; self and 29–30, 41
Turner, D. 58, 64–5, 70, 156
Tyson, J. 133, 148, 171–2, 174

unconscious: Christian symbolism and 13–14; Freud on 20; Klein on 20; Kristeva on 20; religious symbolism and 50; symbolic expressions and 42
Unitarianism 81
unitive ecstasy 88, 90
unresolved grief 125

Varanese *see* Kirkham, Sally
Vazeille, Mary *see* Wesley, Mary Vazeille
Vickers, J. 175
Viney, Richard 97
Vineyard movement 59
von Balthasar, Hans Urs 69
von Zinzendorf, Nikolaus 106

Waddell, Margot 28–9
Wallace, E. 20
Waller, R. 106
Walpole, Horace 99
Ward, Graham 16–17, 67–70, 72
Watson, J. R. 158–60
Wesley, Anne 124
Wesley, Benjamin 124
Wesley, Charles *132*; as Anglican priest 3; beliefs about death 151; brother John and 134–40, 148, 150, 162, 180; brother Samuel and 134–5, 150; character of 142–50; Christian symbolism and 163, 165, 180, 183, 188; conversion and 140–4, 161, 165–7, 169, 179; Cotswold relationships 139, 146; creative activity 161–3, 165; defensive splitting and 88; dependence and conformity of 150; early life of 4, 133–4; education of 134–6; education of children 147; ego and 162, 166; emotional pain of 150–4; empathy and 161; evangelical nurture and 165; fasting by 166; Holy Club and 94, 100, 136; hymn writing and 2, 138, 144, 147, 151–3, 155–63, 165, 176–8, 180, 185–7; illness and 134, 140, 153–4, 175; image of God 162, 166–7, 169, 179; impact of sibling death on 134; internal objects and 161–2; manic-depression and 144; marriage to Sally Gwynne 146–7; Methodism and 3, 21; mother and 135; mysticism and 159, 169–71; opposition to John's marriage 116, 137–8, 148; on ordaining preachers 137–9, 148; pastoral care 144–6; perfection and 172, 174; as preacher 135, 137, 149–50, 153; pre-conversion life 139–40, 153–4; psychological needs 179–80; relationships with women 146–8; religious beliefs in verses of 155–61; religious objects and 179; self-love and 152; sexual misconduct charges 139; sister Emily and 104; suffering and 173–5; symbolic and semiotic in 185; theology of 174; transformational objects and 38; travel to Georgia by 134, 137, 139; triadic spaces 186–7; Trinity and 175–8; verses of 135, 137–8, 173–4, 177; views of growth and goodness 24, 30
Wesley, Charles (correspondence): with John (brother) 140, 146; with mother 165–6
Wesley, Charles (works): *Gloria Patri* 176; *Hymns and Sacred Poems* 165, 169; *Hymns on the Lord's Supper* 165; *Hymns on the Trinity* 176, 178; *Short Hymns on Select Passages of the Holy Scriptures* 174
Wesley, Charley 147
Wesley, Emily 104, 107–9
Wesley family: death of children in 124–5; evangelical nurture and 90, 124; faith of grandfathers in 79; influence of Puritanism on 77–9, 90; poverty of 81, 83
Wesley, Hetty 146

Wesley, John 92; Antinomianism and 102; appearance of 99; beliefs about death 151; Bible and 122–3; biography of 93, 96–8, 106; brother Charles and 134–9, 148, 150, 162, 180; character of 142–3; Christian symbolism and 165, 179–80, 183, 188; conversion and 94–8, 165–8, 172, 179; Cotswold relationships 107–10, 114, 119; defensive splitting and 88; early life of 4; education of 134; evangelical nurture and 165; fasting by 94, 166; fear of the abject 168, 187; Grace Murray and 115–16; health and healing 174–5; Holy Club and 94, 99–100, 109, 123; idealisation and 107–10, 114–16, 118–19, 126, 128; image of God 95–6, 161–2, 166–8, 179, 187–8; image of parents as sexual couple 106–7, 126, 128–9; impact of sibling death on 124–5; influence of 101–4; inner struggles of 95–6, 98–100, 103; internal objects and 126, 161, 180; lack of feeling by 96–9, 102–5, 109, 123, 130, 167–8; marriage to Mary Vazeille 116–17, 123–4, 137; Methodism and 2–3, 21, 101–2; Moravians and 95, 97, 102, 106, 110, 160; Morgan brothers and 123; mother and 87, 98–100, 106–8, 126–7; mysticism and 169–71; ordaining preachers 137–9; paranoid-schizoid position and 129; perfection and 171–4, 188; as preacher 3, 101–5, 110–15, 135, 137, 149, 153, 187–8; pre-conversion life 93–5; providence and 101, 105; psychological defences of 120–4; psychological needs 179–80; relationships with women 96, 105–24, 126–30; religious life of 94–105; religious objects and 179; response to brother's hymns 155, 160–1; salvation and 173, 183; self-destructive impulses 97–8; self-examination and 90, 94–9, 120–1; sex and 106–7, 110–15, 121, 123–4, 126–8, 130; Sophy Hopkey and 110–15, 120–1, 124; suffering and 173–5; supernatural beliefs of 149; theology of 168, 175; transformational objects and 38; travel to Georgia by 95, 110–15, 120–1; Trinity and 175–6, 179; views of growth and goodness 24, 30

Wesley, John (correspondence): with Alexander Knox 96; with Ann Bolton 98, 118–19, 171; with Ann Loxdale 119; with Charles (brother) 97, 100, 115–16, 140; with Elizabeth Briggs 119; with Elizabeth Ritchie 96; with Emily (sister) 108–9; erotic aspects of 109, 119, 123, 128; with Hetty Rogers 118; with James Hutton 117; with John Burton 110; with Martha (sister) 104; with Mary Bishop 118, 175; with Mary Pendarves 109–10; with Mary Stokes 118; with Mary Vazeille 116–17; with mother 98–100; with Richard Morgan Snr. 123; with Richard Viney 97; with Sally Burdock 117; with Samuel (brother) 122–3; with Sarah Crosby 96, 120; with Sarah Ryan 100; with William Law 170; with William Pitt 97; with women 106, 109, 117–20, 123–4

Wesley, John (works): *An Account of an Amour of John Wesley* 105; 'Circumcision of the Heart' 122; *Collection of Hymns* 179; *Hymns and Sacred Poems* 165, 169; *Hymns on the Lord's Supper* 165; 'The New Creation' 175; *Plain Account of Christian Perfection* 171; *Primitive Physick* 174; *A Word to a Condemned Malefactor* 103

Wesley, John Benjamin 124
Wesley, John (deceased brother) 124
Wesley, John (Jacky) 151
Wesley, John, Snr. 77
Wesley, Kezia 86, 133
Wesley, Martha 86, 104
Wesley, Mary Vazeille 116–17, 123–4, 137, 148
Wesley, Sally (daughter) 147–8
Wesley, Sally Gwynne 146–7
Wesley, Samuel, Jnr. 85–6, 104, 124, 133–5, 150
Wesley, Samuel, Snr. *76*; Church of England and 80; disputes of 81–2; marital relationship 81–3; marriage to Susanna Annesley 80; religious convictions of 80–1
Wesley, Susanna *76*; beliefs about death 151; on breaking child's will 84–5, 87; children of 81–2, 86–7; Church of England and 80; correspondence with Charles (son) 86, 165–6; correspondence with John (son)

81–2, 84, 98–100, 107–8, 173; correspondence with Samuel Jnr. (son) 135; death of children 124–5, 134; dedication to God's purpose 98, 135; education of children 83–6; evangelical nurture and 87–8, 90, 124; forgiveness and 87; intellectual capacity of 83–4; interest in Unitarianism 81; love/hate struggle of 87–8; marital relationship 80–3; relationship with father 78, 80, 84; religious convictions of 80–1; sexual attitudes 127; struggle for salvation by 136, 183; tombstone inscription of 106; unacceptable feelings and 103; unresolved grief and 125; on Wesleys 3–4; writings of 83–4

White, John 'Century' 77
White, Mary 77
Whitefield, George 137, 143
Williams, Harris 18, 44, 65, 180
Williams, M. 53
Williams, Rowan 17, 25–8, 30
Williamson, Mr. 113–14
Wimber, John 59–61
Winnicott, D.: on good-enough mother 36, 38; on illusion and creativity 42–3; mother/child interactions 35–6, 38; on negative feelings 35; psychoanalytic concepts of 14; transitional space 42
Word to a Condemned Malefactor, A (Wesley, J.) 103
Wright, K. 14, 19, 35–6, 43